The New English Literatures

The New English Literatures

— cultural nationalism in a changing world

Bruce King

St. Martin's Press
New York

St. Martin's Press, Inc., 175 Fifth Avenue, New York, NY 10010
Printed in Hong Kong
First published in the United States of America in 1980

ISBN 0-312-56655-7

Library of Congress Cataloging in Publication Data

King, Bruce Alvin.
The new English literatures.

Includes bibliographical references and index.
1. English literature — Commonwealth of Nations authors — History and criticism. 2. English literature — 20th century — History and criticism. 3. Nationalism and literature. 4. Civilization, Modern — 20th century — English influences. I. Title.
PR9080.K53 1980 820'.9 80-36847
ISBN 0-312-56655-7

Contents

Other books by Bruce King

Dryden's Major Plays (Oliver and Boyd, 1966)
Marvell's Allegorical Poetry (Oleander Press 1977)

Edited

Twentieth Century Interpretations of All for Love (Prentice Hall, 1968)
Dryden's Mind and Art (Oliver and Boyd, 1969)
Introduction to Nigerian Literature (Evans & Holmes and Meier (USA), 1972)
Literatures of the World in English (Routledge & Kegan Paul, 1974)
A Celebration of Black and African Writing (Oxford University Press, 1976)
West Indian Literature (Macmillan, 1979)

To Jeanne, Bo and Derry

Preface

Many of the best contemporary authors in English come from new nations that not long ago were part of the British Empire. This book is a comparative study of the emergence of the new English literatures and their major authors. It looks at the origins, themes and context of creative writing in newly independent nations, especially the effect of political and social change on culture, and suggests parallels between the literature of the Third World and that of the older dominions of the British Empire. As my subject is the new literatures that have come to international attention since the Second World War, I only occasionally mention similarities to Irish and American writing. Reasons of space also preclude discussion of English literature outside Nigeria, Australia, Canada, India, New Zealand and the West Indies.

My concerns include why the new literatures developed when they did and their relationship to local nationalism, to each other and to international English-speaking culture. It will be found that writers from the new nations often express similar themes and are concerned with analogous problems; sometimes the parallels reflect a common history; often the resemblances are local expressions of movements of western culture or of social changes that took place throughout the English-speaking community during a decade. The recent outburst of creative literature in the new nations can, for example, be attributed to the effects of the last war, the subsequent British withdrawal from their former Empire, self-determination and the continuing problems of decolonisation and nation building. While creativity is closely connected to the growth of nationalism, there were anticipations of such developments since at least the late nineteenth century. The present relevance of writers from new nations to international English literature was anticipated in previous decades by Jean Rhys, Claude McKay, Henry Handel Richardson and Katherine Mansfield, to name some of the better-known authors who came from colonies.

In the first two chapters I summarise the main periods of literary development of the new English-speaking nations from colonies of the British Empire through national independence to the social changes of the 1970s. Although a historical survey of colonial and national development will be useful to many readers, my purpose is to show that the new literatures often began at approximately the same time, followed similar courses of evolution, shared similar styles in each decade, and reflected locally what were international political and social changes within the western world. My third chapter explores the relationship of the new literatures to the social causes that produce nationalist movements. Subsequent chapters treat of separate new national or regional literatures and their major writers. I begin with Nigeria which because of its comparative lateness on the scene of English literature provides a useful example of the evolution of a new literature and its development in response to social change. The Nigerian Wole Soyinka is discussed at length because his work shows one solution to the recurring problem of 'authenticity' and because it reflects later stages of national independence. V. S. Naipaul, Wilson Harris, Derek Walcott and Edward Brathwaite, four major West Indian writers, are studied as different responses to the problems of colonialism, nationalism and decolonisation. Frank Sargeson, of New Zealand, illustrates that the mastery of a colloquial realism is a liberating step in the evolution of a literature. A survey of major Australian writers shows that both nationalists and those identified with high culture have sought to create other sources of values than those produced by modern, urban, middle-class society. It will be found that the characteristics, problems, themes and context of each literature have an applicability to the writing of other nations. Certain topics, therefore, are alluded to throughout the book. The conclusion suggests that the concerns of the new national literatures are related to the problems of modern western culture; analogies are made between developments in the new nations and those within Britain and the United States.

To make this book more useful to students of English, its focus is primarily on works of literature and literary history rather than on the social context of national writing. While the works discussed are among the best of our time, the proportion of this book given to each author is not a reflection of relative value. I am particularly sorry that there is not space to discuss other African literature beyond Nigeria, and the recent development of creative writing in the Pacific islands. As the new English literatures grow and produce significant authors, their comparative history will become increasingly more difficult to summarise.

While I have in previous publications argued for the need to see each of the new national literatures as having its own traditions which reflect local social, political and cultural history, in this book I attempt to define what is common to the new literatures of the English-speaking world. The two approaches are not contradictory. If, for example, a knowledge of Indian spiritualism or Yoruba culture contributes towards an understanding of the works of R. K. Narayan or Wole Soyinka, it is also useful to compare how both writers have used aspects of their local cultures in responding to the effects of colonialism and modernisation on their societies. Although writers from each nation will respond according to their own perspectives, modern means of communication, travel and the effect of industrialisation, urbanisation and western education on most societies result in similar problems.

Although a book of this kind must necessarily be selective, impressionistic, and occasionally assertive, it may offer readers a general introduction to the major writers from the new nations, while placing the new literatures in a historical and cultural perspective.

I want to thank the Rockefeller Foundation for a Humanities Fellowship during 1977–8 which made the research for this book possible.

BRUCE KING

1 Literature and colonial society before the Second World War

As it is commonly said that the British Empire developed by accident, without any imperial plan, it may seem unusual to treat the development of new national literatures as if there were strong similarities to be found between the white dominions of settlement and the colonies in which Europeans did not settle. But from the perspective of a literary and cultural historian, there is a unity to the evolution of the Empire and the Commonwealth of independent states that followed. Nor are the cultural and historical differences between the new nations as great as is sometimes claimed. The Amerindians and Aborigines may form a small part of Canadian and Australian society but the literature of the two nations has been concerned with native inhabitants, if only as symbols of an authentic local culture which colonisation destroyed. If African or Indian writers have idealised the past, so some white Australian and Canadian writers have tried to locate a national culture in pre-colonial history.

Each of the former colonies and dominions, whether white, black or racially mixed, was a product of conquest or imposing British administration over natives, and the result in each case has been a nation of various races, tribes, tongues or blood stocks. While Nigeria has its many tribes of which the Yoruba, Hausa and Ibo are the best known, Canada has its English, French, Eskimos, Amerindians and various large communities of immigrants to whom neither English nor French is a first language. Less than half the Canadian population is of British stock. If Hindu India is an illusion masking the presence of

Muslims, Dravidians and others, white New Zealand has its large Maori minority and Australia has its Aborigines. The West Indies and South Africa also consist of various races, cultures and languages.

The new nations were the consequence of British expansion and international events; although settlement or political subjugation began at different times, the colonial histories and the emergence of new nations reflect the beginnings, growth and break-up of the Empire. England and France had been in competition as world powers throughout the eighteenth century until victory in the Seven Years War (1756–63) left England in control of the seas. A large part of the Caribbean, the South Pacific, Canada and coastal areas of West Africa came under English dominion at this time or were secured as English trading bases. At the end of the Seven Years War England had become the main power in India and leader of the slave trade in West Africa. An important consequence of the war was that the American Middle West, taken from the French, attracted illegal settlement, which in turn meant the need to raise taxes to protect the settlers from the Indians. The resulting outcry in the colonies soon led to the American Declaration of Independence (1776), the need to strengthen Canada as a political unit against possible American expansion and the need to create new colonies to which to transport criminals—which led to the settlement of Australia in 1782. The American Revolution caused the breakdown of the old colonial system and led to the creation of a more centralised, better administered Empire in which some form of local representative government was seen as necessary if other colonies were not to follow the American example. The American Revolution can be said to have precipitated the creation of a Canadian nation (especially with the immigration of forty thousand loyalists north to Ontario and the Maritime provinces), led to the settlement of Australia (and in turn the settlement of New Zealand) and had lasting effects on the West Indies.

While the eighteenth century produced little literature that can be said to be part of the usable histories of the recent new nations, a few writers of African descent began to appear in

England. The cultural and racial tensions noticeable in Olaudah Equiano's *Narrative* (1789) and Francis Williams's poetry anticipate some of the themes that will appear when colonial authors become conscious that they are not Englishmen. The attempts by early white settlers to write poetry in the colonies reveal the problems which result from transporting European literary styles to dissimilar, often inappropriate environments.

The rapid growth of the Empire during the nineteenth century followed from British dominance of the seas, which increased maritime trade; the profits from trade provided the basis of the Industrial Revolution which in turn gave England such a lead over other nations, until later challenged by Germany, that what began as a commercial venture became the Victorian *Pax Britannica*. Imperialism brought the modern state, modern scientific thought, modern technology and what is known as westernisation to other continents and eventually created the basis of the new nations, especially as industrialisation, education and the creation of an administrative cadre produced local elites, politicians and urbanised masses who saw themselves as members of a country dominated by foreigners.

The abolition of the slave trade (1807) and the abolition of slavery through the Empire (1833) produced the paradoxical result of increased British involvement within Africa. Some freed slaves resettled in what became early colonies along the West African coast; it was from such early coastal settlements as Freetown (1790) that a new elite developed which was later to provide the early nationalist leaders. The attempt to stop other European powers from carrying on the slave trade, which disrupted the newly profitable trade in materials and products, necessitated more naval bases and forts. The protection of local enclaves and the support given to local anti-slavery rulers resulted in a further presence, spheres of influence and eventually crown colonies.

The incorporation of many parts of the Empire, either as crown colonies or through annexation, took place during a sixty-year period of the nineteenth century, as did the start of an English educational system. Capetown was taken in 1806 to protect the route to India against the French; with victory over Napoleon the Cape of Good Hope became British property and the British became involved in South Africa. In 1833 the British government purchased the East India Company and opened the Indian market to free trade. The Hudson Bay Company sold its claims to sovereign power and monopoly to the Canadian government in 1865. Natal became a colony in 1844. Except for a few areas, Australian settlement mostly occurred after 1830; New Zealand was annexed and settlement started in 1840. Between 1825 and 1850 Brisbane, Melbourne, Perth, Christchurch and Wellington were founded in Australia and New Zealand, and the Vancouver Island Colony (1849) established in Canada. By the middle of the century a system of schools had been founded in Australia and universities established at Sydney (1852) and Melbourne (1853). A South African college was founded in 1829, which later became the University of Cape Town. In India the Hindu College (1816) included English language and literature among its subjects. It was after the Macaulay Minute (1835) recommending the study of English and European culture that universities in Bombay, Calcutta and Madras started (1857). By the mid-nineteenth century universities had been established in New Brunswick, Toronto, Kingston and Ottawa in Canada. The decision to promote English schooling in the West Indies for the descendants of the freed slaves belongs to this period of educational expansion, as does the founding of the first missionary schools in Nigeria. By the 1870s the universities of Otago and Canterbury had been started in New Zealand. Fourah Bay College in 1876 was affiliated with the University of Durham, and provided the elite that was to dominate the professions, trade and missionary activities, and to spread European values along the coast of West Africa.

The colonial literature of the first half of the nineteenth century is generally uninteresting and derivative. There are diaries, journals and reports from the colonies, often written by the wives of British administrators—*Lady Nugent's Journals* (West Indies, 1839)—or of early settlers—Susanna Moodie's *Rough-*

ing It in the Bush (Canada, 1852). Often the histories of exploration are more interesting than the creative writing. The high proportion of female authors in the early writing of the colonies can be explained by the presence of educated immigrant wives who recorded their strange surroundings in autobiographies or in letters to England. In pioneer societies the arts are likely to be women's occupations: the continued prominence of women writers in many Commonwealth countries may reflect a continuing prejudice towards the arts as feminine and impractical. Early Australian, Canadian and Indian poets followed English models; Augustan verse forms and Wordsworthian descriptions of nature predominated, with the substitution of local names for European references. Even descriptions seem more appropriate for the settled woods of England than the different landscapes of the colonies. Charles Harpur's *Thoughts: A Series of Sonnets* (1845) reveals a feeling for Australian landscape, but the style is artificial and bookish in the late eighteenth-century manner. One of the earliest Indian poets, Henry Derozio, a teacher at Hindu College, of Eurasian origin, wrote the kind of patriotic and inspirational verses that could be found throughout the Empire until the actual attainment of national independence. If such imitativeness was an attempt by Englishmen to carry their culture abroad, for the non-European it was a means of assimilating oneself to the dominant colonial culture. National consciousness, or even clear physical boundaries of the state, often did not exist.

If it is easy to laugh at Judge Barron Field with his poetic exclamations to the Australian kangaroo ('Kangaroo, Kangaroo!/Thou Spirit of Australia,/That redeems from utter failure'), early Indian poets often imitated Lord Byron or Sir Walter Scott. 'Except for a name here and there, the events might just as well have taken place in the Scottish borderland.'[1] Many early Canadian novels, such as Major John Richardson's *Wacousta* (1832), are also influenced by Scott, as is the Australian romantic novel, *Robbery Under Arms* (1888) by Rolf Boldrewood. A common theme of American writing, which will appear in many of the new nations, is expressed by the Canadian Oliver Goldsmith's *The Rising Village* (1825): the decay of the Old and the virtue of the New World. Perhaps the only notable writer of this period is Thomas Chandler Haliburton, whose Sam Slick stories (1835) reflect the somewhat ironic relationship that had developed between the long-settled Maritime provinces and the American New England states to which they were culturally and historically related. Although a Tory in spirit, Haliburton was aware that colonial dependence had left the Nova Scotian unable to help himself during a period of economic depression. His humorous stories of an American pedlar contrast Yankee with English ways; while both are found wanting, the stories inculcate the need for thrift, industry and self-help.

With the Industrial Revolution the colonies were becoming increasingly useful to England as sources of raw material and for trade. West Africa supplied palm-oil and ground nuts, Australia supplied wood, and New Zealand exported wood, butter and cheese. During the nineteenth century England's population doubled and the colonies provided a new start for millions of the working class. Towards the end of the century the labour unions were among the main supporters of the new imperialism. The 1870s and '80s saw massive emigration from Europe to North America and the British colonies; a product of the increased population and urbanisation in the colonies was unemployment during the depression of the 1880s and the rise of trade unionism and radicalism during the 1890s. The discovery of gold in Australia, New Zealand, West and South Africa and Canada during the second half of the century also helped to attract new immigrants and to make the colonies economically stronger. In New Zealand, for example, the population of the South Island more than tripled during the 1860s, mostly as a result of the discovery of gold.

By the middle of the nineteenth century the British had begun to invest in the colonies. Improved communications increased trade and helped centralise administration and finances, while speeding the development of the colonies. Steamships cut the time of travel from England to India from six to two months. Electric telegraphs and railways opened up and unified the colonies. By 1870 cables were laid under the ocean linking Canada, India, New Zealand and Australia with London. Refrigerated cargoes became common in the 1880s. It now became possible for officials to travel between England and the colonies on leave, and to bring their families with them. A new social class was created, mostly products of the public schools, which manned the Empire and which, both to the African native and to the working-class immigrant, was to appear the oppressor. The consolidation of the colonies under centralised administrations is noticeable from the mid-century onward. After the mutiny of 1857 India was brought under crown rule. Lagos became a crown colony in 1861, the Gold Coast in 1874. The Union of New Zealand was formed in 1876. In 1867 the British North American colonies confederated and became the Dominion of Canada. British Columbia was added in 1871.

The period from the third quarter of the nineteenth century until the First World War coincided with the rise of liberal economic imperialism. This is the period of Disraeli's New Imperialism and the move towards Imperial Federation. At the 1897 Imperial Conference a programme of federation was proposed. British colonisation had created schools and colleges; cities now had histories; settlement had increased to the point that the comforts of western middle-class life were possible for an elite; a local intelligentsia had started to develop among doctors, lawyers and colonial clerks. Samuel Ajayi Crowther was appointed Bishop of the Anglican Church in Nigeria in 1864. In Lagos by 1875 the Head of Police, Head of Posts and Telegraph, the Collector of Customs and the Registrar of the Supreme Court were all Nigerians.[2]

The growing consolidation of the Empire, and its expansion into Africa, was paralleled by the development of nationalist cultural movements. Aestheticism and naturalism developed alongside a colloquial realism in literature. Aestheticism and regionalism were both products of the Romantic movement.

If the new imperialism of the late nineteenth century partly resulted from the ability of the colonies to absorb immigrants, there were also economic reasons. England's early start in the Industrial Revolution had been caught up by other countries, particularly Germany and the United States. Instead of free trade being to British advantage, it now seemed preferable to turn towards protectionism and guaranteed markets. While the colonies and new dominions saw in imperialism a threat to their established trading patterns, they were interested in the possibility of expanding their own industries and trade within a closed economic community. The liberalism which had earlier created the Empire was superseded for a time by thoughts of the benefits that might be gained from closer links.

While it is often said that the Boer War ended plans for an Imperial Federation, the same developments that had turned the colonies into thriving states had started to produce strong nationalist sentiments, often in opposition to imperial ideas. The Indian National Congress was formed in 1885. The Australian Labour Federation (with its demand to stop immigration, keep Australia white and employ Australians) was founded in 1890. Dominion status and the completion of the Canadian Pacific Railway (1886) had brought a new patriotism to Canada (which once more felt threatened by its southern neighbour). The spread of various progressive ideas and movements during the last decades of the century also contributed to nationalism. If the newly enfranchised worker was in favour of the Empire as providing living space for his class, the intellectuals, whether Marxist or Fabian, were often anti-imperial. With improved communications and travel, their attitudes spread to the colonies. The Pan-Negro movements of the age are similar to the Indian National Congress as an expression of the new native elites who had begun to demand political and cultural recognition. The West Indian Edward Blyden settled in West Africa where he wrote books arguing the uniqueness and dignity of traditional African culture at a time when a new professional class of African lawyers, clergymen and teachers was beginning to demand a role in local government and to discuss the possibility of a West African nation.

Both imperialist and nationalist sympathies can be seen in the literature of the period. And it is noteworthy that there was a considerable body of good literature. The progress that made the Empire of economic interest also began to produce political and creative literature. Henry Kendall's *Leaves from Australian*

Forests (1869) is representative of how Romantic descriptions of nature had become assertions of national consciousness. Charles G. D. Roberts and the post-Confederation poets were associated with the Canada-First movement. They wrote nature poetry meant to express the spirit and history of the nation through its landscape and legend. Isabella Valancy Crawford tried to be Canadian by writing about pioneers and Indians. The concern with legend, history and folk culture, however, was part of the sensibility of the time and was international. Each colony produced its own version. The close relationship between nationalism and imperialism is shown by the paradox of the Canada-First movement of the 1870s later transforming itself into the Imperialist movement. Another well-known movement was formed around *The Bulletin* (1880) in Australia, and included Henry Lawson, Joseph Furphy and 'Banjo' Paterson.

The *Bulletin* writers of the nineties believed in Australia as the salvation of the working classes and in the value of matesmanship. Significantly, the *Bulletin* writers often were urban, intellectual, bohemian, while the myth they proclaimed was based upon the pioneer frontier life of previous generations. At the turn of the century two-thirds of the Australian population lived in cities. The literary ballads of the nineties were imitations of what was once a folk art, and might be seen in terms of an international interest in folk song at the time. The minstrel-influenced black American dialect verse of Paul Lawrence Dunbar, a northerner who wrote of life on the southern plantations, is an instance of a similar literary sensibility, as is the dialect verse of the Jamaican Claude McKay, published in 1912. The incongruity of matesmanship to an increasingly urban Australia may be seen by the fact that near the height of the bush ballad period Christopher Brennan was writing complex, esoteric symbolist poetry influenced by Mallarmé and Novalis. It would be possible to say that the intellectual climate at the turn of the century has been the primary source for many later Australian writers: the ballads and matesmanship, the edenic new land corrupted by the importation of European values, the various blendings of and variations on evolutionary socialism, Fabianism and Nietzschean doctrines, and the attraction to symbolist poetry are still surprisingly present in Australian literature.

The myths of Australia which developed at the turn of the century are similar to those in other new nations. The Australian outback was the equivalent of the American frontier; the bush was the real Australia, as was the American West; the working classes the real Australians in contrast to the Anglophile middle and upper classes; the new land an Eden threatened by European society. Australian nationalism and patriotism were seen as working-class movements, while the wealthy and educated saw themselves as Englishmen or Austral Britons. The claim that 'socialism is only matesmanship' shows how late nineteenth-century European radicalism had been exported to Australia and indigenised. The direct influence of Fabian, Marxist and other radicals and reformers is noticeable throughout the British colonies at the turn of the century. The American radical Henry George, then almost as influential as Marx, visited Australia in 1889. Australia early in the century was at the forefront of progressive legislation, a Scandinavia of its age. Old age and invalid pensions, a democratic electoral franchise, the right of women to vote, strong labour unions, and a Labour Party Prime Minister—all before 1908—created hopes for a Utopia of the working classes.

The first effective body of Indian writing also was published during the 1880s and '90s. It was towards the end of the nineteenth century that Indian nationalism began to develop; significantly this was the period when Indians had established themselves as part of the intellectual and literary life of London. Toru Dutt, Romesh Chunder Dutt and Manmohan Ghose may now appear insignificant but their reputations were then often treated seriously. If some Indians were highly praised by English critics for their ability to write poetry in the latest style, Indian spirituality was also fashionable among intellectuals. As later happened in Africa, it was the research of European scholars into the culture of the past that gave the cultural nationalist the evidence and tools to reassert traditional, non-western values. It was in prose that the new nationalism was first observable: the prose narration of legends and tales, autobiographies, domestic sketches, Indian scenes. Such works as Lal Behari Day's *The Folk-Tales of Bengal* (1883), P. V. Ramaswami Raju's *Indian Fables* (1889) and Manmatha Nath Dutt's *Gleanings from Indian Classics* (1893–4) represent an interest in local culture and an attempt at formulating a national identity parallel to that, say, of the Australian *Bulletin* and Canadian and Irish creative writers of the period.

The founding of the Indian National Congress in 1885 coincided with the Berlin Conference (1884–5) at which the European powers divided Africa among themselves. Imperialism went hand in hand with the rise of nationalism and spread new ideas about local culture, democracy and self-government. In West Africa during the 1890s a generation of local nationalists had developed; Reverend Carl Christian Reindorf was writing the *History of the Gold Coast and Asanti* (1889); J. E. Casely-Hayford wrote *Gold Coast Native Institutions* (1903). In 1897 the Gold Coast Aborigines Rights Protection Society was formed. The 1890s in South Africa saw some of the earliest creative literature written in local languages by mission-educated Africans.

Generally the turn of the century was marked by tall tales, sketches, ballads and a colloquial local realism that had been developed earlier in the United States by Mark Twain and Bret Harte. Already the national writers were, at least superficially, dividing into 'natives' who used local subject-matter, local colour and dialect, and those who were internationalists and closer to the English or European tradition. Sara Jeannette Duncan, author of *An American Girl in London* (1891) and other Jamesian stories of cultural contrast, is perhaps the best of the pro-imperialist Canadian novelists of the period. While Olive Schreiner's *The Story of an African Farm* (1883) gains part of its strength from local realism, it is also a product of romanticism and of the Cape tradition of liberalism in contrast to narrow Afrikaner nationalism and puritanism. In London Olive Schreiner was immediately seen as an example of the New Woman and became part of the international scene. If local realism was usually associated with nationalism, and aestheticism with an English or European bias, Schreiner's work shows that such distinctions are not watertight and that the best writing usually combines both local and international cultural movements of the time. Schreiner interestingly depicts both a girl's rejection of social convention and a man's acceptance of his inability to impose European order on the African land. Similarly the Irish Renaissance of the period blended the techniques and attitudes of symbolism and the *avant-garde* with cultural nationalism and the affirmation of Celtic folk ways.

It was only in the first two decades of this century that 'pacification' of reluctant tribes and the imposition of European administration took place in Africa. Often African missionaries from coastal cities, which had been colonised for generations, brought Christianity and the English language to their surprised tribesmen in the hinterland. British education, modern communications and a modern economic system began to spread throughout the countryside. Since the last quarter of the nineteenth century poetry was being published in West African newspapers. In South Africa the African National Congress was founded (1912) and West Africa produced its first novel, J. E. Casely-Hayford's *Ethiopia Unbound* (1911). Reflecting the international Pan-Negroism of the period, it is set in both London and West Africa—London where black intellectuals from many nations met to discuss their situation, West Africa where a new class was affirming traditional local culture and values.

New Zealand became a dominion in 1907. In 1910 the Union of South Africa was formed and made a dominion. In both countries writing was largely divided between those who treated local material as exotic and those who attempted realistic descriptions of settler life. From 1895 until the First World War there was economic prosperity; this was a period when the farmer was comfortable and small towns became politically influential. In Canada, Ontario had been long settled and its small towns provided the comedy of Stephen Leacock's sketches and stories. The attempt to create a realistic tradition of fiction in Jamaica by Thomas MacDermot and

H. G. de Lisser petered out for lack of an audience and sufficient local writers of ability. (Many black West Indian intellectuals of the period emigrated to Harlem.) While local realism, the ballad tradition and the contemporary imitation of Romantic and Victorian verse were typical of colonial literature, the first decades of the twentieth century also saw a transformation of *fin-de-siècle* French decadence into a new international hedonism and bohemianism. Norman Lindsay's *A Curate in Bohemia* (1913) and Hugh McCrae's *Satyrs and Sunlight* (1909) attempted to make the new paganism adaptable to Australia. McCrae's poetic centaurs, dryads, fauns and Pans were lusty, galloping, energetic, exuberant and sensual. The late Victorian gothic and medieval sensibility was turned into humorous, playful fancy.

Colonial society had become sufficiently settled and aware of culture to produce the first generation of writers of international stature; local society, however, was insufficiently cosmopolitan to keep the best writers at home, where there was no audience or market for the work of a full-time professional, serious author. Feeling that their talent would be stifled in the colonies, Henry Handel Richardson, Katherine Mansfield, Claude McKay, Jean Rhys, left Australia, New Zealand, Jamaica and Dominica for the cultural opportunities offered abroad; their work is international in style and subject, although often marked by a feeling of being outsiders. In general colonial society was still largely raw, philistine, satisfied with material comforts and antagonistic towards the arts. It will not be until the expansion of education after the Second World War that a sophisticated local audience will exist for writers from the new nations.

During the First World War the colonies and dominions were often divided, sometimes rebellious, in responding to the need to contribute soldiers to the British army (a reluctance felt alike by the Irish, French, Indians and Afrikaners, whether in Australia, Canada, India or South Africa). Although the war effort helped to industrialise the economy of each of the colonies, it contributed to the rise of nationalism. Local minorities and trade unionists objected to conscription, while intellectuals questioned the wisdom of involvement in what was seen as a foreign war between European interests. At the Versailles Peace Conference, the war-time importance of the Empire was shown by the inclusion of Australia, New Zealand, Canada and India among the representatives. Wilson's Fourteen Points included self-determination. Suddenly European nationalism was seen as applicable elsewhere. A Pan-African Congress, with British West African representatives, met in Paris while the Versailles negotiations were taking place. The League of Nations mandated former German colonies to the Allies until the colonies could stand on their own feet. Australia and New Zealand were given such mandates.

The First World War was followed throughout the Empire by disillusionment with Europe and its culture and later by an interest in Russian Communism. The war was also followed by a distinct anti-imperialist mood. The Empire had become identified with the military and upper-class administrators. Anti-militarist and anti-establishment feelings reinforced the rejection of imperialism. Democracy and Empire seemed incompatible. It is often claimed that Britain never really recovered from the First World War and lost its will to rule others. Liberal imperialistic free trade depended on stable conservative finances; such economic conservatism was seen as conflicting with the conditions that promised full employment. With the growing division of Britain into Them against Us, the Empire was increasingly seen as anti-democratic, anti-working class. The recession of 1926 and the Great Depression which began in 1929 made the Empire seem increasingly irrelevant to the masses. The Balfour Declaration (1926) recognised dominions of Empire as autonomous Commonwealths, equal in status, in no way subordinate to each other. The Statute of Westminster (1931) gave legal force to equal status. Australia, Canada, New Zealand and South Africa now had sovereign power, and India was viewed as a future dominion within the Empire. In actual practice the older dominions remained culturally, economically and even politically tied to England until after the Second World War. Although the dominions were granted the right to be self-governing, the Balfour Declaration assumes a common allegiance 'within the British Empire'. A distinction was made between legal status and the actual 'function' on such matters as international diplomacy and defence. Although in theory the dominions could be independent, the Statute of Westminster was not adopted by Australia until 1942 or by New Zealand until 1947.

The West African National Congress was founded in 1918 and held in Accra during 1920 one of the earliest Pan-African conferences. South Africa industrialised during the 1920s and West Africa became economically significant for cocoa. During the 1920s there was a government-sponsored expansion of education in Africa and major railways and harbours were started. Britain, under both local and international pressure, accepted that its colonies had to be prepared for eventual self-government.

After the First World War there was a noticeable cultural change throughout the Empire. Writers attacked provinciality, middle-class gentility, and asserted the self, sexuality and a bohemian style of life. Concern with the individual, with experience, often led to expatriation. Trends included an interest in art for its own sake, a rise in literary standards, an experimentation which leads into modernism, and the development of pro-Negro sentiments and the spread of the influence of the Harlem Renaissance. Rejecting their society and being rejected by it, the artists of the time saw their home as Paris, London or New York. Those who could usually emigrated to Europe; those who stayed at home tried to create artist bohemias in the colonies. Aestheticism, hedonism, revolt against social convention and a concern with craft are as noticeable in the better colonial writers as in their European and American counterparts.

The earlier bohemianism and decadence was transformed into the international rejection of Victorianism in Katherine Mansfield's *Bliss* (New Zealand, 1921), *The Garden Party* (1922) and *In a German Pension* (1926). West Indian contributions included W. A. Roberts's Parnassian poetry, *Pierrot Wounded* (1919) and *Pan and Peacocks* (1928), Jean Rhys's *The Left Bank and Other Stories* (1927) and Claude McKay's novels of expatriation, *Home to Harlem* (1928) and *Banjo* (1929).

J. E. Clare McFarlane says of Una Marson's 'Confession' that it reflects the spirit of post-First World War Jamaica with its feverish search for sensation.[3] An editorial in the second issue of *Trinidad* (1930) commented: 'The *Zeit Geist* is one of revolt against established customs and organic loyalties. Since the War, the revolt has been directed not so much against the Puritanism of the sixteenth century as against a degenerate form of it popularly known as Victorianism.'[4] Canada was represented by the early stories of Morley Callaghan and the modern anti-Maple-Leaf poetry of F. R. Scott, A. M. Klein and A. J. M. Smith. Significantly they felt the need of emancipation from Victorianism as a step towards articulating national life. In New Zealand Georgian verse was written by R. A. K. Mason. South Africa saw William Plomer's novel *Turbotte Wolfe* (1926) and Roy Campbell's early poems. The internationalism of the period is shown by Hemingway and Rhys in Paris and Sarah Gertrude Millin in South Africa each writing a simplified, stripped-down prose.

In contrast to the aestheticism, bohemianism and metropolitanism of the post-First World War period, there was a continuing minor current of local naturalism, usually focused on rural, provincial, pioneer and immigrant lives. The early socialist tradition was given a new lease by the Russian Revolution and many of the realistic prose writers were politically on the left, although some, such as the South African Pauline Smith in *The Karoo* (1925), were merely describing local life. Representative is the Canadian F. P. Grove with *Over Prairie Trails* (1922), *Settlers of the March* (1925) and *Our Daily Bread* (1928). In Australia there were Katharine Susannah Prichard's *The Pioneers* (1915) and *Working Bullocks* (1926), a novel of the timber country. It was partly from such naturalism that the social realism of the 1930s evolved. A significant literary development starting in the late 1920s was the rise of a modern narrative poetry based on the earlier ballad tradition, but more sophisticated, even sceptical, which will later appear to be a form of national epic. Again Canada, as represented by E. J. Pratt, and Australia by Kenneth Slessor, were in the lead, although some New Zealand writers, such as A. R. D. Fairburn, also attempted to develop the form. The influence of international modernist poetry helped move colonial writers from imitating older, out-of-date English verse forms and subject-matter. In Canada, Australia, New Zealand and South Africa poetry was written in the modern idiom against accepted colonial middle-class values. Although the viewpoint was international and universal, such poetry freed colonial verse from provinciality and it laid the foundation for later writers who could develop their own voice and vision.

The Great Depression of the 1930s hit each of the colonies and dominions. In the West Indies there were unemployment marches, strikes and riots as the new labour unions, nationalists and left intellectuals turned against the colonial administration. The older Jamaican poet, J. E. Clare McFarlane, writing in the 1950s, claimed that since the 1930s 'extreme nationalism had grown strident everywhere',[5] and says that the earlier Jamaican poets 'grew to maturity in another kind of world; a world which had some appreciation of universal values'. McFarlane praises a poem entitled 'The Empire's Flag' and comments: 'To me . . . the Commonwealth, or Empire is fraught with deep meaning.'[6]

The economic crisis turned intellectuals and artists into dissidents. If they became nationalists, in contrast to imperialists, they were also anti-government, anti-establishment. The new nationalism of the 1930s was represented in Australia by such writers as Eleanor Dark and Xavier Herbert, just as the contemporary Marxism was represented by Christina Stead, who combined the modern fictional techniques of the 1920s with radical politics. A provincial naturalism was being replaced by a more exciting style of historical novel, critical of the colonial establishment, or by an emphasis on urban life and speech.

The main development of the 1930s was a protest literature, often influenced by socialism and sociology, in which identification was made between the authentic nation and the folk or poor. The former distance between high culture and the masses had been narrowed. The new mood had been anticipated in the early thirties by the Trinidadian journal *The Beacon*, with its leftish critique of the colonial establishment and its realistic dialect stories sympathetic towards the poor non-whites. It was interested in the Russian Revolution and the Indian national movement. An editorial in *The Beacon* demanded that local writers 'break away as far as possible from the English tradition. . . . One has only to glance through the various periodicals published in this and other islands to see what slaves we still are to English culture and tradition.'[7] Novels followed which focused on lower-class lives. Often such writing reflected middle-class intellectuals turning against their own background. Anti-elite and anti-colonial, the West Indian literature of the period expressed the writer's dissatisfaction with middle-class society and his sympathies with the populace—Claude McKay's *Banana Bottom* (1933), Alfred Mendes's *Pitch Lake* (1934), and C. L. R. James's *Minty Alley* (1936).

During the 1930s New Zealand produced its own leftist writers, John Lee and Robyn Hyde, who attacked the comfortable suburbs; but more significant was the appearance of Frank Sargeson's *Conversations with My Uncle* (1936). Rejecting his middle-class, puritanical family, Sargeson turned towards the lower-class casual worker for his subject-matter and attitudes. He adapted the streamlined modern realism of Joyce and Hemingway to local speech and conditions, creating what is often felt to be the first authentically New Zealand fiction—authentic in the way that Mark Twain's *Huckleberry Finn* is more 'native' than any preceding American novel.

The Indian civil disobedience movement led by Gandhi during the early 1930s provoked the Government of India Act of 1935 and the elections of 1937 when the Congress Party and its allies won a majority of provincial government ministries. In the period 1921–39 the number of degree colleges increased from 231 to 285; many of them were teaching institutions, not mere examining boards. The rapid expansion of Indian education during this period is relevant, since a nationalist movement and its literature depend on a developing educated class. When education and the degrees necessary to pass Civil Service tests were only available in England, Indians became English. When it was possible to obtain qualifications at home, they remained Indian, although English remained the language of the political and professional classes who formed the leadership of the nationalists.

The effect of the First World War, of Wilson's Fourteen Points and the Russian Revolution was to create a sense that colonialism was not inevitable and that social justice would follow national independence. Such an idea of justice is part of any colonial political movement and transforms it from an elite wanting equality with its masters to a mass movement. Gandhi's mixture of Christianity and humanism with Hindu values crossed Indian caste lines and made the untouchables and lower classes part of Indian nationalism. Gandhi upset traditional Hindu society with his campaign to eradicate untouchability. Westernisation is thus part of a nationalist movement and often the basis of its demands for justice.

It is with the rise of the Gandhi-led nationalist movement, with its mixture of Hindu culture and western social and political ideas, in the 1930s, that a modern Indian English literature developed, through the novel. Many of the writers took part in, or used as subject-matter, the nationalist movement. Representative titles of 1935 include K. S. Venkataramani's *Kanden, the Patriot—A Novel of the New India in the Making*, Malk Raj Anand's *Untouchable* and R. K. Narayan's *Swami and Friends*. They are often written in a consciously 'Indian' style and reflect the political and cultural mood of the time. Indianisation of the novel in the 1930s is parallel to the emphasis in the West Indian literature of that period on the poor and the 'yards' and is similar to the local focus in Canadian and New Zealand writing during the Depression. The same feelings that turned many writers towards Communism also found expression in a concern with the culture of the poor. Many Indian poets of the period, however, resorted to Victorian rhetorical inflation in attempting to write mystical and epic verse inspired by traditional culture. Poets generally find it more difficult to create an appropriate local style and it will not be until independence is gained that Indian poets will realise that modern verse is the best gateway to authenticity. It is also significant, if to be expected, that the same people who were most westernised should be among those most strongly in favour of a return to Hindu culture, by which in practice they meant a national culture to be selected from parts of the local past. Gandhi himself was shocked by many existing traditional social practices when he returned to India.

Throughout the Commonwealth the years preceding the Second World War were marked by political movements that might be described as nationalist, although the specific purpose of such movements was often the expression of economic grievances. The Depression of the thirties and the radical politics of the era brought about a consciousness of the need for social reform. Usually British colonial policy was seen as defending the status quo and the local Anglophile establishment; regardless of whether there were active local nationalist movements, a national consciousness had been created in opposition to what were felt to be the values of the Empire and British rule. During the 1930s a new class of educated Nigerians began to appear in contrast to the older Creole and coastal Yoruba elite. Nnamdi Azikiwe's return from America in 1937 began a period of nationalist agitation. The well-off and educated in the older dominions might still regard Britain as 'home', but farmers and industrial workers, as well as those of non-European blood, increasingly felt Canadian, Australian or Trinidadian.

Influenced by the social realism of the 1930s with its emphasis on dialect, urban slums, small towns, poverty-stricken lives, local conditions, minorities, underdogs and social injustices, literature shifted its focus from European elite culture to that of the majority of the inhabitants of the colony or dominion. Such writing in its subject-matter, themes, language and empathy laid the foundations for the national literature that began to emerge during the war years. The Australian Xavier Herbert's *Capricornia* (1938), with its protest at the treatment of the Aborigines and use of allegory, anticipates the Canadian Hugh MacLennan's *Barometer Rising* (1941) and *Two Solitudes* (1945), which show how the refocusing of literature on local problems evolved into consciously national writing. Such writing brought to the folk-realist and naturalist tradition of the previous fifty years a more direct involvement with the central immediacies of national life and a range of literary techniques, such as symbolism, which were formerly regarded as part of the modernist international tradition.

The historical narrative poetry of E. J. Pratt in Canada and Robert FitzGerald in Australia also assumed a sense of national community and a culturally usable historical past. The change in poetry using local scenery as its setting is also significant. Late nineteenth and early twentieth-century poems in the romantic Wordsworthian vein were primarily attempts to record the local colour of Canada, Australia, New Zealand and the West Indies. As in colonial poetry, often nothing was particularly national to them except the local variety of trees or birds. As poets learned to become more exact in their descriptions, the scene became usable as a 'symbol' for personal emotions or a means to contrast the external with the subjective. Throughout the Commonwealth of the late thirties and forties poets use landscapes or seascapes as a starting point for meditative verse about the self.

The inter-war years were not, however, the exclusive preserve of nationalists, local realists, and the political left. The internationalism of the previous decade continued. Anticipating a theme sometimes found in recent writing, such expatriates from the colonies often felt outsiders to North American or European society. McKay and Rhys might nostalgically romanticise the West Indies, but other lands were where life really happens. The Australian novelist Martin Boyd is representative of the position of the colonial upper classes during a period of radicalisation, when anti-establishment views were popular. Connected to wealthy English and Australian families, Boyd felt that art and good taste were the product of breeding and of freedom from the need to earn a living. Australia had wealth but not breeding or taste; England had the refinement and aristocratic independence necessary for a good life. The progressive weakening of the European aristocracy through mass democracy, the influence of commercial interests, and the politicisation of art were signs that the western culture was endangered. Boyd's two major novels, *Nuns in Jeopardy* (1940) and *Lucinda Brayford* (1946), suggest that the good life is only possible within a long tradition supported by religion.

2 Literature and new nations: the Second World War and after

Wars breed revolutions and the effects of the Second World War on the Empire were felt equally strongly in, say, Australia and Ghana. If the war stimulated the sympathies of many individuals towards Britain, its general effect was to set the stage for the dissolution of the Empire. Isolation from Britain, the spectre of possible British defeat in Europe, increased American influence, the creation of local industries and the rhetoric of national liberation provided the psychological, social and ideological conditions for independence. Each of the colonies and dominions underwent rapid social, economic and psychological changes during the war. Africans fought alongside white soldiers who did not have the attitudes and privileges of colonial administrators. Canada became a major industrialised nation, but, because of the Francophonic Canadian resentment of conscription, avoided direct involvement of conscripts in the European battle theatre. India became a supply centre for the Middle East war and after 1941 a base for hostilities against Japan. The Indian Army expanded to two million; industry was stimulated, especially iron, steel, cement, mica and aluminium; mechanisation produced technicians; the Women's Auxiliaries helped to westernise a new class of women. The German threat to the British navy in the West Indies and the establishment of American bases on the islands created great psychological and social changes in what had been an impoverished economy. The industrialisation of Southern Rhodesia took place during the war. The West African economy was stimulated by the demand for strategic war material and the presence of foreign soldiers and bases; the monopoly of the old trading companies was broken by the new governmental purchasing agents and marketing boards which partly transformed the peasant economy. British inability to defend the Pacific produced in Australia a sense of isolation. It has been said that Australia almost grew out of the Empire during the war. The war effort, which stimulated the Australian universities to increase scientific research, was followed by scholarships for returning servicemen and the creation of the Australian National University in 1948.[1]

Not only did the war radically weaken British prestige and power, stimulate the local economy and bring about rapid social changes, but as war aims became defined the defence of Empire was replaced by ideals of independent democratic states. The American involvement in the war against the Axis powers, the rhetoric of liberation and the subsequent Cold War against Russia resulted in a climate of world opinion in which colonial empires were no longer felt to be acceptable. The Atlantic Charter included among Allied war aims the right of all people to choose the form of government under which they live. The United Nations Charter specified that the aims of trusteeship were 'to develop self-government, to take due account of the political aspirations of the peoples, and to assist them in the progressive development of their free political institutions'.[2]

If the Cold War which developed following the Allied victory in 1945 soon made such ideals appear slogans under which both the West and the East could manoeuvre for world-wide influence, it should not be assumed that the Atlantic and United Nations Charters were framed for propaganda purposes. The Axis powers aimed at world conquest and consequently the Second World War took on for the West .the character of a struggle for national liberation and self-government.

The mood of decolonisation that developed during the war can be illustrated from Doris Lessing's novel about Southern Rhodesia, *Ripples From the Storm*, where there is a public meeting of trade unionists, RAF service men, liberals and Communists supporting Indian independence; Jack Dobie, the union leader, energetically says 'Having bled India dry for hundreds of years it is our moral duty'; 'The women fanned themselves with programmes emblazoned: "Let India Go Free!"' Lessing says 'The meeting, in short, was like all the meetings of that short epoch 1942–1945.' 'Words like liberty, freedom, democracy, revolution drove one brave sentence into the next.'[3] Such democratic sentiments were consistent with American ideas of government and with the declared policy of Franklin Roosevelt during the war. If Churchill had no wish to dismantle the Empire, his views were hardly shared by the Labour Party members of the war-time government, or by the Labour government which followed in 1945, which sympathised with local national independence movements. In any case, the desire to turn Britain into a welfare state ran contrary to the social hierarchy and expense needed to maintain an empire. Faced by great war debts, Britain hastened to relieve itself of responsibility towards its colonies.

Older dominions of settlement and newly created African nations rapidly became fully independent; Canada asserted separate citizenship in 1946, and was soon followed by Australia and New Zealand. The British withdrawal from India in 1947 meant that a sixth of the world population gained independence overnight. Ghana, the first black African country to become independent in 1957, was followed by Nigeria (1960), Sierra Leone (1961), Tanganyika (1961), Uganda (1962) and Kenya (1963). The founding of the short-lived West Indian Federation and its first federal elections took place in 1958. Self-government and independence did not always have desirable results. In 1948 apartheid became official policy in the Union of South Africa, although it was not until 1961 that the South African Republic left what had become a multiracial Commonwealth of nations. It is symbolic of the changing roles in the post-war world that leadership towards the development of a multiracial Commonwealth was provided by Canada.

The early short stories of Cyprian Ekwensi show the effect of rapid urbanisation and social change in Nigeria. There were disputes during the war about land on which to build military bases, and between labour unions and the government. A Yoruba theatre had evolved from religious pageants to historical and protest drama treating of political and national events. Such was the background from which Ekwensi's novel, *People of the City* (1954), developed.

The same modernisation which created the new nation also produced its emerging literary tradition. An early sign that the rapid industrialisation and nationalism brought on by the Second World War was to produce new literatures can be found in South Africa where Peter Abrahams's *Mine Boy* (1946) and Alan Paton's *Cry, the Beloved Country* (1948) are transitional between an earlier kind of protest fiction and the new social conditions and resulting literary themes of the post-war period. The increased international importance of the mines, of South Africa as a dominion of settlement, the wave of immigration during the thirties, especially from middle Europe, bringing new intellectual energies, the increasing urbanisation of society and the development of industries, the rise of the labour movement, the spread of socialist and Marxist ideas, and the development of articulate, educated black Africans and Coloured in the urban townships meant that by the 1940s South Africa was a modern society and its English literature had begun to join world literature. Abraham's *Dark Testament* (1942) and *Son of the City* (1945), Paton's *Meditation for a Young Boy Confirmed* (1944) and *Too Late the Phalanthrope* (1953), Ezekiel Mphahlele's *Man Must Live* (1947), and Nadine Gordimer's *Face to Face* (1949) are a partial listing of titles that indicate development of creative writing during the war years and immediately after.

In the Union as elsewhere, the protest idiom of the late depression years was transformed into the vocabulary of a search for national identity. Protest at mistreatment of non-whites developed, with the early novels of Lessing and Gordimer, into an exploration of the colonial structure and inheritance of local society, and subsequently into studies of identity set within the context of cultural and political crisis. As often occurs in such early national literature, autobiography and autobiographical novels provided means to record consciousness of social and moral confusions. Lessing and Gordimer share with Mphahlele and many black African writers a strong tendency towards autobiography and the factual depiction of a rapidly changing society. In South Africa rapid industrialisation and consequent urbanisation of black Africans ran into conflict with a still crude capitalism and the rise of Afrikaner nationalism which took power in 1947. While Afrikaner nationalism is unusual in that a minority rules over a majority (a reversal of the normal result of independence), the British leaving of South Africa to its fate was no different from what happened elsewhere at the end of the war. The Muslims and Hindus of India were told that whether or not they composed their differences the British intended to withdraw within a year.

In the literature of the war years and the period immediately preceding independence, there is a mood of national cultural assertion. Local intellectual and literary journals came into being—*Meanjin* was founded in Australia (1940), and *Bim* (1942), *Kyk-over-al* (1945) and *Focus* (1943) in the Caribbean. Characteristics of the period include the re-investigation of national history, identification with minorities, and criticism of the ruling power structure. Eleanor Dark's *The Timeless Land* (1941) included sympathy for the effects of colonialism on the Australian Aborigines. In the West Indies Edgar Mittelholzer's *Corentyne Thunder* (1941) brought attention to the rural East Indian in contrast to the urban middle-class creole. George Campbell's *First Poems* (1945) sang of the black man, while V. S. Reid's *New Day* (1949) used dialect to recall a significant moment in Jamaican history when the colonial elite returned its rights of self-government to the Crown rather than risk increased black participation. *The Hills Were Joyful Together* (1953) by Roger Mais studied the lives of the Kingston poor. Doris Lessing's first novel, *The Grass is Singing* (1950), set in Rhodesia, was another naturalist study in the effects of colonial history; it tells of a poor farmer destroyed by capitalist exploitation of the land, and his wife driven insane by the isolation of her life and her fear of black Africans.

Whereas nationalism in Canada, which produced the Massey Report (1951), created the Canada Council (1957) and led to the founding of the journal *Canadian Literature* (1959), was directly reflected in the novels of Hugh MacLennan, it produced a more subtle response in Australia where many writers, whether nationalists or cosmopolitans, rejected the conformist middle-class suburban culture. Judith Wright looked nostalgically back towards the pioneers and early settlers and mystically towards the land. Patrick White looked wistfully if sceptically towards heroic qualities in the early explorers, settlers and eccentrics, while satirising modern urban culture. A. D. Hope turned against the nationalist literary movement as provincial and tried to realign Australian poetry within the tradition of English and European verse, while adding his disparagement to the attack on Australian mass culture. Frank Hardy's *Power Without Glory* (1950) uses the techniques of an earlier naturalism to show the rise of the Australian labour establishment from poor immigrants to corrupt political bosses.

The complex relationship of literature to nationalism and internationalism is shown by P. Lal's creation of a modernist poetic style in India at the time of independence. Whereas earlier poetry was consciously nationalistic and reflected the spiritualism and epic literature of Hindu culture, the new poetry began from the example of T. S. Eliot and other modernists to evolve a contemporary style, more attuned to the immediacies of Indian urban and intellectual life. What at the time appeared an imitation of cosmopolitan literature can now be seen as a necessary step in the transformation of Anglo-Indian poetry from romantic spiritualism, divorced from reality, to a more direct engagement with what educated Indians actually think, feel and do.

The breakdown of the isolation of ethnic communities, the loss of control by the older colonial establishments and the rapid urbanisation of the war period led to a search for national roots and for personal identity. Faced by an oversimplistic nationalism, but aware that they were not Englishmen, writers of the 1950s tended both towards the exploration of national identity and towards examining the historical sources of their present condition. Derek Walcott wrote, 'That sun which would never set until its twilight became a withdrawal of Empire and the beginning of our doubt.'[4] Many writers sought ideals in the past. Consequently novels became increasingly psychological, poetic, or even epic, when treating historical material formerly thought proper to realism. In the West Indies Derek Walcott's early verse plays gave a grandeur both to the local folk and to former Caribbean black leaders, while his poems, after a period of protest, explored his divided cultural heritage. Samuel Selvon's *A Brighter Sun* (1952) is representative in showing the increased contact between the various races of the West Indies, the depiction of a new American influence as a result of the war, the setting of the individual life within a historical context, an awakened nationalism and the uncertainty of what the next step is, of what one should be. George Lamming's *In the Castle of My Skin* (1953) sensitively records the passing of local feudally organised society, the new social awareness brought by the labour movement of the thirties, the replacing of the old elite by a new local bourgeoisie, and a young man's awareness that education has uprooted him from his village and that he is black in a dominant white culture. Edgar Mittelholzer's *Children of Kaywana* (1952) begins an epic trilogy about the mixed, confused cultural and racial past of Guyana.

The best example of the sensitive recreation of the past being used as a source of identity is Chinua Achebe's *Things Fall Apart* (1958). Besides teaching Nigerians that they had a usable history, the novel is notable for the many techniques that create an 'African' reality within its narrative. The naturalism, dialect and emphasis on a community, observable in earlier nationalist literature, have been developed into a much more sophisticated portrayal of local culture in which such features as the passing of time and the narrative point of view reproduce the texture of tribal society. Ngugi wa Thiong'o's *River Between* (1965, but written earlier) combines nostalgia for tradition with an awareness of the difficulty of building a Kenyan nation from various tribes and religions.

The early classics of the independence period were followed by a literature of cultural confusion and conflict. In South Africa,

India, Nigeria and the West Indies opposing traditions and values seemed irreconcilable. Humour often afforded the means of bridging the distance between nationalist values of the past and the actuality of the modern nation inhabited by the writer. N. Chaudhuri's *Autobiography of an Unknown Indian* (1951), Balachandra Rajan's *The Dark Dancer* (1959) and *Too Long in the West* (1961) and even R. K. Narayan's ambiguous spiritual comedy, The Man-Eater of Malgudi (1961), offered variations on the East-West conflict. Within the West Indies, John Hearne's novels recorded the awareness of the newly emergent middle class that their values were not necessarily those of the local black majority. If in *The Leopard* (1958) V. S. Reid turned towards Africa as a source of identity, many West Indian novels of the period, of which Denis Williams's poetic *Other Leopards* (1963) is the most impressive, are concerned with the differences between the New World black and the black African. V. S. Naipaul's *A House for Mr Biswas* (1961), based upon the life of his father, is ambiguous and could be seen as an epic record of the struggles of the East Indian immigrants in Trinidad to become part of the new national community, or it could be seen as a record of displacement, isolation, dispossession, and the subsequent disillusionments of integration into a society which remained chaotic, directionless, and without the prospect of significant material and spiritual satisfactions.

Within Africa the contrasts between tribal and western values or between English and local values were the subject of Nadine Gordimer's *A World of Strangers* (1953), Achebe's *No Longer at Ease* (1960), T. Aluko's *One Man, One Wife* (1959), and Lenrie Peters's *The Second Round* (1965). Often the literature of the early and mid-sixties, such as Wole Soyinka's *The Interpreters* (1965), poetically described the search for a new code of values which would bridge past and present.

The political optimism of the post-war period was often followed by disillusionment. The West Indian Federation, founded in 1958, broke up in 1962. The Western Region crisis in Nigeria followed a few years after independence and led to a civil war. Self-government sometimes brought to power corrupt, inefficient and uncultured politicians who were viewed with suspicion by the young writers, graduates of the new local universities or educated abroad. V. S. Naipaul's early satiric novels of the decay of East Indian culture in Trinidad—*The Mystic Masseur* (1957) and *The Suffrage of Elvira* (1958)—included absurdly unprincipled politics among the effects of self-government. In Nigeria novels by Aluko and Ekwensi warned against the rise of demagogy and corruption. Soyinka's play *A Dance of the Forests* (1960) greeted the celebration of Nigerian independence with a reminder that the past was often inglorious and that the present would probably be a continuation of the same greed, pride and evil found in former ages.

In the mid-1960s, Soyinka's *Kongi's Harvest* (1967) and Achebe's *A Man of the People* (1966) in Nigeria, and Ayi Kwei Armah's *The Beautyful Ones Are Not Yet Born* (1968) in Ghana attack their governments as radically corrupt, tyrannical and inauthentic. Independence brought disillusionment and with it writers turned from glorification of the community to the depiction of individuals who remained loyal to their conscience. A more profound scepticism of independence can be seen in V. S. Naipaul's *Mimic Men* (1967), where it is implied that the new nations lack the material and cultural resources to stand on their own feet.

The increasing use of allegory, parody, or fragmented narrative forms is noticeable as writers try to find an appropriate expression for the complexities that had replaced simpler assertions and social comedy. Another characteristic of the sixties is the increasing use of myth as a means of offering imaginative order where nationalism had brought disorder. Soyinka's drama *The Road* (1965) and long poem *Idanre* (1967) are the first sustained presentation of what has become his private vision of the truth behind reality. Wilson Harris's novels, beginning with *Palace of the Peacock* (1960), introduce a period of Caribbean writing in which integrative myths are used to transcend the cultural chaos, injustice and poverty of the region. While the intense, sometimes bloody, conflict between those of East Indian and those of African descent made such symbolic integration particularly necessary to Guyana, myth became a favoured means within the new nations of finding spiritual harmony where actual society was either cacophonous or dispirited. Walcott's poems beginning with 'Crusoe's Island' (1962) are a further instance of new cultural myths which argue against the simplicities of nationalism and colonialism. The increased Canadian interest in literature as myth, represented by the criticism of Northrop Frye and the novels of Robertson Davies, might also be seen as a desire to find patterns of truth within a confused national mosaic. In Australia James McAuley's *Captain Quiros* (1960), an epic poem, offered a glimpse of a former time when men could believe in divine purpose; A. D. Hope often based poems on the Renaissance harmonious vision of the world, and Judith Wright explored various mystical notions of a world in process yet spiritually whole.

The writers mentioned until now have been primarily concerned with colonialism, nationalism, and such issues as high versus low culture and European versus national society, the relationship of the past to the present, and national versus personal identity. From the mid-1960s onward there is a different perspective among some new authors who write of local life from within their community. Such fiction is realistic, makes use of local speech, detail and characters, but its significance is not explained to outsiders. Its themes concern average people in their daily routines. Rather than the large issues of nationalism, the concerns are more with coming to terms with oneself, with adapting, or with the repressed part of an individual's life. While the realism of such novels as Margaret Laurence's *The Fire-Dwellers* (Canada, 1969) and Michael Anthony's *A Year in San Fernando* (Trinidad, 1965) is akin to naturalism, the novels themselves tend towards the subjective and poetic. Some Nigerian novels also reveal similar characteristics. I think such writing shows that for many writers the problems of colonialism and independence have passed. Local society is apprehended from within rather than by a dialectic of national and imperial values. The realistic portrayal of society is consequently subsumed by a sensitive record of personal, subjective impressions of the kind formerly found in novels of elite values or divided cultural heritage. It could be argued that such a literature concerned with the problems of ordinary, in contrast to representative, lives shows that cultural decolonialisation has finally occurred. Such a view would not be accurate. While psychological realism reflects the fact that after the excitement of independence a literature will develop concerned primarily with recording and expressing the lives of ordinary people, alongside such work, existing simultaneously, the writing of intellectuals continues to treat of cultural crisis and assertion.

The need to fulfil mass expectations after independence led, during the affluent sixties, to rapid industrialisation, expansion of education, and other forms of modernisation which once more disrupted existing social traditions (whether in Canada, Australia, or Nigeria) and which, ironically, required the importation of foreign, often American, experts, advisers, teachers and businessmen. The nineteenth-century British Empire developed as a result of free trade and the advantages that England had over other nations because of its early place in the Industrial Revolution; the American 'empire' of the 1950s and '60s similarly was a result of economic liberalism, the technological superiority which followed the Second World War and the leadership of the West during the Cold War. The departure of British administrators, advisers and teachers during the period was often followed by the arrival of a greater number of Americans or a new generation of British experts who were necessary to the rapid growth of the local economy. Education was rapidly expanded. In Australia between 1955 and 1970 the number of university students increased from 30,000 to 120,000. In Canada the province of Ontario alone created nine new universities during the 1960s in an attempt to fill the expanding economy with its own nationals. Often the new universities could only be staffed with foreigners, usually from Britain or the United States. Soon the new graduates saw their advancement blocked by foreign experts. A new nationalism began, often with the American presence and 'neo-colonialism' as its target.

As the training of new graduates was often American-influenced, and as modernisation increasingly meant Americanisation, the new forms of protest were inspired by, similar to, or linked with protest movements within the United States. The black civil rights movement in the United States, the anti-establishment mood associated with the 'counter culture' of the young, and the rise of a 'new left' resulted in identification with 'the people' and with 'ethnic' rather than British values. Thus the strangely un-Canadian anger, in a nation which prided itself on blandness, of the late 1960s and early '70s. The Black Power riots in the Caribbean during the same period appeared to imitate the anti-war protests, the drop outs, and the Black Power movement in America. In spite of the rise of black consciousness and talk of revolution, the only major literary text directly to sympathise with such causes is Edward Brathwaite's *The Arrivants: A New World Trilogy* (1967–69), although N. D. Williams's *Ikael Torass* (1977) should be mentioned as a promising first novel showing a young man's progress from the West Indian elite through disillusion with his class to neo-nationalist identification with the urban poor. Derek Walcott's play *Dream on Monkey Mountain* (1967) reflects in its plot and themes, while being critical of, the radical mood. V. S. Naipaul's *In a Free State* (1971) and *Guerrillas* (1975) examine the implications of the withdrawal of British power, the confusions which followed, and the effect of the indirect American imperialism on the new nations.

It is an example of the increased communication within the modern world that the radicalism and neo-nationalism of the late 1960s and early '70s existed throughout most of the Commonwealth. In Africa radicalisation and anger are noticeable in Soyinka's novel *Season of Anomy* (1973), play *Death and the King's Horseman* (1975) and poem *Ogun Abibimañ* (1976), and in *Petals of Blood* (1977) by the Kenyan novelist Ngugi wa Thiong'o. Often the literature of the period echoed the themes and methods of American writing. The basic style is slangy, oral, experimental, bright, mythic, angry and influenced by advertising and American ways of life. Canadian examples of neo-nationalism include David Godfrey's *Death Goes Better with Coca-Cola* (1967) and *The New Ancestors* (1970), and Margaret Atwood's novel *Surfacing* (1972) and *Survival* (1972), a thematic study of Canadian literature. The increasing

Americanisation of Australian society is noted in Frank Moorhouse's rather American-styled short stories of urban Sydney, *The Americans, Baby* (1972).

While the growth of literary criticism and historical scholarship may appear extraneous to creative writing, they do offer evidence of when national or regional literatures were recognised as academic disciplines. A comparison between dates of the recognition of various literatures is useful towards understanding recent cultural changes.

Studies of African literature begin in the 1960s. Significantly most of them treat of the continent and the first works are more concerned with culture than creative writing. Literary criticism soon follows: Gerald Moore, *Seven African Writers* (1962), Judith Gleason, *This Africa* (1965), Janheinz Jahn, *A History of Neo-African Literature* (1966), Ulli Beier, *Introduction to African Literature* (1967), and Oladele Taiwo, *An Introduction to West African Literature* (1967). If Taiwo's was the first book of literary criticism to distinguish West Africa from the rest of the continent, Margaret Laurence's *Long Drums and Cannons* (1968) was the first to survey the literature of a single nation, Nigeria, and G. D. Killam's *The Novels of Chinua Achebe* (1969) was the first book on an individual author. In other words an awareness of African literature as a separate literary field developed during the 1960s. Moore's book followed four years after the publication of Achebe's *Things Fall Apart*, the first novel which could have formed the basis for a national tradition in contrast to the earlier novels of Amos Tutuola and Cyprian Ekwensi.

In the West Indies where there was a longer history of creative writing and where there was a larger body of writers during the 1950s, the significant dates are slightly later than in Nigeria. This may be due to the confused political situation which resulted from the breakup of the Federation. G. R. Coulthard's *Race and Colour in Caribbean Literature* (1962) treated more of Spanish and French literature than English. 1966 might be considered a better starting point with Wilson Harris's polemic *Tradition and the West Indian Novel*, followed by Louis James's *The Islands in Between* (1968), the publication of Ivan Van Sertima's radio broadcasts under the title of *Caribbean Writing* (1968), Gerald Moore's *The Chosen Tongue* (1969)—a comparison of West Indian and African writing—and Kenneth Ramchand's *The West Indian Novel and its Background* (1970). It is not until the 1970s that the first books devoted to individual writers, such as V. S. Naipaul and Wilson Harris, begin to appear.

India has a longer literary tradition than many of the Commonwealth countries and should have a longer history of national literary criticism. While one can find in bibliographies early, now seldom mentioned, surveys—Behramji Malabari's *The Indian Muse in English Garb* (1877), Lotika Basu's *Indian Writers of English Verse* (1933)—the study of contemporary literature in English began shortly before the period of independence with K. R. Srinivasa Iyengar's *Indo-Anglian Literature* (1943) and *The Indian Contribution to English Literature* (1945). Despite the pioneering scholarship of Iyengar, it is only in the 1960s and '70s that modern critical studies begin: John B. Alphonso-Karkala's *Indo-English Literature in the Nineteenth Century* (1970), Meenakshi Mukherjee's *The Twice Born Fiction* (1971). It is only in the 1970s that monographs on individual authors appear.

It can be seen that critical attention to African, West Indian and Indian literature was a reflection of political independence, that study really began in the 1960s, and that it is only in the past few years that monographs on single authors, the real test of research and evaluation, have been published. Nigerian, Indian and West Indian literatures were only seen as existing after the Second World War. While significant Nigerian creative writing was a product of the post-Second World War years, the same cannot be said of India which had a long literary tradition stretching back into the mid-nineteenth century, or of the West Indies, which in de Lisser, McKay, Rhys, Eric Walrond and others had a small but significant body of internationally known writing before the 1940s. The recognition of the national or regional literatures has been part of the same mood of self-determination that found expression in the setting up of the United Nations and that resulted in the independence of most former colonies.

In the older settled dominions there is a similar pattern. A count of book titles of both criticism and anthologies in William H. New's *Critical Writings on Commonwealth Literatures*[5] shows that while there were such occasional publications celebrating contemporaries in the nineteenth century as G. B. Barton's anthology, *The Poets and Prose Writers of New South Wales* (1866) and Arthur Patchett Martin's *The Beginnings of Australian Literature* (1899), the first attempt at criticism occurs in the 1920s with Zora B. M. Cross's *An Introduction to the Study of Australian Literature* (1922), followed by little else until the late 1930s when A. J. Coombe's *Some Australian Poets* (1938) and M. B. Eldershaw's *Essays in Australian Fiction* (1938) appeared alongside the flare-up of nationalism that preceded the war.

Despite the long history of Australian literature, and the early nationalism that found literary expression in the 1890s, there were less than a dozen books of criticism on Australian writing published before 1940. The 1940s marked the change, with more works on Australian literature published in that decade than in the previous eighty years. In the fifties the situation continued with a slight increase over the forties, but it is in the sixties when the real explosion of publications on Australia occurs. By my rough count there were one and a half times as many books published on Australian literature and culture during the 1960s as in all previous decades combined! Even allowing for the expansion of the book trade during the 1960s, the increase is staggering.

The pattern in the critical study of Australian literature is therefore similar to that of India: a few celebrations of contemporaries in the late-nineteenth century, a few attempts to claim a national literature in the 1920s and '30s, a sudden development in the awareness of a national literature in the 1940s, followed by an explosion of academic studies and textbooks during the 1960s, parallel to the recognition of other Commonwealth literatures and the sudden development of an educational market with the introduction of courses of study in

Australian, African and Commonwealth literature at the new universities. The most significant pointer is John P. Matthew's *Tradition in Exile: A Comparative Study of Social Influences in the Development of Australian and Canadian Poetry in the Nineteenth Century* (1962).

The pattern of the critical and historical study of Canadian literature is straightforward and except for minor variations of emphasis does not differ significantly from that seen elsewhere in the Commonwealth. The nineteenth century produced such expected items as John G. Bourinot's *Our Intellectual Strength and Weakness: A Short Historical and Critical Review of Literature, Art and Education in Canada* (1893). The first real studies of the national literature began in the 1920s. There were somewhat more Canadian works of this period than in Australia or India. Mention might be made of Lionel Stevenson's *Appraisals of Canadian Literature* (1926). Whereas elsewhere with the Depression the literary nationalism of the twenties somewhat abated, in Canada studies continued to be written and led directly to E. K. Brown's *On Canadian Poetry* (1943).

Basically, however, the revival of interest in Canadian writing began in the 1950s and developed into the neo-nationalist criticism of the late 1960s. Some representative titles are: Desmond Pacey, *Creative Writing in Canada* (1952); Harold Adams Innis, *The Strategy of Culture, with Special Reference to Canadian Literature* (1952); A. J. M. Smith, *The Book of Canadian Poetry* (1957); Carl F. Klinck, editor, *Literary History of Canada* (1965); Sheila Egoff, *The Republic of Childhood: A Critical Guide to Canadian Children's Literature in English* (1967); D. G. Jones, *Butterfly on Rock: A Study of Themes and Images in Canadian Literature* (1970).

For all practical purposes, an anthology of verse published in 1906 and republished in 1926 being the exception, the study of New Zealand literature is parallel to that of Australia or Canada: E. H. McCormick, *Letters and Art in New Zealand* (1940); J. C. Reid, *Creative Writing in New Zealand* (1946). The proper study of New Zealand writing begins in the 1950s and, as with other Commonwealth literatures, is mainly a product of the 1960s; E. H. McCormick, *New Zealand Literature: A Survey* (1959); Allen Curnow, *The Penguin Book of New Zea-*

land Verse (1960); Joan Stevens, *The New Zealand Novel, 1860–1960* (1961).

While the production of literary criticism, anthologies and surveys somewhat reflects the quality and quantity of literature of a period, the main causes are political and economic. Before Australian, Indian, Canadian or West Indian literature was taught at schools and universities, there was little reason to do research and little prestige to be gained from, or market for, books on national literature. With political independence, cultural nationalism, the creation of new local universities, and the study of local literature in the universities and schools, a market was created, research was done, and prestige could be earned by being a critic or scholar in the new literatures. Such a process is self-perpetuating. Courses of study create a demand for more books by and about local writers. As more students become interested in reading national authors, they create a demand for further courses in, production by, and studies of, local writers. Once national writing begins to challenge the centrality of the British tradition, other new literatures are used to reinforce the demand that British studies be replaced with courses in national or other new cultures. And as the same social and political forces that created the new nations are also the energy behind the achievement of the writers from those countries, the attention given local authors and authors from other recently independent countries is indeed the study of some of the best contemporary literature.

3 New literatures and nationalisms

The new nations of the Commonwealth are a recent development of what has been a changing notion of a political state; the notion of a national literature would not, for example, have been appropriate when Europe was culturally unified through Rome and the use of Latin, nor are tribal oral literatures the equivalent of the written literature of a modern state with its diverse population and values. The same process of nation-building that led to the creation of national vernacular European literatures can be said to be still in progress in the new English-language states. I use the term 'state' purposely because the English literatures under discussion have emerged during a period when nation-states formed as a result of British imperialism are attempting to transform themselves into nations having the shared history, myths, habits and values of a people with a common culture. The large immigrant populations of Canada and Australia, the diverse racial stocks of India and the West Indies, the many tribes of Africa, the existence of large native populations within the white dominions of settlement, the problem of Francophonic Quebec in Canada, and the continuing conflict between settlers and Africans in South Africa are evidence that the newly independent English-speaking nation-states are still in the process of evolving towards the cultural and political homogeneity of long established nations. At the same time older nations have been shaken by ethnic, regional and micro-nationalist pressures which have challenged their supposed unity.

A brief examination of the modern concept of a nation

shows shared assumptions inherent to the new literatures. The evolution of feudal society into the European nation-states of the late Renaissance with their mythologies of divine kingship was followed by contractual theories of government during the seventeenth and eighteenth centuries. A poet, such as John Dryden in *Absalom and Achitophel* (1681), might attempt to refute the contractual argument by using the new High Tory myth that the king was the father of his people and inherited his rights from Adam's dominion over the earth, but the sacramental view of monarchy that had prevailed during Elizabethan and Jacobean rule was no longer accepted in England. Significantly, mythologies of the sun king or the patriarchal origins of government appeared during a time when government was being centralised. Rationalism and political changes destroyed the mythologies of divine appointment and required that the state be seen as a secular creation. Thomas Hobbes claimed the power of government derived from conquest or from the protection offered the ruled by the ruler. John Locke assumed the origin of government in those powerful, especially propertied interests who established an authority for their mutual benefit. As in Hobbes's theory of government, the implied assumption is that man naturally is at war with others to further his interests and that government is a contract accepted by society to contain man's predatory instincts.

It is perhaps only in seventeenth-century radical Protestant thought that an ideology of the state as representative of 'the people' is articulated. It was more common to see the state as a legal fiction having its origins in the utility of its functions. Thus in the late eighteenth century Samuel Johnson could assume that as people naturally come together to create societies for the mutual benefits derived, so they will create some form of government. Here again utility is the main theory for a state. In *Taxation No Tyranny* (1775) Johnson ridiculed the American demands for self-government. As a colony was established by the state for its own benefit, the colonial settler had no natural rights beyond those of any citizen either to accept the protection offered by the government or to rebel against established power and re-enter the state of nature where all men have equal right to all possessions.

That Johnson so strongly rejected natural rights as a basis of government shows that mid-seventeenth century radical theories of government derived from the consent of the people were becoming influential towards the end of the eighteenth century. The American Revolution, followed by the French Revolution, established the modern ideal of the state as an expression of the majority of the population. In Paris the Place du Trône was changed to the Place de la Nation. The representative and democratic ideas which began to predominate from the late eighteenth century onward were themselves reinforced by a mythology of the 'folk' and 'nation' which was part of Romanticism. Urbanisation and industrialisation had created a new, modern working class; such social change was accompanied by a nostalgia for rural life in contrast to the evils of industrialisation. Or, looked at more sceptically, the demand for representation by the new classes threatened the prerogatives of established society which in turn created a mythology of the rural peasantry as belonging to an organic, harmonious community destroyed by city life. Thus the radical demand for social justice for the people was paralleled by a romantic nostalgia for a folk culture unimpaired by industrialism.

For Europe the nineteenth century was the main period of the creation of nations. There was the long process of assembling Germany from its various states, the Greek struggle for independence, the emergence throughout the century of nations in Eastern Europe. Often the writers and intellectuals of the period sympathised with, even fought for, the independence of the smaller nations from their imposed governments and foreign dominance. Boswell championing Corsican independence, Byron in Greece, Shelley in Ireland are a few examples of what might be described as the association that developed between the Romantic writer and the right to national independence. By the late nineteenth century such Romantic involvement in national liberation had become stereotyped and was satirised in G. B. Shaw's *Arms and the Man* (1894), where the unheroic, unpatriotic but efficient Swiss middle class is contrasted to the sentimentalities of Byronism and nationalism.

It was not, however, until after the First World War that many of the nations of modern Europe became independent; the subsequent annexation of territory by Germany under Hitler and by the Soviet Union shows that the question of what is a nation remained still unsettled. In both Western and Eastern Europe there are today strong movements wanting a separate and independent nation for their region or language group. The independence of Malta, the incorporation of Estonia and Lithuania within the Soviet Union, the partition of Germany, and the activity of nationalist movements in Wales, Scotland, Brittany, Corsica, parts of Spain, Yugoslavia and Czechoslovakia show that nationalism remains a problem to Europe.

Nationalism often results from rapid urbanisation and industrialisation when a section of those who have participated in social changes challenge those in power. Nationalism is an urban movement which identifies with the rural areas as a source of authenticity, finding in the 'folk' the attitudes, beliefs, customs and language to create a sense of national unity among people who have other loyalties or who feel threatened by the conflicts and alienation of urban life. Nationalism aims at group solidarity, cultural purity and dignity, a typicality in the lower orders (worker or peasant) and rejection of cosmopolitan upper classes, intellectuals and others likely to be influenced by foreign ideas. Nationalist movements attempt to define a 'little tradition' of the folk or the past which will serve as a basis for a mass culture. Images of a noble past will be used to overcome a modern sense of fragmentation and loss of identity.[1] By stressing authenticity nationalist movements attempt to legitimatise demands for unity both of purpose and of communality. Nationalism attempts to overcome the division of labour and the loss of older stable identities in modern society, although nationalism is in itself a means of modernising mass society, especially through the appeal of participation.

Nationalism develops after there has been social disruption

through industrialisation, war, rapid increases of wealth, rapid accumulation of population into large cities, or whatever combination of events disrupts traditional social relationships. Industrialisation, urbanisation and new wealth particularly create new classes which will demand political power. Doctrines of equality, the rights of man and the sovereignty of the people have strongly contributed to modern nationalism. As rising expectations are not met, nationalist groups form which turn to the general population to support demands for more participation and the sharing of the fruits of production.

The catalysts of nationalism are proto-elites who are or feel excluded from power. Usually they activate the urban lower-middle and lower classes, bringing together people who might not otherwise feel they share a similar historical background. The proto-elites organise the masses, synthesise various elements into a national culture and separate the 'folk' from those who do not share in the new communal goals. To achieve synthesis nationalists need scholarship to find symbolisms, evidence of a folk culture, a usable history. Often these proto-elites come from other backgrounds than the masses; they have been educated abroad or belong to groups that are marginal to the rural and ethnic population. It is this difference which creates their need to identify with the people or nation.

Nationalism develops in the cities because it is there that social change and dislocation is most pronounced. It is also in rapidly expanding cities that rural ethnic groups come into conflict with foreigners or culturally 'foreign' natives who control the economy and dominant positions of status. As new workers gather in the cities as a result of industrialisation, nationalism spreads from the intellectuals to the middle classes to the urban proletariat, and from industrial centres to the towns. Eventually the movement is brought to rural areas which, unlike the cities, retain a local traditional culture undisturbed by modernisation and therefore feel no need for nationalism. Nationalism is thus an urban movement with a built-in conflict between modernisation and the positing of authentic culture in the past, rural areas, or pre-industrialised groups.

It is the conflict within nationalism between modernisation

and authenticity which produces the well-known phenomenon in developing nations of wanting western industry, science and material goods while rejecting European culture or the kind of secular, rational, sceptical mentality that has usually accompanied industrialisation. But as its claim to authenticity is the defence of traditional culture, and as it needs the symbols of tradition to obtain and remain in power, a nationalist movement will find itself imprisoned in a paradox which in turn provides its dynamism, its despair and its outbursts of rage.

Once self-government is obtained, advances which bring about increased standards of living, higher literacy, participation of the masses in elections and other forms of modernisation weaken what remains of traditional culture and therefore weaken the supposed authenticity of the newly independent state. Moreover, the masses who were enlisted in the struggle for freedom have gained a new consciousness of themselves as the nation and are likely to expect social and material advances that the government cannot provide. Social anomy, bitterness, reaction and various forms of demagogy, repression or state-led nationalism (as the ruling elite attempts to regain the leadership role it had before independence) are likely to follow.

While such traumas are more likely in recently created nations, in which independence was obtained from a foreign power, and where the state has no long tradition of authority, they will also occur less dramatically, and in more moderate forms, in other nations where rising expectations can only be met by the importation of foreign capital, industry, experts, professors and skilled labour. An often observed consequence of national independence is that as colonial administrators depart they are replaced by twice as many international experts needed by the new nation as part of its development. In recent practice this has usually meant Americans replacing Englishmen, although in some nations the new class of foreign experts may come from such nations as Canada, Australia or Nigeria. This new class and the industrial development with which it is associated is seen as a neo-colonialism and produces a neo-nationalist reaction. Because of the inherent dialectic between progress and authenticity within a new nation, there will be cycles of nationalism followed by internationalism, followed by more nationalism. Periods of rapid industrial growth, new wealth or disruptive social change will usually be followed by retreats into a search for roots, national values and traditions. Large-scale immigration, accompanied by a need to acculturate the new populace, will also breed nationalist phases. With the expansion of international trade, nationalism is likely to occur in many countries simultaneously.

The writer in a new nation usually is a member of the proto-elite that led the drive for independence. As one of the educated, the writer belongs to the group that is created by the ruling power to inherit the machinery of the state; but even more than the lawyer, politician or doctor, the writer is likely to feel an intensification of the conflict between the values of tradition and those of the colonising power. Most writers in modern times come from the bourgeoisie; in a colonial society the writer is likely to belong to the rising new class which, having obtained education or urban careers, is in the vanguard of the nationalist movement.

It will often be found that writers are produced by families that themselves have links with cultural traditions. Often in Africa the writer has a father or grandfather who was a teller of traditional tales, a tribal priest, or a member of a traditional cultural elite. The family has converted to Christianity within recent generations and has emphasised European behaviour. It is in rebellion against such 'gentility' that the writer turns towards the 'little tradition' of the folk, the past, or towards an internationalism. In the older dominions of settlement, writers often have teachers for parents, an amateur writer for a father, or a painter for a brother, and are likely to come from older, settled stock in contrast to new immigrants. (Jewish writers are an exception.)

For the writer the 'little tradition' of the people, with its folk songs, dialect, dances, popular ballads and regional customs will be in contrast to the 'great tradition' of English literature, with its formalism, standard English usage and European humanism. While the specific adjustment each writer will make to this conflict will be shaped primarily by personal and national circumstances, his or her creativity is likely to be a result of the attempt at resolution and the continuing tensions within it. Those unable to find the substance of art or to be at ease within the community in the 'little tradition', will remain outsiders, nostalgic for elite values of the past. The writings of V. S. Naipaul are perhaps the classic case of the latter situation, but such a perspective is also noticeable in the work of T. S. Eliot and Henry James among American authors. If the romanticisation of a foreign high culture leads to expatriation, a similar nostalgia also exists in writers who posit values or ideals in the local past. Chinua Achebe's village novels of Nigerian tribal life, Patrick White's ironic celebrations of the early Australian explorers and settlers, James McAuley's concern with Australian Pacific history, and E. J. Pratt's Canadian historical narratives are each in its own way an attempt to locate heroic values in national history in contrast to the cities and the middle classes. Middle-class life is usually seen as devitalised, inorganic, alien and yet provincial. Examples of such a response to the urban conditions which produce nationalism can be seen in the nineteenth-century American literature that idealised the frontier and in the 'Irish Revival' with its identification of nation with myth, land, folk and the untouched islands of the west. (Thus such writers as Mark Twain or J. M. Synge will often be found to have influenced New Zealand, Canadian, Australian, West Indian and African authors.)

Since nationalism starts in the cities as a modernising movement and seeks its symbols of authenticity in the countryside and in the past, there are unresolvable tensions within it, although leaders, governments and philosophers will seek forms of rhetorical resolution in which increased standards of living, industrialisation, the expansion of education and the training of more modern workers will somehow be reconciled with traditional, non-urban or folk values. While it is tempting to argue that a national literature comes of age when it begins to treat the modern city realistically, and as a symbol of national culture, instead of the land and the past, this would be only partly true. The fiction of Cyprian Ekwensi in Nigeria,

Morley Callaghan in Canada and H. G. de Lisser in Jamaica treats of urban subject-matter. The romanticisation of the peasant, village and past as the true sources of national life often follows a period of urban literature and is a reaction to recent social change. It is, however, true that as a national literature develops it will focus increasingly on the problems of modern urban life or judge concepts of authenticity by contemporary standards. The subject-matter of the novel moves from exoticism and history to realism, protest, cultural assertion and then to the treatment of the psychology of individuals and personal problems.

This progress of literature from the exotic to realism to the individual is, however, complicated by the dialectic within nationalism of rural and urban, past and modern. If later writing is less assertive of the past as the authentic national culture, it will continue to explore history nostalgically for 'roots', 'seeds', or usable cultural myths. The neo-nationalism of the later 1960s and early 1970s, with its concern for ecology, conservation and community participation, is a period swing from identification with the modern state to a search for more 'authentic' values in the national or ethnic past. Margaret Atwood's *Surfacing* (1972) in Canada, Edward Brathwaite's poetry in the West Indies, Wole Soyinka's *Season of Anomy* (1973) in Nigeria and Nadine Gordimer's *Conservationist* (1974) in South Africa are examples of a recent radicalism which has located authenticity or the source of contemporary problems in the national past. If nationalism rejects the colonial culture of the elite, neo-nationalism sees the modern state as neo-colonial and an expression of a lingering or a new foreign imperialism. The city, which was once the symbol of foreign values, in contrast to the rural peasantry, once more becomes the image of national corruption, a Babylon and the source of injustices resulting from international capitalism. In *Surfacing* the main character leaves the city for northern Quebec in what becomes an exploration of the sources of her identity, while *Season of Anomy* concludes with a cleansing journey back towards the communalistic tribal village. In Kenya Samuel Kahiga sets his novel of disillusionment, *Girl From Abroad* (1974), in the capital, while Ngugi wa Thiong'o's *Petals of Blood* explicitly contrasts the African countryside with the city of the corrupt ruling elite.

The expansion of education is influential in the development of nationalism and national literatures. When qualifications for elite positions can only be obtained abroad and when there are few local graduates in government and professional careers, the model for social and cultural advancement will be the imperial power which staffs elite positions. With the expansion of local education, proto-elites are created who, in demanding advancement, resort to national symbols. As the proto-elite gains power and must fulfil raised mass expectations, education will be further expanded. This brings into modern urban society classes which formerly were outside the channels of power and which become producers and consumers of a new national culture. Each stage in the development of the new literatures has been marked both by an increase in education and by urbanisation. The post-war years, for example, not only saw universities established in Nigeria and the West Indies; new universities were created in Australia, New Zealand and Canada. Such universities produced graduates who did not feel that they had to imitate British models to gain social and professional advancement.[2] Often the literature of England was foreign to them. (Sometimes American literature was closer to their style of life or aspirations.) This new class wanted recognition of their own national culture, and, most important, provided a market for local writing.

There is a close relationship between economic conditions, society, politics and new literatures. Culture requires an elite of producers and consumers. Writers, literary critics and teachers are specialists. In a colonial society in which the urban educated population is small there is little market for the arts and an insufficient density of talent for specialisation. If some of the leading African writers have also been scholars, trade-union leaders, politicians, or even presidents of their country, many early Australian, Indian and New Zealand writers also were all-rounders, or amateurs, for whom literature was but one means of expression and often a means of political expression. The handful of local graduates had to fulfil many functions in their society—from political leaders to artists—without there being a sufficient local market for their work in the arts. With urbanisation, the expansion of education and the development of a local educated class, specialisation becomes possible and a market develops for its products. Urbanisation and the expansion of education therefore produce writers, a public, and a local professional class who will identify with the literature as national, in contrast to the past when literature was either imported as part of the culture of the ruler or when local writing appeared to belong to a small group of amateurs who supposedly could not make the grade in foreign metropolitan centres.

While the appearance of professional literary criticism and university courses of study is essential for the spread of the reputation of local writers to the community, an awareness of a national literature depends on a reader's sense of belonging to a nation. Canadian literature, for example, was marked by a feeling of regions and provinces before the rise of post-Second World War nationalism.

Similarly, West Indian authors and literary critics were often associated with a specific country, such as Jamaica or Guyana, before the West Indian Federation of 1958–62 brought about an awareness of a broader community. The effect of inter-island communications in the West Indies (in the form of the B.B.C. *Caribbean Voices* programme and the publication of authors from throughout the region by the Barbados-based journal *Bim*) can probably be paralleled elsewhere. It was only after there were national radio networks, national television and easy means of transportation by road and air that a sense of national identity could be felt by those separated by great distances in Australia, Canada or New Zealand, or by religion, language or clan in Nigeria and India. But the rapidity of modern communications and travel also brings the nation more closely into contact with the rest of the modern world. The same empathy and involvement with other people needed for modernisation will standardise values and cause a reaction; fear of integration results in the assertion of differences. The communications network necessary for a new nation also contributes to its cultural self-consciousness.

A national literature in English is thus in part the product of urbanisation and modernisation. Oral African literature, Indian spirituality or Australian outback ballads may shape style and themes of a local literature in English, but a national literature in English involves the transplant of European literature to foreign lands, the creation of local elites who imitate that literature, adopt it for their purposes, and reshape it in accordance to local life, as their perspective of what is significant is transformed from European to national society. This perspective may at first be self-conscious and limited to local colour, protest and cultural assertion; eventually as local society becomes aware of itself the perspective will become less self-conscious, more natural and concerned with individual lives, although changing social conditions will create neo-nationalist movements which will influence literature. Such writers as Michael Anthony in Trinidad, Margaret Laurence in Canada, and Kamala Das in India, write about the problems of society or themselves without the self-conscious nationalist cultural assertion evident in earlier literature.

Although a new literature evolves with the rise of a local, urban, educated middle class, it will often turn against the local bourgeoisie. In this it is not different from other movements of modern literature which in recent centuries have been anti-middle class. Even those writers who reject nationalist values will attack middle-class life as devitalised and will seek value in universals, myth or some 'great tradition'. Literary nationalism is a local branch of the general revolt in European and westernised culture against the effects of industrialism and urbanisation. Instead of the division of labour, highly specialised, often monotonous jobs, increased social divisions, and feelings of cultural confusion and the anomy of the city, the writer seeks an organic, vital, authentic, satisfying vision of life in other cultural ideas. The more sophisticated the writer the more complex, and probably ironic, will be the treatment of such ideals. Achebe's nostalgia for an organic tribal culture acknowledges that there were injustices in the villages and that even former African societies underwent social changes and divisions of opinion; Patrick White's unconventional Australian heroes are often treated with irony. It is the shared awareness of the modern existential condition, in which there are no fixed values, and the desire for an ideal or harmonious vision of reality that give the new national literatures an apparently universal relevance while treating local subject-matter.

The neo-nationalism of recent decades is international. The nationalism which followed the Second World War was a direct product of the war, with its rhetoric of self-determination, the Atlantic and United Nations Charters, the British Labour government, the collapse of British power internationally, and the increased influence of the United States during the Cold War. The independence of the older dominions was accompanied or followed by the handing over of power in India and Africa. The mood of decolonisation, including the examples of liberation struggles in Cuba, Algeria and elsewhere in the Third World, returned to the United States and provided an example for black Americans and other ethnic groups at a time when the war in Vietnam and American involvement throughout the world had created extreme disillusionment with the values of the government and western liberalism. Liberalism, with its dynamic of international free trade, expanding capitalism, and cultural relativism, tends towards an indirect form of imperialism. The techniques of international trade, investment and modernisation export the values, methods and educational system of the stronger nation to the weaker, making the latter economically and culturally imitative of the former. The reliance of developing nations upon international corporations and experts creates a situation where independence does not necessarily lead to economic and cultural self-determination and may, indeed, result in a greater entanglement with foreign powers. But at the same time imperial expansion leads to a relativism which questions its own values. Thus disillusionment with the ruling liberal establishment within the United States and throughout the West paralleled disillusionment with independence in new nations. As a result of modern communication, travel and study, anti-establishment attitudes and ideas spread quickly throughout the world, influenced by the supposedly successful communalism of Cuba, China and other Third World socialist states. The demands of the 1960s and '70s for a 'popular-folk' culture and for social justice for the masses erupted along with anti-Americanism, anti-white attitudes, demands for local government, the assertion of non-Northern-European, non-elite, ethnic 'roots', and neo-nationalisms. While local circumstances shaped the exact form of this wave of protest, the demands for greater democracy, ethnicity, authenticity and folk power were international.

As often in the past, nationalism was part of what might be described as an international movement. Its source of power was among the young in the cities and universities, and its method of leadership and propaganda depended upon the mass media. Once again the cities and the educated had created a nationalist movement in protest against the ruling establishments. And it is observable that once more nationalism or the demand for ethnicity was part of a wave of social change in which urban groups that felt excluded from power challenged the older ruling elites and mobilised support by championing power for the poor, mass participation in government and culture, and the usual aims of nationalist and ethnic movements.

If nationalism is based on an internal conflict between modernisation (which essentially means urbanisation, industrialisation, internationalism and metropolitan standards) and ethnic traditionalism, and if literary creativity is often dependent upon education within the 'great tradition', it is not surprising that the writers of the new nations have taken a variety of positions towards national and international cultures. These range from V. S. Naipaul's early desire to be part of a great cultural tradition, or A. D. Hope's attempt to integrate Australian poetry to the mainstream of western culture, to the emphasis on tribal culture in the works of Achebe, Soyinka and Brathwaite. Whereas many writers have tried to identify national culture with the landscape, the folk, or some protest movement, the major writers have envisaged encompassing myths to overcome the fragmentation of culture brought about by modernisation and social change. Such myths, whether of a lost organic African culture or of eternal universal processes, are personal and national responses to the effects of industrialisation, urbanisation and middle-class styles of life.

In the European movements of the nineteenth century language mattered greatly to nationalists. Usually a language used in a rural region or by the peasantry was elevated into a symbol of identification with the authentic nation in contrast to the alien language of the rulers. In the new English-speaking nations, the choice of language is also controversial. Nigeria and India would use a local language if it were possible, but it has proved impossible since whatever language is chosen will be as alien as English to a large portion of the population and will therefore represent the domination of a tribe, religion or section of the nation over others. For writers in the new English-speaking nations, whether Nigeria or Australia, the problem is local versus standard British usage. In colonial countries standard British usage was associated with the wealthy, the educated and those in power. Those who spoke a dialect or pidgin or used a local accent were looked down upon as uneducated, uncivilised or lower class. The nationalist consequently attempts to reverse the status of local and standard English, seeing in the former the language of the people and in the latter the language of the coloniser.

While the nationalist writer will seldom use a pure folk dialect, which would make him unintelligible to his middle-class and often foreign readership, he will attempt to create a literary form that approximates indigenous speech. Thus the Jamaican English of V. S. Reid's *New Day*, the Igboised English of Achebe, the Yorubaised poetry of Soyinka, the New Zealand colloquialism of Sargeson, and the Indianised English of Rao and Anand. While the creation of a local literary language is an attack on middle-class 'alien' values, it is an essential step in the creation of a new literature. When local writers must be careful to write 'correct' British English, they feel a divorce of the written language from their own speech, and being overly conscious of foreign standards will be imitative. Before a major writer shows how to use local speech successfully, the national literature will be hampered by attempts to write educated English and the inartistic use of dialect, usually as part of local colour. Once a writer, such as Achebe or Sargeson, has shown how local speech can be used seriously and artistically, the problem of language will no longer be of prime importance, although it will remain an issue for nationalist politicians and intellectuals. The writer will have a range of options available from standard British English to various registers of local speech which he can use as appropriate to his needs, characters and inclinations.[3] Soyinka's plays or Narayan's novels are unpredictable, even inconsistent in their use of registers of English. While it is incorrect to assume that a national literature must be based on local forms of English, it is necessary for writers to be freed from their 'bondage' to standard British usage before they can feel free to use their own voice and to imitate the community.

Because of the wish to shift the focus of the arts to the 'people', nationalist literature is often narrated from the perspective of the community, or places the main character's life against national events or within a highly visible local society. Such African and West Indian writers as Achebe, Ngugi, Selvon, Errol John, C. L. R. James and Roger Mais have used variations of the communal narrative form. Achebe's creation of a narrative perspective which reflects the values of the tribal village is discussed in Chapter 4. In the older dominions, such as Australia and New Zealand, 'authenticity' has more often been portrayed through the imitation of the speech and thoughts of an uneducated man and, usually, his 'mate', who lives close to the land, outside middle-class society. This is discussed more fully in Chapter 8.

It would appear that the new English literatures have developed during periods of nationalism and are related to the same social and economic conditions which produce nationalism. Nationalism is, in itself, a recurring political phenomenon which is often influenced by the effects of international political developments on local society. The writer is usually a member of the middle class, or someone educated into the colonial elite, who questions or rejects the values of his class and seeks a more rewarding way of life either in the 'little tradition' (of the local past, the peasants, the land) or the 'great tradition' (of imperial, European or international modern culture). The appearance of significant writers is often related to a local journal and some intellectual group that is either associated with political movements or an expression of cultural aspirations reflecting social changes. In the West Indies, for example, the main periods of literary creativity began with the MacDermot, de Lisser and McKay circle in pre-First World War Jamaica, followed by the *Trinidad* and *Beacon* groups of middle-class rebels in Trinidad during the early 1930s. *Bim* (1942–) started in Barbados as a journal for progressive middle-class intellectuals. Both *Kyk-over-al* in Guyana (1945–61) and Edna Manley's *Focus* (1943, '48, '56, '60) were linked to local political movements. More recently the Caribbean Artists Movement and their journal *Savacou* have been associated with such writers as Edward Brathwaite and Andrew Salkey. In West Africa *Black Orpheus* and the Mbari club and its publications were influential to the emergence of Nigerian writing. *The Bulletin* in Australia during the 1890s is another instance of such a publication, as are *Southerly* (1939–) and *Meanjin* (1940–) during the Second World War. Sometimes the publications and circle of writers are associated with a newly founded college or university, such as the University of the West Indies or Ibadan University, both founded in 1948.

While it may be felt that my comments about the social foundations of the new national literatures are largely based upon events during recent decades, especially in the Third World, it will be found that they are applicable, with minor modifications, to colonial writing. The social and psychological setting of Thomas Chandler Haliburton, perhaps the first significant Canadian writer, is analogous to that which provided the context of, say, Nigerian literature. The northern emigration of loyalists to the Maritimes during and after the American Revolution radically 'transformed what was essentially a scattered frontier of New England farmers, giving it a varied class structure, a multiplication of specialized trades, a temporary influx of capital, and a new political and cultural orientation'.[4] Bitterly anti-American, often better educated than the local Presbyterian farmers, the loyalists became a Tory Anglican gentry and founded King's College at Windsor. During the next fifty years the population of Nova Scotia increased by 500 per cent; but from 1815 to the middle of the 1830s Nova Scotia underwent an economic and social crisis which caused increased dependence upon the government and demands for reforms.

Haliburton, who was educated at King's College, came from a Tory family. His father was of pre-loyalist Nova Scotian stock; his mother was the daughter of loyalists. A member of the Legislative Assembly, he sensed the need for change but distrusted the reformers. He wanted to be an eighteenth-century conservative while arguing for the need to adopt American enterprise. To make Nova Scotians aware of their heritage and resources he wrote *A General Description of Nova Scotia* (1823) and *An Historical and Statistical Account of Nova Scotia* (1829). A member of the Literary Club of Halifax, he met Joseph Howe, editor of the *Novascotian*, in whose paper he first published serially *The Clockmaker; or, the Sayings and Doings of Samuel Slick* (1835). *The Clockmaker*'s combination of early eighteenth-century essay with American folk humour reflects the author's attitudes behind the anecdotes, a mixture of Burkean social conservatism and the propagandising of Yankee values of thrift, industry and practicality. The anecdotal form, use of Yankee dialect, and humorous satire made Haliburton internationally famous and contributed to the development of one tradition of North American comic literature.

The new national literatures are influenced by, and often express if only to reject, the same economic and social changes that create the nationalist movements which develop from time to time within a country. As such movements are themselves often influenced by international political and economic forces, the new literatures are also influenced by the prevailing sensibility within the English-speaking community of nations—besides being influenced by fashionable literary models or techniques. Literary style and social change are often related.

Thus the new national English literatures are part of international western culture and go through similar literary movements. There are two opposite leanings within each national literature, towards local assertion and towards a metropolitan point of view; this reflects the dialectic within nationalist movements of traditionalism and modernism. A national literature swings back and forth between these two tendencies. The most achieved writing tends to be either metropolitan-oriented or explores the problem of nationalism in sophisticated ways. Nationalism tends towards realistic and naturalistic styles and has generally been associated with the political left or occasionally with the extreme right. Poets, however, are unable to develop colloquial and realistic styles into a useful idiom for high levels of achievement. They are more likely to need an *avant-garde* mode to express their views of authenticity.

Nationalism and naturalism are continuing literary forces even after independence; the contradictions within nationalism are likely to result in the development of new, more extreme nationalist positions at the same time as the nation achieves 'modernisation'. A reversal then takes place in which elite writers will explore myth and use *avant-garde* styles as a means of asserting authenticity, while a bourgeois realist literature will develop concerned more with recording the problems of modern lives than with treating of large cultural themes. As a literature evolves, the elite or high cultural tradition will progressively utilise more of the techniques associated with nationalists. It is likely that the previous tendencies will continue, as they reflect common aspirations and instincts inherent within any culture: the affirmation of local dignity and traditions, the exploration of the problems of modern society, and the attraction towards a cosmopolitan sophistication and a place in world culture.

4 Nigeria I: the beginnings and Achebe

Poems and stories appeared in newspapers along the coast of West Africa from the late nineteenth century onward, and in 1911 the Ghanaian nationalist leader J. E. Casely-Hayford, influenced by Edward Blyden, published a novel of ideas, *Ethiopia Unbound*, which, in arguing for the value of tribal culture and for the need to create universities which express the authentic African personality, anticipated many of the topics found in later nationalist writing. If the newspapers published no lasting literature, they had in Nigeria by the 1920s and '30s printed, as serials, a few novels of interest as reflections of their time—Isaac Thomas's *Segilola* and Mohammed Duse's *A Daughter of the Pharaohs*. Dennis Chukude Osadebay's *Africa Sings* (1952) includes verse he had written between 1930 and 1950. It might be considered representative of what J. P. Clark has called 'pioneer poetry in English by Africans'. The style consists of hand-me-down phrases, generalisations and pious thoughts. Osadebay's Africa is generalised; there are no details, no precise descriptions. Clark has described such early African poetry:

> The very name Africa is 'like a bell to toll' them back to their glorious past of 'tall palm trees', 'cool breezes wafting over pleasant lagoons', 'bare-breasted virgins, and simple trusting men of brains and brawn treacherously lured into slavery abroad' and loss of 'human dignity' at home.[1]

By contrast the poetry published in the 1960s by Clark and Christopher Okigbo was closer in style to Gerald Manley Hopkins, Ezra Pound, T. S. Eliot and other modern poets. Beginning with an *avant-garde* idiom they gradually incorporated characteristics of oral literature into their later verse.

The seeds of modern Nigerian literature were planted by the social changes that took place in West Africa during the Second World War. As a result of the expansion of the economy during and after the war, such cities as Lagos, Port Harcourt, Enugu and Kano grew quickly, while labour unions rapidly developed from 4,300 members in 1940 to 30,000 in 1955.[2] The rapid industrialisation and urbanisation led to increased prices, strikes, nationalist activity, and constitutional reform. In 1944 the National Council of Nigeria was formed, bringing together trade unions, intellectuals, tribal unions and politicians into a nationalist movement. By 1954 Nigeria was on the way towards self-government. Economic expansion created more participation in the modern society and led to the extension of the system of highways which linked up what had been distant parts of the country to national commerce. Internal airlines contributed to communication. The growth of the economy and the need to staff the government with Nigerians led to the rapid development of educational opportunities at all levels. A new elite was created which wanted a return to African cultural values.

In Ghana, R. E. Obeng's *Eighteen Pence* (1941)[3] appeared with its haphazard mixture of moral tales, adventures, descriptions of African customs and illustrations of the usefulness of western educational and agricultural methods. The digressions, the meandering story of the hero's rise from poverty to riches, and the triumph of Christianity anticipate Amos Tutuola's narratives and are an expression of the many Africans at the time making the transition from traditional to modern society. Obeng's fluent but unidiomatic English is similar to the novel, a sign of someone between two cultures.

A few years later there was a spurt of pamphlet literature published in Onitsha, the main Igbo commercial city in eastern Nigeria. E. N. Obiechina explains that the appearance of this popular literature coincided with an expansion of literacy, 'the sudden population explosion, the drift of a large number of people from the villages into the towns, the rapid increase in Nigerian-owned and operated printing presses'[4] during and after the Second World War. The material in the pamphlets ranges from instruction manuals to fiction. The common link between the publications is that they show how to survive or get ahead in modern westernised society. They are written for the semi-educated, new city-dweller who wants to know how to write applications, pass examinations, speak at a meeting, carry on a love affair, and how city people are expected to behave.

Although they were not published until later, Cyprian Ekwensi started writing short stories during the mid-1940s. A graduate of Government College, Ibadan, Yaba Higher College, Lagos, and Achimota College, Ghana, Ekwensi's first book was a collection, *Ikola the Wrestler and Other Ibo Tales* (1947), based on stories he had learned from his parents. The same year he was commissioned to write and broadcast stories, usually of urban life, for Radio Nigeria. He joined the newly founded Scribblers' Club in Lagos, which included T. M. Aluko and Mabel Dove-Danquah. Their first publication, *African New Writing* (1947), included fourteen short stories.[5] A Lagos bookshop commissioned Ekwensi to write *When Love Whispers* (1948), a forty-four page romantic story which was published in Onitsha. It sold over two thousand copies and is among the early examples of Onitsha marketplace literature.

From his short stories of urban life Ekwensi pieced together the first modern realistic novel published in English-speaking West Africa, *People of the City* (1954). It was the first West African novel written in English to describe the cultural and moral confusion that had developed among those who had moved to the cities. Sango, a reporter and dance-band leader, is a bachelor with a 'desire to forge ahead'; 'beneath his gay exterior lay a nature serious and determined to carve for itself a place of renown in this city of opportunities'. 'To him the past was dead. A man made a promise to a girl yesterday because he was selfish and wanted her *yesterday*. Today was a new day.'[6]

The girls Sango meets and loves are motivated by similar ambitions for advancement and experience regardless of the cost. The move from country to city, the attempt to live a foreign style of life, results in a loss of values. Ekwensi, fascinated by such a life, is implicitly a moralist who makes the reader conscious that the attractions of the city are paid for by spiritual loss. The city is cruel, violent and corrupt. But the city is also representative of a new nation that will soon become independent.

Sango's exploration of urban life is set against a backdrop of an emerging national political consciousness. The two are related. Demands for justice and freedom have become mixed with the fight for political power. The independence movement of the period is sketched in: 'The British have given us a new constitution . . . Yes, things are gradually passing into African hands. Soon all power will be in our hands . . . Politics is life . . . and one day we'll get what we're fighting for: complete autonomy.' The now often forgotten role of the unions, especially the miners, in the rise of nationalism is noted: 'Sango had heard of the coal crisis which broke out in the Eastern Greens, of the twenty-one miners who had been shot down by policemen under orders from "the imperialists".' 'Sango discovered that this shooting had become a cementing factor for the nation. The whole country, north, east and west of the Great River, had united and with one loud voice condemned the action of the British Government in being so trigger-happy and hasty. Rival political parties had united in the emergency and were acting for the entire nation.' It is significant of the symbolic effect of Gandhi and the Indian nationalist movement to West Africa that the death in the novel of De Pereira, 'the greatest nationalist of all time', is compared with Gandhi's: '"It's like the death of Gandhi," Sango said. "De Pereira was, after all, our own Gandhi!"'

Set against the new nationalist forces with which Sango identifies are the old order of upper-class Africans who hold chieftaincies, who became wealthy under colonialism, and who profit from national corruption. Beatrice's father belongs to the Ufemfe society, which demands the blood sacrifice of the eldest son as the price of membership:

> He believed in the Realisation Party, though people accused it of belonging to the 'upper classes'. And why not? Was he himself not of the upper classes? . . . 'I believe in the past,' the old man said, when the meal was over. It is when you know the past that you can appreciate the present. We need something like the Realisation Party to preserve our kingship, our music, art and religion!'

A noticeable feature of African literature just before and after independence is the clash of generations. The old are usually corrupt, traditionalist, poorly educated and pawns of the colonisers. The young, more western in education and style of living, are progressive and sympathetic to the poor. Later, in *Jagua Nana* (1961), the story of a Lagos prostitute, Ekwensi will record the extreme violence and corruption that entered Nigerian politics with independence.

The publication in 1952 of Amos Tutuola's *The Palm-Wine Drinkard* (written 1946) suddenly put Nigeria on the English-speaking literary map. Here was something unexpected, odd, and clearly African. Chief D. O. Fagunwa had established a reputation among his tribesmen for 'expanding the Yoruba folk-tale into an extended story',[7] using a mixture of stylish Yoruba prose and Christian precepts. Tutuola, whose education ended shortly after primary school, tried something similar in English, although his English was insecure and he often relied upon the direct transliteration of Yoruba idioms into strange combinations of English words. Clearly influenced by his reading of Fagunwa's stories, *Pilgrim's Progress*, the Bible, and probably *Gulliver's Travels*, and by his familiarity with Yoruba story-telling, Tutuola clustered together various adventures around the traditional quest motif common to many folk literatures. His basic rhetorical devices are those of the story-teller, and the main tale, the quest for the dead palm-wine tapper, is linked to a sacrificial myth involving the pacification of the heavens to end famine. Around this core there are riddles, creation myths, moral parables, wonders, personifications, and other materials common to many folk cultures. There are also such revealing instances of westernisation influencing folk culture as: 'The middle of the ashes rose up suddenly and at the same time there appeared a half-bodied baby, he was talking with a lower voice like a telephone.'[8]

While it is tempting to dismiss *The Palm-Wine Drinkard* as an odd mutant of two cultures, it is similar to Obeng's novel in reflecting the transition between tradition and modernisation. Tutuola's novels and Onitsha marketplace literature developed from a large class of people who lacked the formal education to enter the westernised middle classes, but who, by virtue of some education and by living in cities, inhabited a world no longer limited to tribal culture. Tutuola represents a link between the Yoruba tales of Fagunwa and the later imaginative use of Yoruba myth in the writings of Wole Soyinka.

Although drama had been performed in Lagos since the late nineteenth century, it was in the 1940s, beginning with Hubert Ogunde, that theatre became nationally important; this was the consequence of touring companies performing political plays in Yoruba, and later in Yoruba and English. Such vernacular theatre was an expression of post-war nationalism. Ogunde's plays included *Strike and Hunger* (1945), *Worse than Crime* (1945), *Towards Liberty* (1947) and *Bread and Bullets* (1950).[9]

By contrast, the first published Nigerian dramatist in English wrote plays, to be used in West African schools, which preached the need for westernisation. In his 'Preface' to the three plays in *This Is Our Chance*, James Ene Henshawe complains that even the best foreign drama lacks immediacy for African audiences. Although his plays make use of what were to become the usual themes of early Nigerian literature—cultural and generational conflict—they lack any African texture beyond setting and a few customs. Just as Henshawe's preface fails to distinguish between Nigeria and West Africa, so two of the three plays are set in a West African village that could be anywhere. Such vagueness was common in English-speaking Africa in the 1950s before national independence fixed the borders firmly between the former colonies, and is analogous to the regionalism found in other new literatures before the emergence of a national society. The title play, *This Is Our Chance*, is a plea for the virtues of progress and modernity and for the Christian virtue of turning the other cheek. 'The world outside moves fast, my Lord, and we must move with it. This is our chance.'[10] The conflict between authenticity and progress is portrayed as a generational conflict, with the sons and daughters holding westernised values.

The opening of University College, Ibadan (now the University of Ibadan) in 1948 was influential in the development of Nigerian literature. Soyinka, Clark, Achebe and Okigbo were among those who attended. The University brought together a national elite before the independence period and provided a setting for new developments in the arts. There is a deeper awareness of cultural issues and of the standards of serious literature among the Ibadan graduates than previous writers. A significant event in the emergence of Nigerian literature before the publication of Achebe's *Things Fall Apart* (1958) was the founding by J. P. Clark of *The Horn* (1954), a student poetry journal at the University of Ibadan. Christopher Okigbo was among its contributors. Such journals, which might be of little importance in countries with established outlets for young writers, are necessary in new nations. Achebe, for example, began by publishing short stories in the Ibadan *University Herald* as early as 1952. It was not until the appearance of *Black Orpheus* (1957) and the establishment of the Mbari Club and its pamphlets, that a sufficient mass of talents and means of publication were available to create a sense of a dynamic national literature consciously involved in the intellectual movements of its time. *Black Orpheus* and the Mbari Press (1961) became the centre for English-speaking black African writing during the late 1950s and early '60s, and published authors from Ghana and South Africa. Besides Achebe, Clark, Okigbo and Soyinka, such foreign literary critics as Ulli Beier and Gerald Moore were part of the Ibadan circle.

The close relationship between the rapid growth of Nigerian literature and the social, cultural and economic changes in West Africa after the Second World War is indicated by Achebe's comment: 'The nationalist movement in British West Africa after the Second World War brought about a mental revolution which began to reconcile us to ourselves. It suddenly seemed that we too might have a story to tell.'[11] The rising nationalist movement Ekwensi noted in *People of the City* is the origin of the cultural assertion in *Things Fall Apart*.

With the publication of *Things Fall Apart* (1958) Nigeria had the classic book that would serve as a point of reference and comparison for future writing. The novel was not only more competent than anything that had preceded it, but it also introduced techniques that liberated future African novelists from having to imitate the conventions of a western literary genre. The omniscient narrator of the opening paragraphs is representative of the voice of the community and introduces the story with simple, somewhat repetitive sentences in an approximation of a story-teller, thus associating the novel with Igbo traditional oral literature. In contrast to the literary device of a first-person narrator which makes us see events through the eyes of the individual speaker, Achebe's narrator makes us part of the awareness and vision of a small, apparently self-enclosed community of nine villages. We are immediately introduced to the traditions of the community, its history and myths, its arts and crafts:

> Okonkwo was well known throughout the nine villages and even beyond. His fame rested on solid personal achievements. As a young man of eighteen he had brought honour to his village by throwing Amalinze the Cat. Amalinze was the great wrestler who for seven years was unbeaten from Umuofia to Mbaino. He was called the Cat because his back would never touch the earth. It was this man that Okonkwo threw in a fight which the old man agreed was one of the fiercest since the founder of their town engaged a spirit of the wild for seven days and seven nights.
>
> The drums beat and the flutes sang and the spectators held their breath. Amalinze was a wily craftsman, but Okonkwo was as slippery as a fish in water. Every nerve and every muscle stood out on their arms, on their backs and their thighs, and one almost heard them stretching to breaking point. In the end Okonkwo threw the Cat.[12]

The next sentence ends with a simile using two features of the local environment: 'That was many years ago, twenty years or more, and during this time Okonkwo's fame had grown like a bush-fire in the harmattan.'

The apparent simplicity of this passage is deceptive. It is artistry of a radically different order from those—Florence Nwapa, for example—who later tried to write novels of village life limited to repetition and simple sentences. Achebe's purpose is to situate the reader within a community governed by a rich tribal culture which, being a living culture, is undergoing changes, and the continuity of which will be challenged by the intrusions of Christianity and the white man. If his purpose is to show the dignity of traditional African culture, his job as a writer is to make the Igbo village as richly textured with manners and mores as any local community in the novels of Jane Austen or George Eliot. Indeed Achebe's Igbo village novels resemble those of Eliot or Thomas Hardy in showing the tragedy of individuals resulting from the clash between their own strength of character and the unstoppable forces of historical change. Achebe's heroes gain their stature by their excessive virtue in attempting to oppose fate. This is in contrast to the rest of the village community, which changes its ways under pressure and which may be said to illustrate the importance of communal survival in Africa. The rigidity with which Okonkwo upholds traditional values makes him heroic, but such excesses bring self-destruction because temperance and the ability to accept change are necessary with the coming of the powerful Europeans.

Things Fall Apart is remarkable for its complexity of technique and vision. After the deceptive simplicities of the opening pages, the narrator gradually becomes our sharp observer-guide through a foreign land while retaining his identity as the voice of the community. We become aware of the closeness of African village life to the soil, to the movement of the seasons and to the gods who are present in the elements. The tribe has its history, its social divisions, economy, ethics, customs, myth, religion, cosmology, and, most important, its traditional wisdom handed from generation to generation through proverbs. The proverbs, which are the most noticeable feature of Achebe's style, occur mostly in the first part of the novel, before the coming of the white man; they are guides to social and moral behaviour, and represent a kind of wisdom literature. Early in the novel we are told 'Proverbs are the palm-oil with which words are eaten.' Such proverbs as 'If a child washed his hands he could eat with kings' and 'A man who pays respect to the great paves the way for his own greatness' are repositories of social advice. These two proverbs, however, are somewhat contradictory in attitude: one teaches purity of selfhood, the other obedience to those in power. Achebe does not pretend that traditional Igbo culture was totally self-consistent. At various places in the novel it is mentioned that customs important in one village are ignored in the next, and that customs change. Indeed, he wants to show that traditional society was not static. Repugnance at such traditional practices as the killing of twins or the treatment of outcasts made Christianity attractive to many of the villagers. Moreover, Okonkwo, who sees himself as the upholder of traditional values, is himself out of harmony with the village, which has changed considerably during the seven years of his exile. His act of defiance in killing the messenger of the white men is in keeping with his previous excesses and his suicide which follows, is, within tribal custom, a greater crime against his society than that of which he accuses others.

There are two techniques in *Things Fall Apart* that make the novel seminal to Nigerian literature in the way that *Huckleberry Finn* is the beginning of modern American fiction. The first characteristic is Achebe's reshaping of English into a Nigerian prose style. The inclusion of Igbo words and the translation of Igbo proverbs into English has often been commented upon. Equally worthy of notice is the modification of Nigerian spoken English to make it into a literary style; diction and word order are often based more upon Nigerian than British usage: 'I have kola'; 'Unlike his father he could stand the look of blood'; 'Let the kite perch and let the eagle perch too. If one says no to the other, let his wing break'; 'Okonkwo's neighbours heard his wife crying and sent their voices over the compound walls'; 'Their clan is full of the evil spirits of these unburied dead, hungry to do harm to the living'; 'You will blow your eyes out'; 'I cannot yet find a mouth with which to tell the story'. Many of these expressions are transliterations from Igbo, while others sound like contemporary Nigerian usage: 'I tell you that *jigida* and fire are not friends. But you will never hear.' 'Let us go out and whisper together.' The other characteristic is the change in narration of the novel according to the kind of community it describes. The self-enclosed world of the nine villages in the opening pages is accepted on its own valuation and terms. Although Achebe describes traditional Igbo society for the benefit of the reader, recreating a now lost world, he sees it from the inside, accepting its premises.

There are several different perspectives combined within the first half of the book. Achebe as narrator describes traditional Igbo life to the reader, objectively narrates events, acts as the voice of the community and offers comment on the characters which implies judgement. In other places he indirectly presents the psychology of the characters or allows them their individuality through dramatisation. He rapidly alternates techniques to create a consistency of appearance:

> Okonkwo was beginning to feel like his old self again. All that he required was something to occupy his mind. If he had killed Ikemefuna during the busy planting season or harvesting it would not have been so bad; his mind would have been centred on his work. Okonkwo was not a man of thought but of action. But in the absence of work, talking was the next best.
>
> Soon after Ofoedu left, Okonkwo took up his goatskin bag to go.
>
> 'I must go home to tap my palm trees for the afternoon,' he said.
>
> 'Who taps your tall trees for you?' asked Obierika.
>
> 'Umezulike,' replied Okonkwo.
>
> 'Sometimes I wish I had not taken the *ozo* title,' said Obierika. 'It wounds my heart to see these young men killing palm trees in the name of tapping.'
>
> 'It is so indeed,' Okonkwo agreed. 'But the law of the land must be obeyed.'
>
> 'I don't know how we got that law,' said Obierika. 'In many other clans a man of title is not forbidden to climb

the palm tree. Here we say he cannot climb the tall tree but he can tap the short ones standing on the ground. It is like Dimaragana, who would not lend his knife for cutting up dog-meat because the dog was taboo to him, but offered to use his teeth.'

'I think it is good that our clan holds the *ozo* title in high esteem,' said Okonkwo. 'In those other clans you speak of, *ozo* is so low every beggar takes it.'

If the first half of the novel is told from within the psychology of the village, the third part of the novel stylistically reflects the social and psychological changes that have occurred with the coming of the white man. There are fewer proverbs or Igbo words, fewer expressions which appear to be based on Igbo idioms. As the unity of village opinion is lost and division occurs requiring a larger perspective on events, the style becomes more distanced: 'There were many men and women in Umuofia who did not feel as strongly as Okonkwo about the new dispensation. The white man had indeed brought a lunatic religion, but he had also built a trading store and for the first time palm-oil and kernel became things of great price, and much money flowed into Umuofia.'

In the passage describing various reactions to Okonkwo's suicide there are radical shifts of perspective ranging from Obierika's 'That man was one of the greatest men in Umuofia' to the messenger's 'Yes, suh', the latter indicative of the new political order and social hierarchy. This shift from the enclosed tribal word to that of the coloniser is expressed in the irony of the District Commissioner's perspective on Okonkwo's death:

> Every day brought him some new material. The story of this man who had killed a messenger and hanged himself would make interesting reading. One could almost write a whole chapter on him. Perhaps not a whole chapter but a reasonable paragraph, at any rate. There was so much else to include, and one must be firm in cutting out details. He had already chosen the title of the book, after much thought: *The Pacification of the Primitive Tribes of the Lower Niger*.

Things Fall Apart has themes in common with Ekwensi's earlier work. Both record societies in transition in which older values no longer hold, in which adaptability has become necessary for survival; in the novels of both the main character is an ambitious, self-made social climber. Besides the moral chaos present in both works, the presence of dialect in one and a Nigerianised style in the other, the two novels are set against a changing political situation involving, in Ekwensi's case, the approaching end of colonialism, and in Achebe's the beginning of the colonial period. The similarities might be explained by saying that both writers come from the same tribe, and that the kinds of conflict are transformations of the problems and assumptions faced in Onitsha marketplace writing. If the tragedy in *People of the City* and *Things Fall Apart* results from societies undergoing rapid change (and it is difficult not to see the past in *Things Fall Apart* as related to Nigeria in the 1950s, the same Nigeria which produced Henshawe's dramatised pleas for westernised progress), Achebe's novel expresses a cultural nationalism not found in the earlier writers. Since colonial rule was based on the claim that the Africans are backward, it was necessary for Nigerian intellectuals to show that they indeed had a culture which had been misrepresented by their conquerors. The careful depiction of tribal custom by Nigerian writers belongs to this period immediately preceding and following independence.

One year after the publication of *Things Fall Apart*, T. M. Aluko's *One Man, One Wife* (1959) offered a comical treatment of the theme of cultural conflict and the confusions which resulted from partial westernisation. On the opening page, as the 'village Christians gathered' there is lightning and thunder foretelling a storm:

> Shango, the god of lightning and thunder, was registering his anger at this strange talk of a new God taking hold of simple folk who were once unquestioning votaries of his order. This new malady must be nipped in the bud.[13]

As the Teacher urges his audience to repent their sins, 'A heavy peal of thunder which tailed off into rumbling and died out grumbling behind the clouds effectively emphasised the case for repentance.' The novel surveys traditional village society, including folk tales and songs. The time is the 1920s when western education and the knowledge of English have become useful means of social and financial advancement. The translation of the Bible and Hymnal Companion 'was bringing the pleasant by-product of literature in their own Yoruba tongue' to some Christian converts. Aluko shows how absurd Christian doctrine, with the promise of eternal life, sounded to many Nigerians, but his attitude as author is non-traditional in most matters: 'The consequences of refusing to marry Joshua! The girl knew what they were. Parents could exercise the ancient right of giving a disobedient daughter to the Oba as a gift bride.' The village elders and the priests of the various Yoruba gods are treated as corrupt. Those who oppose Christianity are usually seen as villains.

Aluko parodies *Things Fall Apart*: 'My father Joshua was the greatest man in Isolo'; 'I, Joshua, son of Fagbola would like to see the White Man who will come to arrest me. I will show him that at least there is still one man left at Isolo'; 'If the world has not become the world of the White Man, I would cut off Teacher's head, and then kill myself'; 'It contained plenty of coins which represented his savings from the proceeds of several seasons' cocoa sales. This was the oil with which the human machine that would get him the chieftaincy was going to be lubricated.' But if Aluko makes fun of traditionalism he also finds humour in pious Christian platitudes. The absurd situation at the end of the novel is proclaimed by the clergyman as 'one more manifestation of the incomprehensibility of the ways of God'. Aluko's novels show that while the Nigerian writers of the independence period often based their plots on themes of cultural conflict, their interest was in the confusion that resulted from modernisation. The old values no longer hold, but no stable new set of values has become accepted. It is this problem that underlies *Things Fall Apart* and that is treated more explicitly in Achebe's second novel, *No Longer at Ease* (1960).

The story of *No Longer at Ease* concerns Obi Okonkwo, the grandson of the Okonkwo of the first novel, who returns from his studies in England to become a civil servant in Nigeria a few years before independence. The time is 1957 and the Nigerian elite is beginning to hold most civil service and professional positions, which they see as a source of quick riches from bribes. Nor are the villagers immune from shoddy ethics. Although proclaiming traditional clan values, they see the new society as a means of enriching the village through government jobs and various corruptions. The novel traces the social forces that turn Obi Okonkwo from an idealist into another corrupt member of the new society that has emerged in modern Africa. After the opening pages describing Obi's trial, the narrative moves back into the past beginning with the decision to send him to England for further education. This is followed by a straightforward narrative description of his economic and social problems after his return to Nigeria. While putting the normal conclusion of the narrative at the beginning of the book is dramatically effective, its main purpose is to make the subsequent events appear determined. It focuses attention on the narrative as a study in social cause and effect; the opening pages of the novel show us a promising young Nigerian on trial in a corrupt society, and the remainder of the story will show what has made him what he is.

The quotation from T. S. Eliot's 'The Journey of the Magi' is relevant in suggesting that Obi, like the biblical wise men, is caught between two eras: an older Nigeria with its demands of responsibility towards family and clan, and a modern Nigeria, still unborn, in which individuals live their own life, follow their own conscience, and use their money to pay taxes, electricity bills, run automobiles and choose their own wife. Obi says: 'What is a pioneer? Someone who shows the way. That is what I am doing.'[14] He has the worst of both worlds, the responsibilities of the past and the money economy of the present.

But it is perhaps wrong to view Obi as a fallen hero. Achebe has always cast a weary eye on his protagonist and Obi himself warns: 'Real tragedy is never resolved. It goes on hopelessly for ever.' The tragedy in the novel has no real resolution because it began earlier when his father became a Christian, turning against the ways of *his* father, and thus destroying the cultural unity of the family and village. If *No Longer at Ease* is a study in the cultural chaos of Nigeria on the eve of independence, it also shows Achebe's nostalgia for an ordered—if imperfect—past, when there was one accepted code of values.

His third novel, *Arrow of God* (1964), contrasts a strong individual, Ezeulu the Chief Priest of Ulu, with a confused, pliant community. Under the misguided policy that by creating local chiefs where none previously existed it would be possible to rule indirectly, the British imprison Ezeulu—ironically, for refusing appointment as a Warrant Chief. Ezeulu blames the villagers for their lack of support. Divining his god's wish that he refuse to celebrate the New Yam Festival, the celebration of which is necessary before the crop can be harvested, he brings famine on the village and conversion to the less demanding Christian god. The main irony of the novel is that Ezeulu had previously been a voice for the acceptance of social change. Ezeulu is the first in the village to send one of his sons to study at the white man's school and to the Christian church. His favourite expression to signify the need to adjust to social change is 'A man must dance the dance prevalent in his time.'[15]

As in *Things Fall Apart*, we are told that tradition changes and is not static. Tribal facial marks were once customary but are now considered old-fashioned and no longer used. African gods and customs are made for the survival of the clan and are not of transcendent importance in themselves. Ulu, the god for whom Ezeulu is chief priest, was made when previous gods had failed the six villages. If a god fails, he is forgotten or destroyed and another god takes his place.

Ezeulu's tragedy is that he believes his god has told him to punish the villages for being influenced by the priest of the Python god. He sees himself as an arrow of his god scourging the clan. This has made him rigid, and his rigidity necessarily must be rejected by the clan if it is to survive. His excess of will and courage makes him a victim of history. In the preface to the second edition of *Arrow of God,* Achebe speaks of Ezeulu as 'victim, consecrating by his agony—thus raising to the stature of a ritual passage—the defection of his people'. It is perhaps of psychological significance that Achebe's father was a Christian missionary.

While *Arrow of God* takes place after the First World War, in the village colonialism has not radically touched upon custom. The European penetration of Africa has been going on for centuries; there is no sudden demarcation between an African past and conflict with European culture, although in localities conflicts do occur. The catechist of the church in Umuaro is John Jaja Goodcountry: 'His home was in the Niger Delta which had been in contact with Europe and the world for hundreds of years.' 'Mr Goodcountry with his background of the Niger Delta Pastorate which could already count native martyrs like Joshua Hart to its credit was not prepared to compromise with the heathen over such things as sacred animals.' Despite the long period of contact between Europe and Africa and the growing presence of westernised, Christian Nigerians, there is little communication between white and black. They are separated by radically different cultures and by race.

A theme of the novel is the effect of the British policy of indirect rule. Although the intentions are innocent there is, ironically, interference in African ways in the hope of strengthening African self-rule: a corrupt, semi-westernised, English-speaking class (forerunners of the future elite) is created, and old customs are accidentally weakened and destroyed. Mission-educated Africans are appointed chiefs and they use their European-given power to organise vast systems of extortion, taking bribes, creating illegal taxes, and intimidating the villagers. The clan has no means of protecting itself against such chiefs created by the Europeans. And to make matters worse, the government is inconsistent and, because of the distance of the bureaucracy from the local scene, irresponsible.

It is probable that the cultural tensions and confusions of *Arrow of God*, while based on historical fact, reflect the period during which the book was written. It observes the rise of a class of Africans who, working for the state, feel free of tribal ethics, and describes the changes that have occured in Africa as a result of western education, the Christian religion, and the impersonal apparatus of central government. The novel sets the stage for the drama depicted in *No Longer at Ease*, showing the long historical process which created Obi Okonkwo and modern Nigeria. The tension between the six villages, their leaders and their priests is not unlike that between tribes in post-independence Nigeria. There is, however, one supposed difference between the past and the present, shown by the statement made several times in the novel that one man cannot go against the clan. Whether the clan is right or wrong—and it is often wrong—it has its social mechanisms of reconciliation, judgement, sanctions and survival; the new national state produced by colonialism, as seen in *No Longer at Ease* and *A Man of the People*, has no organic unity, no moral sense, no mechanism of purgation; its values follow from the corrupting powers given the warrant chiefs, messengers and police by the colonial government.

One difference between *A Man of the People* (1966) and Achebe's previous novels is the use of a first-person narrator, Odili. Whereas the omniscient narrator of the village novels assumed the perspective and sometimes the voice of the community, the use of the first-person narrator is significant of the lack of traditional communal values in the new nation. The conclusion of the novel makes explicit the difference between the traditional society of the past, with its sense of moral obligation, and the new state, with its uncontrolled corruption and lack of ethical sense:

> 'Koko had taken enough for the owner to see,' said my father to me . . . My father's words struck me because they were the very same words the villages of Anata had spoken of Josiah, the abominated trader. Only in their case the words had meaning. The owner was the village, and the village had a mind; it could say no to sacrilege. But in the affairs of the nation there was no owner, the laws of the village became powerless. Max was avenged not by

> the people's collective will but by one solitary woman who loved him. Had his spirit waited for the people to demand redress it would have been waiting still, in the rain and out in the sun . . . in the fat-dripping, gummy, eat-and-let-eat regime just ended—a regime which inspired the common saying that a man could only be sure of what he had put away safely in his gut or, in language evermore suited to the times: 'you chop, me self I chop, palaver finish'.[16]

The use of pidgin is revealing. The old moral sayings of the Igbos have no relevance to a nation made up of various tribes and cultures; pidgin, a bastard mixture of African and foreign languages, expresses the individualism, immorality and materialism which have resulted from the colonial period and the independent nation which followed.

At the centre of the novel is Chief the Honourable M. A. Nanga, M.P., Minister of Culture, representative figure of the West African politics before and after independence. A former popular school teacher, he entered politics in the early 1950s but only came to prominence in 1960 when the intellectuals were purged from the ruling political party. The Prime Minister whips up fury against 'all university people and highly educated professional men', claiming that an 'expensive university education . . . only alienates an African from his rich and ancient culture' and vows 'Never again must we entrust our destiny and the destiny of Africa to the hybrid class of Western-educated and snobbish intellectuals who will not hesitate to sell their mothers for a mess of pottage.' Nanga, who never attended a university, led the Prime Minister's supporters; 'seeing the empty ministerial seats' he 'had yapped and snarled so shamelessly for the meaty prize'. He is now a rich man living in a government-rented house of seven bedrooms and bathrooms, and although Minister of Culture he has never heard of the nation's best-known writer.

The novel is set in a period of growing social tensions which reflect the political crisis in Nigeria after independence. Mention is made of various strikes, rapid inflation, favouritism towards politically loyal villages and political thuggery.

British companies pay vast bribes to control the economy and American neo-colonialism arrives in the form of aid, investment, willing white women and anti-communism. A radical Marxist party, supported by an Eastern European nation, is formed and its leader killed on election day. As political thuggery gets out of hand and the government loses control, the army takes over. This, Odili tells us, is no triumph of the people over its corrupt leaders. The people themselves 'had become even more cynical than their leaders and were apathetic into the bargain'. While it would be a mistake to equate Odili with Achebe, it is clear that *A Man of the People* not only reflects a growing animosity between the Nigerian intellectuals of the mid-sixties and the government, it shows that disillusionment with independence had set in; the desire of the people for western luxuries appeared as corrupt as the government. With increased political and social changes brought about by independence, the ideal of an organic, communal way of life had even more validity, although now it was used in contrast to the new national society.

5 Nigeria II: Soyinka and Ogun

Soyinka comes from a prominent Yoruba family in Abeokuta, the spiritual centre of the old Oyo Empire, now the capital of Ogun State.[1] After spending two years at the recently founded (1948) University College Ibadan, where he met Achebe and Okigbo, Soyinka went to the University of Leeds, England, took his B.A. and started postgraduate work. At Leeds he studied with the brilliant, unconventional critic, G. Wilson Knight. There was a meeting of like minds. Knight's interpretations of literature discover metaphysical, spiritual and moral patterns based upon ultimate truths of which individual plays often seem exemplifications. Influenced by Nietzsche, Knight claims that heroes and artists go beyond normal ideas of good and evil to bring about a higher good. Besides a common interest in drama and large philosophical ideas, Knight and Soyinka share similarities in their views of the world. Soyinka claims that there is continuity between the spiritual and material worlds which finds expression in tragedy and heroic action. He assumes the artist is a man of action whose involvement is both destructive and creative, the fight against evil having its validation less in conventional ethical behaviour than in its spiritual quest. This does not mean that Soyinka is a follower of Knight. Although there are influences, it would perhaps be more accurate to say that Knight provided Soyinka with means of analysing Yoruba myth to make it applicable to his own needs.

While in England Soyinka had written several plays and, between 1958 and 1960, read drama scripts for the Royal Court

Theatre. On his return to Nigeria he was welcomed with commissions to write plays, opportunities to write for newspapers and broadcast on the radio, and a Rockefeller Fellowship to do research into dramatic elements within Yoruba ritual. There was the *Black Orpheus* journal and Mbari Club, centred upon the lecturers and young writers at the University of Ibadan. Rather than the expected conflict between two worlds, Nigerian independence more often produced generational conflict in which the young university graduates found their idealism opposed by an older generation that already held positions of power, a subject Soyinka later treated in his novel *The Interpreters*.

One of his earliest plays, the humorous *The Lion and the Jewel*, written by 1958 while in England, surprised those who assumed that Soyinka was on the side of modernisation. It might be considered a sophisticated reply to Henshawe's school plays praising progress. Lakunle, the school teacher, who wishes to copy European fashions, is a fool. Dressed in 'an old-style English suit', mouthing love poetry to Sidi but unwilling to pay her bride price, dreaming of transforming her into a 'modern wife' with 'high-heeled shoes' and 'red paint/On her lips',[2] who will dance the waltz and foxtrot, he is a comic figure representing the African with some western education who confuses the superficialities of European middle-class behaviour with progress. In contrast to Lakunle is Baroka, a polygamous chieftain in his sixties who, to protect his power, has bribed a surveyor to keep roads and railways from the village.

The Lion and the Jewel is a comedy of the sexes in which cunning, energy, will and power are celebrated as principles of life in contrast to naiveté, weakness, indecision and honesty. The assumed values are here associated with age, tradition and established village wisdom in contrast to the superficial knowledge brought by Christianity and western education. Whereas Lakunle insults beautiful Sidi, calling her 'Ignorant girl', 'bush girl', 'Uncivilised and primitive', Baroka promises the use of his printing machine to forge postage stamps with her picture. Where the school master rants in clichés against village customs—'A savage custom, barbaric, out-dated/Rejected, denounced, accursed'—Baroka speaks poetry in defending traditional life.

Beneath the apparent opposition between progress and tradition is the more profound theme of mankind's will to conquer. Uninhibited, amoral, Baroka is representative of the life force and especially of the sexual drive. When he pretends, so as to trap Sidi, that he is impotent, his first wife rushes to tell the women that they have won over the men: 'So we did for you too did we? We did for you in the end. Oh high and mighty lion, have we really scotched you? A-ya-ya-ya . . . we women undid you in the end.' 'Not me alone girl. You too.' Sidi leaps into the air shouting: 'We won. We won! Hurray for womankind!' Baroka, however, is not impotent; rather he is a fox, lying in wait for his victim. Having tricked Sidi into coming to laugh at him, he smoothly seduces her and so impresses her with his virility that she decides to become his latest wife: 'It was the secret of God's own draught/A deed for drums and ballads.'

Although *The Lion and the Jewel* portrays a traditional Nigerian village and includes African dances and Yoruba songs, the plot situation and the character of Baroka are based on Ben Jonson's *Volpone,* itself an adaptation of Italian Renaissance dramatic conventions. The battle of the sexes and the celebration of will and energy over weak innocence has its obvious parallels in Restoration comedy and in the plays of George Bernard Shaw and in Nietzsche's philosophy. While the use of dance, song, mime, flashbacks has long been part of the European theatre, Soyinka will increase such features in his plays as part of their African character. The language used in the play is far from Achebe's creation of an African English. Sidi, a supposedly uneducated village girl, says 'Tell your lord that Sidi does not sup with/Married men.' While some of Baroka's speeches give the impression of Yoruba sayings, the majority of his lines have the classical clarity of declarations in Ben Jonson's plays.

The Lion and the Jewel is characteristic of the early stages of a national literature. The Nigerianising of conventional dramatic types, the mocking of those who identify progress with western fashion, the sympathy for and assignment of potency to a cunning, corrupt old village chieftain are similar to the novels of Twain or the plays of Synge in shifting value from European middle-class to local, or native, ways of life. (Soyinka's early play, *The Swamp Dwellers*,[3] appears modelled on the plays of Synge.) Although the setting and details of the drama are local, the scene and particularities are inessential to the significance. With modifications, the play could be transposed to India or Ireland without impairing its meaning. Indeed its attractiveness in part derives from the universality of its themes and vision.

The way Soyinka's scenes fade into each other, the flashbacks and simultaneous events, are essentially radio techniques. Several of his early plays were specifically written for radio, including *Camwood on the Leaves*, broadcast by the Nigerian Broadcasting Corporation in 1960. *Camwood* expresses the conflict between generations throughout West Africa during the independence period. The plot concerns the conflict between Reverend Erinjobi and his son Isola. The Reverend typifies the worst of the westernised Christian Nigerians in his Victorian concern with middle-class values. His son rebels, joining the Yoruba Egungun cult: 'My own son . . . an egungun! You made me the laughing stock of my parish . . . Oh, you were damned from the start . . . playing with gutter children . . . singing heathen songs . . . slipping out at night and nobody knowing what bestiality you would commit before the break of day!'[4] Isola impregnates the only daughter of another respectable family and is forced to leave home. He spends a night in the bush hoping to shoot a boa constrictor, which he names after his mother. Instead he kills his father as the latter enters the bush to take the girl back to her parents. While the theme of *Camwood on the Leaves*—the rebellion of the young—is universal, the play shows the rejection of the Christian middle-class father by a son who prefers traditional Yoruba religion and the forest. Although himself westernised to the point of radical rebellion against his father, Isola has rejected the class, religious and cultural values of the colonial Nigerian elite.

A Dance of the Forests (1963) was written for the Nigerian independence celebration and attacks the romanticising of African culture common to the period. The 'gathering of the tribes' in the play is meant to symbolise the Nigerian independence celebrations; Soyinka offers his own realistic view of African history in contrast to the idealised past that was part of the cultural assertion that accompanied political independence. In *A Dance of the Forests* the human community wishes to celebrate its 'accumulated heritage . . . Mali. Chaka. Songhai. Glory. Empires', for the present is to be a return to such eras of 'greatness'. But when it sees the ancestors who have returned, it tries to ignore 'those obscenities'. 'We were sent the wrong people. We asked for statesmen and we were sent executioners.'[5] A parallel between past and present is established by the recurrence of character types, similar crimes and even the same corruptions.

Soyinka draws analogies between the African empires of the past, the era of the slave trade and the present. We are shown one of the great empires of the twelfth century in which the rulers kill their servants, trade slaves and wage unjust wars. African history is shown to be similar to European, no better or worse. The court historian says, 'War is the only consistency that past ages afford us. It is the legacy which new nations seek to perpetuate.' A warrior complains, 'Unborn generations will, as we have done, eat up one another.' He is sold 'down the river' to a slave-dealer who offers a bribe to a court official so that he may overcrowd sixty slaves into his boat. Centuries later, an official is bribed to allow a passenger lorry to carry seventy people, although it was only built to carry forty. It overturns, killing sixty-five. Soyinka suggests that history repeats itself 'in approximate duplicate of actions'. The cyclical pattern of history is shown by the warrior having also been sold into slavery three hundred years before:

> Three lives I led since first I went away
> But still my first possesses me
> The pattern is unchanged.

If Soyinka looks sceptically at the claims of African past glory, he reminds the audience that the guilt is their own. The warrior was guilty of 'laziness'; instead of actually rebelling he surrendered his manhood, and it is this pattern that is being re-enacted throughout history. The implication is that a heroic action, beyond conventional notions of good and evil, is necessary to break the cycle. (We might remember Nietzsche's recurring cycles and their relationship to the superman.) But the cycle is unlikely to be broken. National independence changes few essentials of human behaviour. The Half-Child laments that she will still be 'born dead' as in the past. The Spirit of Darkness prophesies 'They'll be misled' and 'doomed'. Men will die seeking precious stones, will kill the pachyderms for ivory, and will continue to tread upon the Ants, symbol of the poor. Posterity appears in the play 'fanged and bloody'.

Why should Soyinka write such a play as part of an independence celebration? Forest Head, symbol of Oludumare, the chief Yoruba deity and equivalent to God the Father of Christianity, says 'nothing is ever altered'. It is only by torturing 'awareness' from man's soul that a new beginning might be possible. Soyinka had already formulated his vision of history as unchanging cycles and the roles of the gods, especially Ogun, in human affairs. The Ogun myth or cosmology upon which the play is based is explained in *Myth, Literature and the African World* (1976). Drama represents the 'passage-rites of hero-gods, a projection of man's conflict with forces which challenge his efforts to harmonise with his environment'. These gods 'unquestionably' exist; they are questers or explorers of cosmic reality which man cannot directly approach. Ogun hacked a passage through the primordial chaos which allowed the gods' meeting with mankind. 'His was the first rite of passage.'[6] This journey across 'the Void' resulted in the gods and men offering Ogun kingship. He first refused but after much persuasion became king of the town of Ife. Later he killed both his own followers and their enemies during battle. Thus while Ogun's heroism inaugurated the Yoruba world shared by men and gods, he was unable to settle in the world until he understood that he was both destructive and creative.

Demoke, figure of the artist and worshipper of the god Ogun, has carved the totem which is to be used at the festival. Originally unwilling to accept the burden of the past, and a murderer of his assistant who follows another god, Demoke is made to face the essential truth that destruction is part of creation. His totem which reaches the sky approximates the Ogun myth by forging a link between god and man. Demoke must accept his destructive nature, enter into strife with Eshuoro (the deity representing chance or disorder) over the half-dead child, and become a sacrifice. His transformation from an unwilling participant to active involvement is a ritual passage from despair to regeneration. It is this tragic pattern, based upon Yoruba myth and ritual, which Soyinka has set against the romantic cultural idealism of the independence celebration.

Ways in which *A Dance of the Forests* reflects a nationalistic or African cultural renaissance include the depiction of local gods and their relationship to the present world, the use of a festival in the plot which the play itself mirrors, the use of masquerades, traditional characters from oral literature (such as Madame Tortoise), dances, dirge singing, divination and African children's games. Many of the mime movements are similar to masquerade dances in Nigerian festivals. There are various proverbs, sayings and forms of English that capture the metaphoric style of Yoruba speech. While Soyinka parodies the pretentious use of 'deep Yoruba' proverbs in Agboreko's 'proverb to bones and silence', he gives many of his characters speeches with expressions in the style of Yoruba proverbs: 'Perhaps we will meet. But the reveller doesn't buy a cap before he's invited'; 'The knife doesn't carve its own handle, you know'; 'When the leaves tremble it is no concern of the roots'; 'If the hunter loses his quarry, he looks up to see where the vultures are circling'. Soyinka's plays often contrast characters who use creatively the metaphoric, ellipitic form of Yoruba sayings with stuffy, often corrupt traditionalists who attempt to impress with obscure proverbs.

In *The Strong Breed*, the Ogun myth, Greek rituals and the Christian Passion story are applicable. It is the beginning of a new year and a corrupt society wants a sacrificial scapegoat to carry the burden of its sins. Eman, a young school teacher, objects to an idiot child being made the unwilling sacrifice. 'A village which cannot produce its own carrier contains no men.'[7] To save the child, Eman becomes the scapegoat that is hunted, whipped and killed. He both re-enacts Christ's sacrifice and Ogun's crossing of the abyss between man and the gods. Soyinka does not sentimentalise the act which is shown to be terrifying and horrific both to victim and executioners. By taking on the sacrifice, Eman has not so much cleansed the community of sin as thrown it into a turmoil that challenges the unthinking behaviour of the past. He has left the community ill at ease with itself, although what might be the result is not clear. Soyinka is not against sacrifice; ritual sacrifice is central to Yoruba culture. Eman's family were traditionally sacrificial victims and he, after attempting to run away from his fate, has finally fulfilled his destined role. Soyinka is making a distinction between the communal sacrifice of unwilling victims and the tragic hero who initiates a new cycle of history by acting as a link between the gods and men.

It should be remembered that Soyinka's research at the University of Ibadan was on dramatic elements in Yoruba ritual and that Nigeria already had a tradition of vernacular drama. Among Soyinka's Yoruba tribe, in particular, drama began in the secularisation of ceremonial masquerades, which were eventually expanded into the professional travelling theatres of Hubert Ogunde, Kola Ogunmola and Duro Ladipo. The popular Yoruba dramatic tradition increasingly will influence Soyinka's plays, which will make more use of Yoruba songs, dances and topical political and social allusions.

Although *The Road* (1965) involves a comic fraudulent preacher similar to that in *The Trial of Brother Jero* (1964), such attempts at a syncretic religion should be seen as an expression of the modern mind confusedly seeking ultimate truths. *The Road* is a re-enactment of the Egungun ceremony in which a masquerader becomes possessed and undergoes Ogun's perilous journey from the other to this world. It is similar to T. S. Eliot's *Murder in the Cathedral*, in which the symbolism and structure refer to the Catholic Mass which is itself a re-enactment of the Passion story. Soyinka's play incorporates as part of its action an Egungun masquerade, the play's symbolism and events create an identical moment of ritual possession. This moment is the embodiment of a spiritual mystery and truth which cannot be expressed in words. It is a moment of union with the divine, an illumination which others, particularly the Professor in the play, seek but cannot find because it can only be experienced and not discovered through rational understanding. The play itself is an attempt to express this distinction by contrasting the unlearnable experience with the Professor's failure to find the truth, which he, influenced by Christian religious concepts and western literacy, calls the 'Word'.

The title, *The Road*, refers directly to Ogun who as creator of the bridge between men and gods is the deity of travellers and drivers. Road journeys are re-enactments of Ogun's exploration of the primordial chaos. Although Soyinka uses allusions to suggests a parallel between the events in his works and European mythology and belief, his Yoruba view differs from the Christian in that it is not incarnational; the final ground of being, or truth, is death. Thus Soyinka's note 'For the Producer' refers to Agẹmọ as 'a religious cult of flesh dissolution'.[8] Murano, the personal servant to the Professor, is mute because when in masquerade he has been knocked down by a lorry and therefore possessed by the god Ogun. He has been arrested in a transitional state between life and death, between the human and divine worlds, and therefore knows the Truth but cannot communicate it. The Professor's quest for communion with the Truth is impossible, since it would involve rational comprehension of a divine essence. Such communion is only possible for the masquerader or the artist who undergoes Ogun's journey between worlds. It is because the two planes of reality are separate that *The Road* appears a drama of the Absurd.

Although it uses similar techniques of incongruity, disconnection, repetition, fragmentation, parody and mockery to suggest the lack of continuity between various planes of reality, *The Road* is not a drama of the Absurd. The Professor is not an outsider; he knows the written word, and is adept in manoeuvring among the corruptions of his society. His trade as forger is representative; thus he is a friend of policemen and, typical of the play's comedy, contemplates retiring to prison, where in solitary confinement he could meditate. He is representative of a fractured culture in which a discrepancy has developed between uniforms and employment, between words and the Word. Expelled from his position in the Christian Church because of his pride and financial improprieties, he is a modern Nigerian concerned with money and status, not at ease with Christianity and yet removed from tribal culture. His quest is a search for psychic harmony. That such unity is potentially available, if only in death, distinguishes *The Road* from existentialist or absurdist European literary works. It is because the Professor mistakes truth with literacy, rationality and the externalities of religion that he is trapped in the absurd and his quest towards the truth remains a failure until his death, which brings him enlightenment. This does not mean he has been a failure. The quest itself is necessary; it gives life meaning since it imitates Ogun's journey through chaos.

Soyinka early made his direction clear in his literary criticism. 'From a Common Back Cloth' attacks the anthropological novel of village life and the theme of cultural conflict as falsifying the multiplicity of contemporary Africa. Instead he praises Amos Tutuola both for reflecting the modern experience and for his 'largeness' of life. *The Palm-Wine Drinkard* exhibits a 'progression from physical insufficiency, through the Quest into the very psyche of Nature. *The Palm-Wine Drinkard*, as with Fagunwa's *Ogboju Ode* and universal myth, is the epic of man's eternal restlessness, symbolised as always in a Search.'[9] In 'And After the Narcissist' Soyinka criticises the Negritude writer as an exhibitionist. While such Narcissism may for a time be useful, a new African writer has emerged who 'rejects the novel's fascination, seeks his path through experience, through liberation, through self-surrender'. Soyinka offers Christopher Okigbo as an example of such a quest and criticises Gabriel Okara's *The Voice* in which 'there is no communication of the psychic drive which sets a man on a course of single-minded enquiry into the heart of matter of existence'.[10]

Soyinka's first novel, *The Interpreters* (1965), offers impressions of modern Nigerian society shortly after independence, as seen through the eyes of a group of graduates who have returned from their university education abroad. It makes many of the same satiric criticisms found in other Nigerian novels of the period and portrays a financially corrupt governing elite which demands bribes; a dishonest press which will not publish stories embarrassing to politicians; African university professors who imitate European 'civilisation' to the extent of decorating their houses with plastic fruit; fraudulent popular religious prophets; and a broad range of hypocrisies, cruelties and evils. The older generation of Nigerians in positions of power and authority is portrayed as disgusting and cynical.

If *The Interpreters* offers a disillusioning view of post-independence Nigeria, Soyinka's focus is a group of former school friends as they develop into individuals who must make decisions and take on responsibilities. Egbo, for example, is torn between keeping his government post and returning to his grandfather's clan as the 'enlightened' ruler they desire; his irresolution parallels his indecision whether to stay with Simi, a beautiful courtesan who introduced him to sexual pleasure, or marry a student whom he has made pregnant and who represents 'the new woman of my generation, proud of the gift of mind'.[11] If the break-up of the group, the going of separate ways, represents the end of youth, it is also a sign of a generation learning that it no longer has shared values; graduation, like national independence, is followed by the need to find new, appropriate ways of living.

The quest for 'a new law for living' is the main theme of *The Interpreters* (reflected in the group's involvement with Lazarus's strange religious sect). There is the problem of the relationship of the past to the present. Imagery of bridges and domes recurs throughout the book because they represent continuity and wholeness in contrast to apparent fragmentation and chaos. Similarly the narration gives the appearance of chaos but is linked by images, associations, and what is essentially a straightforward time scheme of about two months. The many flashbacks (sometimes memories within memories) give an appearance of discontinuity, but build bridges between past and present. Sekoni says that to make distinctions between the past and present disrupts 'the dome of continuity, which is what life is'. Bridges face two directions, forward and backward; 'there is no direction'.[12] Presumably such mysticism answers Egbo's worry that 'life might be sheer creek-surface bearing the burdens of fools, a mere passage'. Each character is confronted with the need to undergo Ogun's journey bridging two worlds if they are to pass from despair to creation. Early in the novel Egbo is angry at 'his failure to bury the abortive quest' with its promise of 'salvation' and in the nightclub during the storm is depressed. Sagoe also says 'I am low. Damn it, I *am* low. . . . They depressed me.' Will, experience, engagement and love prove necessary. It is significant that at the centre of the novel, in Chapter 9, Egbo, after having lost his virginity to Simi, undergoes a mystical experience by the Ogun river with its bridge. The scene is similar to the psychic rebirth Soyinka has described as part of the Ogun mystery. Sleeping by the river, Egbo feels in the morning that the bridge is a rainbow: 'A rainbow of planed grey steel and rock-spun girders lifting on pillars from the bowels of the earth. Egbo rose and looked around him, bathing and wondering at life, for it seemed to him that he was born again, he felt night now as a womb of the gods and a passage for travellers.' Later he will take 'the new woman' to the same place and their love-making will be seen as ritualistic: 'The centre pure ran raw red blood, spilling on the toes of the god'.

The Interpreters is more than a criticism of modern Nigeria and more than a study of the independence generation. Problems of identity are set against a vision of pattern within apparent chaos—chaos and destruction being necessary parts of creation and therefore the creative process. (The Yoruba myth of creation in which unity is shattered is recalled at the beginning of Chapter 16.) While the novel shows the quest and not regeneration, the various decisions concerning love and marriage in the final chapter should be seen in the light of Sekoni's claim that love is a path to the Universal Dome.

Despite the various attacks on Negritude during the course of the novel, and despite its use of modern literary techniques, *The Interpreters*, like Soyinka's plays, has Yoruba myth and cosmology at its core. Kola's painting of a 'Pantheon' of Yoruba gods points directly to Soyinka's method in his writing.

Although *Kongi's Harvest* (1967) is usually understood as an attack on Nkrumah's rule in Ghana, Soyinka has indicated that there were homegrown Nigerian politicians propagandising their own 'isms' or ideologies who were more the object of his satire. Kongi's relevance to Nigeria was the tyrannical reign of Chief Akintola during what is known as the Western Region Crisis. The split in the main Yoruba political party leading to a state of emergency, the imprisonment of many Yoruba leaders, a regional tyranny, and the breakdown of law and order led directly to the first coup d'état and military takeover in Nigeria, which in turn resulted in the massacre of Igbos and the civil war. *Kongi's Harvest* is the first of Soyinka's major works to reflect directly on the Nigerian political situation. Subsequently most of his writing will concern national or international politics.

The play takes place on 'the eve and the day of the national celebrations of Isma'.[13] The satire on made-up ideologies or 'isms' is similar to Soyinka's wry celebration of national independence in *A Dance of the Forests*, and shows the artist's new function after independence as a critic of the ruling elite, especially of the politicians. Although the satire is primarily directed at Kongi, President of Isma, who has attempted to take on himself the symbolism and authority of traditional rulers, it is also directed at the tribal chiefs. Oba Danlola is pompous, ineffective, and more concerned with his comforts than with liberty or government. Although condemned, Oba Danlola's lechery is likeable. The traditional rulers were far from ideal, but they have been replaced by those who blaspheme against African traditional culture.

It is customary in many West African cultures that a priest or ruler should eat the first yam during a harvest festival; in Achebe's *Arrow of God*, the refusal of the priest symbolically to consecrate the yam leads to the village's conversion to Christianity. The action of Soyinka's play focuses on Kongi's attempt to replace Oba Danlola as the ruler who is offered and eats the first yam, thereby consecrating the new crop. By doing so Kongi would succeed to the traditional ruler's authority. It is significant that opposition to Kongi comes rather from Daodu, an educated 'been to' of the younger generation, than from the Oba and his followers.

The attempt to replace traditional customs by the modern ideology is challenged in the play by the younger generation which has its own communal farm, combining modern agricultural techniques with what is understood to be traditional African socialism. The festival of the New Yam turns from a celebration into a disaster when Kongi is served, instead of the symbolic yam, the head of a man whom he ordered executed. A new cycle has begun. Kongi harvests death, not life. Since mankind is doomed to recurrent cycles or patterns of history, including tyranny, there will always be authoritarian power; but the difference between traditional government and the modern state is that the tribes had means to change their rulers, whereas the modern dictator is much harder to depose. The attempt in *Kongi's Harvest* may result in worse repression; even Kongi's closest aides flee from his wrath.

Why do Segi and Daodu participate in the Harvest Festival after they learn that their plot to assassinate Kongi has failed? Daodu performs a sacrifice and imitates Ogun's mythic journey through chaos towards creativity. Daodu is like the artist, a mouthpiece of the gods, who is redeemed by undergoing a potentially destructive experience. His behaviour represents the will and risk-taking necessary if the *Karma* of man's destiny is to be broken and the hope of a new age brought about.

The first poems in *Idanre and Other Poems* (1967), printed under the title 'of the road', show the modern highway as an embodiment of the cosmic journey Ogun made through chaos to find a pathway between the gods and man. The road is a symbol, a sign of continuity between life and death, and a psychic drama in which one risks destruction to bring creativity. 'Abiku' is based on the belief common to many Nigerians that a child who dies will return and die again until the spell is broken. An Abiku child illustrates Soyinka's cyclical view of history and the hope of escaping from it. Although several of the poems are strikingly effective—particularly 'Death in the Dawn', 'In Memory of Segun Awolowo', and 'Abiku'—there is a strong tendency for language to be wrenched syntactically and semantically. Soyinka is, I think, trying to make English operate like 'deep Yoruba', metaphorically, imagistically, allusively. This style will become increasingly developed in his later work, especially in *Shuttle in the Crypt* (1972). The writing at times is surprisingly insensitive to the limits of English. If the style is partly a result of 'Yorubaising' English, it also results from expressing a sacramental vision in a language, and during an era, which lacks acceptable equivalents for the concepts being evoked.

Idanre itself is an attempt to write a *Paradise Lost*, an inspired vision of the Yoruba cosmic scheme. From the perspective of Yoruba myth it relates the genesis of the world, the story of Ogun—especially his journey to mankind and his slaughter of his own followers—and offers a view of history as a recurring 'eternal cycle of karmas that has become the evil history of man'. The preface to *Idanre* speaks of a 'pattern of awareness' that began with Soyinka's writing of *A Dance of the Forests* and which in the 'context of my society' has been shown in the Western Region uprising and the events that led to the massacre of the Igbos. Using the mathematical figure of a Mobius strip, Soyinka sees eternity as offering an illusion, 'a poetic one' of 'a possible centrifugal escape' from 'the doom of repetition'.[14]

Idanre recalls a visionary experience first felt when visiting the Idanre hills and later re-experienced in a forest during a rainy night. The storm is imagined as representing a battle between the gods Ogun and Sango, in which Sango, as lightning and electricity, is caught by Ogun, who as god of iron conducts 'him down to earth'. Inspired and possessed by Ogun Soyinka enters ('*I earth my being*') the accompanying 'palm wine girl', whose wine makes her symbolic 'priestess'. The sexual experience complements the vision of the god who

'Drew warring elements to a union of being'.

In the 'pilgrimage' section, Idanre's 'boulder complex' recalls the Yoruba myth of the division of the world from its original unity:

> Union they had known until the Boulder
> Rolling down the hill of the Beginning
> Shred the kernel to a million lights.

The poet experiences the history of the gods, especially Ogun's journey from the gods to man. This forms the subject of section IV, 'the beginning': 'And this pledge he gave the heavens I will clear a path to man', which concludes with warnings of the dangers that follow from man's involvement with such a heroic deity. The men of Ire persuade Ogun to be their king and warlord with the result, told in section V, that during battle the god kills both the enemy and his own followers: 'To bring a god to supper is devout, yet/A wise host keeps his distance.' Soyinka turns his vision from the god's remorse as Ogun becomes aware of the carnage he has created. But such knowledge as has been felt cannot be forgotten. The poet cannot abdicate the truth he knows. He has himself experienced Ogun's passage through chaos, his carnage and guilt. He must celebrate both the past and its eternal recurrence in the present and future. Soyinka's vision has affinities with Indian belief, but, unlike the Indians he does not accept fate nor, despite its attractions, withdraw into meditation. There are *Karmas*, but no release from the bondage of history.

During the Nigerian civil war Soyinka was imprisoned in 1967 and held in solitary confinement for nearly two years by the government which claimed that he had aided the Biafran secessionist movement. Much of his subsequent writing has treated of his experience during these years or, by allusion, of the events connected with them. *The Man Died* (1972) is an autobiographical account of his arrest and imprisonment. Shortly after his arrest Soyinka is interrogated by Mallam D. 'When the government has already laid down a policy, what makes you think you know better? You are intellectuals living in a dream world, yet you think you know better than men who have weighed out so many factors and come to a decision.'[15]

At the time Soyinka felt that the populace who follow the government are 'Brain-washed, gullible fools, many-headed multitudes'. However, 'I caution myself and try substituting peoples for nations. . . . In moments of grave doubts it is essential to cling to the reality of peoples; these cannot vanish, they have no questionable *a priori*—they exist.' Soyinka hoped to build 'a socialist state'; 'I think, after all, there is only one common definition for a people and a nation—a unit of humanity bound together by a common ideology.'

Soyinka has claimed that his African mythic perspective provides a unified view of reality which has been lost to the West as a result of fragmentation proceeding from rationalist and materialistic thought. The power of his writing results from the obsessive vision which permeates his work regardless of its explicit subject-matter. In his prison poems, *A Shuttle in the Crypt* (1972), the sequence 'Chimes of Silence' in compressed form makes use of the analogy found in *The Man Died* between Ogun's passing through chaos and the author's will to survive imprisonment. Hezzy Maduakor has said: 'Ogun's trials in the abyss of disintegration have their parallels in the private experience of every individual. Man must pass through the crucibles of experience like Ogun, and one's manhood is proven by the degree to which he summons the inner resources of his being to dare and overcome the abyss of dissolution.'[16] The early poems in the sequence both locate the experience in the prison and show the fatality of those who attempt to survive by prayer, compliance or acceptance. 'Purgatory' shows the absurdity of law with its supposed function of restoring man to society through punishment. Those who punish are themselves villains or perverts; the imprisoned include 'the mad', 'the damned': 'Epileptics, seers and visionaries', all 'Trudging the lifelong road to a dread/Judicial sentence'. Seeing the pain suffered by those who hope for reprieve, 'The mind retreats behind a calloused shelter/Of walls, self-censor on the freedom of remembrance'. The emasculation of hope and desire brings the 'comfort of a gelded sanity'.[17] Where will such loneliness end? 'Recession (*Mahapralaya*)' tells of the dissolution of the self from relationship with the world. Such negation or destruction is necessary before there can be liberation and renewal. Soyinka's footnote to *Mahapralaya* reads: 'In Hindu Metaphysics, the return of the universe to its womb; here, expressed as the consoling experience of man in the moment of death, the freeing of his being from the death of the world.' The poems that follow speak of psychic renewal. Noah and the Dove are invoked in 'Space': 'His mind was boundless when out/He flew.' Rebirth in 'Seed' is suggested by 'Roll away the stone', the reference to Lazarus, the images of 'splitting wood-grains' and 'gentle rain'.

In *Season of Anomy* (1973), Soyinka's second novel, Aiyéró is the self-governing, self-policing village, a Utopia, often portrayed in African literature as the culture of the past, before colonialism. All property is held in common. Its 'religion of the Grain' is a 'way of life', a 'philosophy' and consists of observances, rituals and a communal socialism. Although the community does not believe in aggression, it makes guns to defend itself and grants 'Ogun pride of place' among the gods. Ofeyi sees in Aiyéró the communal way of life which he had planned to teach his country as a result of studying Marxism abroad.

In contrast to Aiyéró the nation is violently ruled by a corrupt elite, business interests and army misusing authority and governmental powers to enrich themselves and stay in office at all costs. Ofeyi enlists the support of Aiyéró to undermine the ruling 'Cartel'. The resulting repression, wave of terror, massacre of the people of Aiyéró in the Cross Rivers, and kidnapping, rape and imprisonment of Iriyese (symbol of Nigeria) allude to the events in Nigeria beginning with the Western Region Crisis, the military takeover, the massacre of the Igbos in the north, and Soyinka's own imprisonment. The hero and heroine, Ofeyi and Iriyise, are a Nigerian Orpheus and Eurydice. The Jeroko prison (recognisably the prison in *The Man Died* and *Shuttle*) from which Ofeyi rescues Iriyise, with its three circles of prisoners, lepers and lunatics, represents hell: 'Abandon hope all who enter.'[18] Ofeyi must go into the depths of the prison with its grotesque parody of the greed, injustice and corruption of the nation before beginning his journey towards life and the political and moral salvation represented by Aiyéró. Ofeyi, former advertising man and writer of songs, has journeyed through hell, like Orpheus, and through the abyss like Ogun. The dangerous journey at the end of the book back to Aiyéró represents the hope, or spores, of a new beginning, or at least a new cycle of history. It 'is a cleansing act. It will purify our present polluted humanity and cure our survivors of the dangers of self-pity.'

While *Season of Anomy* is based on events in post-independence Nigeria, it has similarities to neo-nationalist writing of the period. Westernisation and independence have created a modern state with close links between government and giant industrial interests. The wealth of the rulers is based on exploiting the workers and, through advertising, creating a market for a nutritionally worthless beverage. The government pays lip-service to ideas of national revolution, but is seen as the successor to those Africans who profited from the slave trade; its vision of Africa is alien. By way of contrast there is Aiyéró, the communal rural Utopia from which an authentic culture can be born.

One characteristic of neo-nationalism is its empathy with similar movements elsewhere and the recreation of a 'Pan' perspective of the kind that often existed before national independence. *Ogun Abibimañ* (1976) is a poem prophesying the liberation of South Africa. During March 1976, 'Samora Machel, Leader of the People of Mozambique . . . placed [the nation] in a state of war against white-ruled Rhodesia.' Soyinka sees this as the beginning of the continent's struggle against apartheid South Africa, a struggle which he envisages as ordained to success: 'It *has* happened. The rest is history.'[19] The poem celebrates an 'in-gathering' of the African tribes to battle. Ogun, god of war, creativity, metals and the road, is now envisaged as restorer of rights. He joins forces with Shaka, the most famous warrior in South African history, to complete the liberation of Abibimañ, an Akan (Ghanaian) word for the black nation. (The mixture of three national or tribal cultures, while appropriate to the Pan-Africanism of the late 1970s, seems forced.) Using a technique common both to the epic and African oral literature, Soyinka is inspired to recall the past and retells parts of the Shaka legend as a praise-song. This is followed by what might be described as a war cry; warnings against weakness and memories of injustice: 'Remember Sharpeville—not as aberrations/Of the single hour, but years, and generations.' The poem concludes with a vision of 'the clans' 'massed' 'from hill to hill/Where Ogun stood' dancing to Shaka's war cry '*Sigidi*'. Such a summary oversimplifies a complex blend of modernist, traditional African, prophetic and political poetry; but it will indicate how far Soyinka has travelled in his attempt to shape a supreme fiction from aspects of Yoruba mythology.

Whether or not Soyinka has modified the significance of the Ogun ritual for his own purpose, the extension of the myth to all areas of behaviour is similar to the integration of the modern with the traditional noticeable in many of the new national literatures. While the desire for authenticity is another, more local version of the post-Renaissance wish to harmonise experience and recover the sacramental, the impetus to overcome cultural fragmentation is particularly strong where colonialism has intensified consciousness of the atomised quality of modern society, with its division of labour, separation of the secular from the spiritual, and specialised, often conflicting analyses of experience. Soyinka's affirmation of the Ogun ritual as a re-enactment of the meeting of divine and human and as the psychology of creativity and heroic action has similarities to the attempt of such writers as A. D. Hope, Robertson Davies, R. K. Narayan and Wilson Harris to relate contemporary life to the universal and eternal.

6 West Indies I: Naipaul, Harris and history

To discuss Caribbean writing in English as if it were a national literature may seem unusual. The West Indian Federation collapsed in 1962 and the region now consists of small nations and some remaining political dependencies of Britain. While national traditions are observable, unfortunately no one country has yet produced a sufficient number of major writers to speak of its own literature.[1] Because of the similarities between the various islands, their common history, and the fact that the emergence of West Indian literature occurred during the period when hopes of federation were prevalent, many writers see themselves as belonging more to the region than to a specific country.

West Indian literature follows the same stages of development that can be found in other former colonial English-speaking societies. The eighteenth and nineteenth centuries were marked by the journals and diaries of visiting foreigners, by vaguely descriptive verse, by imitations of older English literary forms, and by collections of 'folk' songs and tales. During the first decade of the new century an attempt was made to write and publish novels in Jamaica. The novels of Thomas MacDermot ('Tom Redcam') and H. G. de Lisser are significant in their occasional use of dialect and inclusion of poor blacks as sympathetic characters. The post-First World War years saw the rejection of provincialism and a flight by the younger generation to metropolitan centres which offered a more sophisticated style of life. Claude McKay and other black West Indians contributed to the Harlem Renaissance and the exportation of an interest in black culture throughout the western world. Jean Rhys's *The Left Bank and Other Stories* (1927) records the international bohemia of the period. By the late 1920s the desire to shock the bourgeoisie was being transformed into politics. Sympathies for the Russian Revolution and the Indian nationalist movement were strengthened by the Great Depression. Such journals as *Trinidad* and *The Beacon* reflected this new mood in urging that fiction be concerned with local lives and written in an appropriate manner.[2] The realistic fiction that developed abroad had its West Indian counterpart in the novels of Alfred Mendes—*Pitch Lake* (1934) and *Black Fauns* (1935)—and C. L. R. James—*Minty Alley* (1936). Questions of cultural identity developed alongside the political tensions of the late 1930s. Edgar Mittelholzer's *Corentyne Thunder* (1941) sympathetically described the rural East Indian who suffered and was left behind as his children began to assimilate into the nation's urban creole society. The novel also records the conflicts of cultural identity among the children of the Guyanese middle class, a concern often expressed in terms of mixed racial and national blood stock and of past family guilt.

During the mid-1940s and early 1950s new sources of local publication contributed to an increased consciousness of West Indian culture. *Bim* (1942–), a Barbadian journal, and the weekly B.B.C. *Caribbean Voices* radio 'magazine' gave writers a wider audience and created a link between London and the region. A literary career, formerly viewed as beyond the reach of a colonial, now seemed possible. *Focus* (1943, '48, '56, '60), an occasional publication edited by Edna Manley, had its roots in nationalist and cultural movements in Jamaica. Closely associated with local radical politics, it published realistic fiction about the impoverished slum dwellers. Writers associated with *Focus* included V. S. Reid (*New Day*, 1949) and Roger Mais (*The Hills Were Joyful Together*, 1953). *Kyk-over-al* (1945–61) in Guyana, edited by Arthur Seymour, was concerned with the multiracial cultural heritage of the country and gave prominence to survivals of the Amerindian past.

The American presence in the islands during the war, the collapse of the Empire after the war and the granting of self-government quickened the social changes that had started during the 1930s. Samuel Selvon's *A Brighter Sun* (1952) recorded the transformations within Trinidad during the war years. George Lamming's *In the Castle of My Skin* (1953) is a poetic evocation of a boy's memories of growing up in Barbados during the mid-1930s and the early 1940s. The narrator's careful recording of family and village life is set within a consciousness of the island's social and political history. The boy's evolving consciousness progressively takes on wider horizons. Towards the novel's conclusion, as the narrator prepares to leave for Trinidad, he becomes aware of race and colour prejudice. His friend Trumper tells him of discrimination in America. Trumper 'was a Negro and he was proud. Now he could walk in the sun or stand on the highest hill and proclaim himself the blackest evidence of the white man's denial of conscience.'[3] The literature of the early 1950s was concerned with identity, race and nationalism. It reflected the emergence of a local professional, often coloured, middle class to positions of power. John Hearne's novels showed the cultural assurance of the middle class and their concern that the discontent of the excluded masses threatened established society. In the 1960s West Indian literature began a period in which myth, allegory and other symbolic and poetic forms were used in response to the problems of historical determinism and cultural identity the region had inherited from colonialism. An affirmation of African roots coincided with the Black Power riots and the growing radicalisation of West Indian politics in the late 1960s and early '70s.

V. S. Naipaul's writing reflects his background in the East Indian Trinidadian community. Indian indentured labour was brought to Trinidad during the mid-nineteenth century after the emancipation of the slaves. Settlement in rural areas soon followed.[4] The East Indians were from the first treated by the Europeans and blacks as the bottom of the social ladder, being recent immigrants, usually impoverished farmers who, because they did not speak English, had no western education and brought their native culture and religions with them. The separation of the East Indians from the rest of society—by race, poverty, language, religion and culture—remained constant throughout the nineteenth and early twentieth century. Various stereotypes developed of the East Indian as a 'coolie', heathen, money-grabber and savage. The East Indians remained in rural occupations and settlements, were denied the vote and other legal rights that had been given to those of African descent and were generally regarded as foreigners. Such attitudes were reinforced by the Indians' desire to retain their own culture, which necessitated keeping their children away from English schools, often run by church missions.

It was only after the First World War that the East Indians began entering West Indian national society, their most significant involvement being the labour riots on various islands during the late thirties, when Indian and Negro leaders co-operated politically for the first time. Such co-operation weakened during the 1940s, when under the influence of the Indian independence movement there was a rise of Indian cultural nationalism. The quarrels over enfranchisement and the fear of a permanent black majority furthered the division between Indians and Negroes at the time of the first popular elections and during the granting of national independence. To some extent the Indian still saw himself as part of an Indian community while those of African descent were nationalists. To the Indian, nationalism meant creolisation and eventual assimilation with the Negro. Despite the increasing cultural creolisation of the Indian community and the emergence of Indian business and labour leaders, the problems of racial and cultural identity within the predominantly black society of the region remain. The Guyanese race riots, the Trinidadian Black Power riots of 1970, and such polemics in favour of creolisation as Edward Brathwaite's *Contradictory Omens* (1974) suggest that the continuing rise of black consciousness in the West Indies plays a part in the Indian–Negro conflict.[5] The growth of the East Indian population, making it the largest group in Guyana and Trinidad, although the governments are dominated by blacks, is likely to produce further conflict.

V. S. Naipaul's father, Seepersad Naipaul, was a first-generation Trinidadian, raised in an impoverished Hindi-speaking household. As he was a Brahmin by caste, he married into an important local East Indian family. He became a reporter for the Trinidad *Guardian* and subsequently published his own small collection of short stories, *Gurudeva and Other Indian Stories* (1943).[6] Written at a time of East Indian assertion (in response to the Indian nationalist movement), the stories record the growing chaos and decay of Hindu culture in the region. They show an immigrant society losing its cohesion and purpose, and the young, lacking the stabilising influences of a settled community, turning towards violence as a means of self-assertion. The style is precise, flat, and subtly ironic, although without comment. Such writing is the opposite of most protest literature written by the middle class for the middle class; it does not play on class or racial guilt and it attempts to record accurately, with slight caricaturisation and irony, how representative lives are shaped by the conditions of their society, a method developed into sophisticated fiction by Seepersad's son, V. S. Naipaul.

V. S. Naipaul's early novels primarily treat of the confusions in Hindu society in Trinidad, both the ossification of a culture into ritual and the loss of traditional culture within a multiracial society. It would be possible to rearrange the subject-matter of Naipaul's fiction into a selected but chronological history of the fortunes of the Trinidadian Hindu community.[7] *A House for Mr Biswas* (1961) traces a life from the isolated, totally Indian rural community of the first decade of the century through its gradual contact with a larger society, culminating for Mr Biswas in his rise to becoming a reporter and houseowner in urban, multiracial Port of Spain. The later part of the novel is concerned with the education of children, which allows Mr Biswas's sons to earn scholarships to study in England. If the novel is a success story of immigrant life and New World assimilation, it also records the failure of Hindu culture to survive in the West Indies.

Naipaul, whose family has been influential in Trinidadian politics and Indian cultural movements, has often written of the lack of future of the East Indian community in the Caribbean; such despair is behind the social comedy of *The Mystic Masseur* (1957) and *The Suffrage of Elvira* (1958). Both novels treat of the electoral process. The life of Pundit Ganeesh, in *The*

Mystic Masseur, can be seen as a humorous success story during a time of social and political change, but it also illustrates a rapid deterioration of Hindu culture which, historically, parallels the movement towards self-government in the colony. If Pundit Ganeesh is a colourful figure, he is without cultural or moral standards. He unashamedly surrounds himself with symbols from many religions when he seeks business as a faith healer; he appeals to Hindu nationalism, however, to win an election. After a period as a radical firebrand, he becomes a supporter of the colonial government and receives a knighthood. Similarly, the election in *The Suffrage of Elvira* is marked by the buying of votes and other forms of sharp dealing. Although religious practices have become creolised, a confused stew of various beliefs, symbols and practices, each ethnic group votes as a block.

For Naipaul the West Indies consists of races that have been uprooted from their original society and that have not produced a new culture to replace what was lost. They have been abandoned on Trinidad, with little in common and without the various resources needed to create an energetic new society. There is no creativity, no achievement; the middle classes are parasites, mimicking the ideas and activities of metropolitan societies; each group or race continues to think of foreign lands as 'home'. Although Naipaul's early fiction is centred on the Indian community, it is clear from his non-fiction that he saw the other ethnic groups in analogous situations. The European settlers drank and ate grossly, were uninterested in education and the arts, and created nothing; as a result their only claim to status was their race. The brown middle class copied the English and was uninterested in Africa. In *The Middle Passage* (1962) and *The Loss of Eldorado* (1965) Naipaul sees slavery as one historical cause which determined the limited development of the region. Slavery left a heritage of distinctions based rather on racial pride than individual or group achievement; it left those of African descent cut off from any viable cultural traditions but desirous of the privileges of European status which they were denied. The linked short stories in *Miguel Street* (1959) show a society of failures, in which nothing is achieved and in which eccentricity, brutality and violence are the usual means of asserting identity in a small, impoverished colony. The young narrator at first wants to be one of the gang and finds their eccentricity and big talk interesting. As he grows up he begins to understand that the code of the street masks communal and individual failure.

Naipaul's early views can be seen as part of the continuing conflict found in all societies between those who seek a better world abroad and those who stay at home and find sufficient cultural nourishment in their local community. He appears to be a writer who has preferred exile to home, but continues to write about home and its problems. Home, however, is rather different for Naipaul than for most writers. He is a product of three cultures: the West Indies, India and England. For many years he thought of home not as England but as India. The fantasy he mocks of the West Indian dreaming of being an Aryan horseman on the northern Indian mountains was his own. While other writers have attempted to set down roots in London, Paris or Accra, Naipaul attempted to settle in India. The experience of that failure is recorded in *An Area of Darkness* (1964), where Naipaul discovers that, despite his Indian upbringing, he is essentially western. The East shocks him with its disregard for individual dignity, its fatalism, its mystical retreat from reality, its lack of energy and its preference for myths to actualities. He is shocked by Indian uncleanliness, feudalism and disregard for facts. Where he had expected a land of achievements based on a long tradition, he found a fractured culture, the vitality of which had ended before the English conquest and which was now a mixture of mimicry of western ideas with an oriental resignation to fate and self-absorption in timeless spiritual destiny. The contradictions, incompetence and ritualism which might charm tourists left him angered. Another home had failed. Naipaul compared his search for identity with a piece of patterned cloth that one unweaves to trace the figures and that ends by being a heap of tangled threads.

It is Naipaul's disillusionment with India and growing awareness that he is a product of a complex world that form the basis of *The Mimic Men* (1967). The main character is similar to Naipaul in his respect for security, traditions, order and long-established culture. But significantly his attitudes of superiority are not approved by the author. While the narrator's despairing analysis of the problems of the Third World is probably more accurate than most liberals would admit, his own withdrawal from activity and his air of civilised superiority is implied to be a personal failure to come to terms with reality. If his career is representative of the post-independence Third World politicians, his longings for a comfortable, settled society verge on a parody of Naipaul's own often expressed feelings. And, of course, his name, Ralph Kripal Singh, points to the element of self-parody; besides being representative of the independence leaders of the Third World, he is also one of Naipaul's many characters who engage in writing. The accusation of mimicry applies equally to the narrator and to the other West Indians in the novel.

Although the analysis of post-colonial society has application to the Third World in general, *The Mimic Men* could be said to be another study in the progress of the Trinidadian East Indian community. The narrator's adventures in England, his English wife, business success at home, position as government minister in an ethnically pluralistic new nation which is not genuinely multiracial, followed by being deposed from office and exile abroad, might be said to represent both the fate of the bourgeoisie of the new nations and Naipaul's picture of the emergence of the East Indian into West Indian upper-middle-class society and his possible fate. The middle-class, westernised East Indian has no real authenticity. His power has been given to him by his former colonial masters and does not grow out of the actual structure of society. He is cut off from the rural Indian labourer. He has none of the ability, experience or means of command found in those who govern older societies. Mr Biswas's badly built, mortgaged house symbolically anticipates the problem of the Hindu in Trinidad and the instability of the nation itself. The rise of black consciousness finds a political base in lower-class poverty. The resulting radicalism will quickly depose the independence rulers and initiate a period of political instability. In impoverished newly created nations the struggle for the spoils of office soon becomes a war of the jungle in which the winner takes all and must brutally fight off the many who seek immediate wealth, which is unobtainable outside government and its corruption.

Seeking escape from the uncertainties of the Third World Kripal Singh remains exiled in London, admiring a society with its comforting folk songs, nursery tales and secure traditions. But England also deceives; London is a city of private cells for those who long for the ideal city of their imagination. Singh's dream of a noble society is both tragic and pathetic. Tragic because the intelligent and sensitive naturally wish to live in a metropolis governed by higher ideals, distinguished by taste and achievement. Pathetic because Singh's feelings are those of a colonial who imagines real life as being lived elsewhere and who devalues his own experience; he has become a cripple incapable of the independence, energy, cunning and will that are required to make any city or nation fit his longings. Indeed in all of his experiences, whether sexual or political, his fastidiousness prevents enjoyment. He is the ultimate mimic man, a neo-platonist for whom reality will always be an idea.

Naipaul's novels after *The Mimic Men* are different. Satiric disdain has been replaced by concern; oddly the objectivity of style contrasts with the commitment towards the subject matter. The later novels are notable for their mosaic organisation, their cool pointillist style, their concern with the lives of the poverty-stricken in the Third World, and their despair at the possibility of current liberal, radical or nationalist slogans in any way improving the conditions that have caused such hardships. *In a Free State* (1971) and *Guerrillas* (1975) might be described as studies in the conditions of freedom where decolonisation has left social and cultural disorder and where the resources, will and knowledge to create a new order are lacking.

An implicit theme of Naipaul's has been the problems resulting from modern freedom. The Tulsi Hindu household has its horrors, but Mr Biswas's attempt to escape into individuality brings anxieties and terrors before he can establish a house of his own. In the process he has lost the security of an extended Indian family. Even settled in his own house he is insecure. The house has a mortgage to be paid off, means must be found to pay for his children's education, and because of illness he loses his job. Modern capitalist society offers a sense of individual worth, but it offers few protections. With Biswas's illness his salary as a journalist stops. His son goes to England and soon loses contact with him. If freedom brings individual, in contrast to caste, dignity, it also brings anxieties, responsibilities and personal humiliations. There is no extended family, caste or community as an escape, no rituals through which one can be cleansed. Each person fights on his or her own. On a ship to Egypt Naipaul sees an English vagabond humiliated by some Greek businessmen. In Egypt Naipaul tries to stop a tourist guide from beating some beggar children, but no one cares. Both autobiographical incidents in *In a Free State* are linked to the themes of the short stories in the book. The frustrations felt by those who have been uprooted from a closed community and forced to survive in the chaos of western freedom are amply indicated by the title of one story, 'Tell Me Who to Kill'. The title story, 'In a Free State', shows the effects of such freedom in post-colonial Africa. A civil war rages, the army is leaderless and commits atrocities, the expatriates are rootless and irresponsible, the political and economic structure is unrelated to the actual society. The independent country is not a real nation but a collection of mutually hostile tribes that have been forced into a nation-state by colonial boundaries. When the colonial power withdraws there is no basis for a society. Such government as exists is based on raw power, tribalism and the support of foreign nations.

Guerrillas looks at the Black Power movements in the West Indies during the late 1960s and early '70s. Here the ideology is imported from abroad, a more fashionable mimicry which replaces the English manners of the colonial period. But the island is run by blacks and the psychological injuries of the past cannot be healed by aimless riots that drive the existing sources of employment from the island. In such an angry, confused nation there is no community, only private injuries to be revenged. Jimmy Ahmed, himself torn between hatred and love of white English culture, says: 'When everybody wants to fight there's nothing to fight for. Everybody wants to fight his own little war, everybody is a guerrilla.'

There has always been a strong autobiographical element in Naipaul's fiction. While the novels and short stories have seldom been about himself, they have reflected the various stages of his disillusionment with Trinidad, his despair with India and, more recently, his concern with being a homeless ex-colonial, a citizen of the western and Third World during a time of rapid social change. He seems to feel in his isolation, his uprootedness, an analogy to the breakdown of a central cultural and political authority in the modern world. Thus the portraits of modern moral anarchy in his recent novels.

In *The Loss of Eldorado* Naipaul examined the confused history of Trinidad. The precariousness of the original settlement was followed by rapidly changing occupying powers. Misguided schemes of settlement, the introduction of African slaves, an influx of refugees from South America and other islands resulted, after the West Indies were no longer of strategic or economic importance to Britain, in a poverty-stricken, unhomogenous, racially conscious nation on the outer fringes of the world community. Despite the objective presentation of facts and the analytic power brought to bear on examining the historical causes of Trinidadian economic and cultural poverty, Naipaul's book shares in the anger at colonialism common to West Indian writers of his generation. There is a feeling that the past has determined the present; the effects of slavery, the introduction of oriental labour, the plantation system, the mixture of races, and a history of political instability, corruption and tyranny have left Trinidad permanently disabled.

If such a vision of the region is common to many West Indian writers, Wilson Harris's strange novels are an attempt to find the seeds for growth and achievement within such apparent displacement. They turn the arguments of the social historian on their head and show how the confused, brutal, provincial past of Guyana, rather than determining the failure of the nation, provides the basis and freedom for a new society, perhaps superior to that of Europe. In a sense the difference between Naipaul and Harris is a regional, more complex variation on a once common topic of American literature, the debate whether the New World is a fall into cultural barbarity or a restoration of man to his original potentiality. But Harris is not a young Walt Whitman singing celebrations of a new society. There is sufficient recognition of guilt, barbarity, cruelty and the ironies of idealism in his novels to suggest a kinship rather with Herman Melville, a novelist whom he has often praised as the beginning of the literature of the Americas. But whereas Melville's novels might be understood as cautionary, Harris envisages continual change, even tragic change, as a process of renewal, a liberation from ossified categories of thought. His novels are experiments in writing without fixed characterisation, logical narrative sequence, or other means of classifying and postulating the relationship between cause and effect. They attempt to show the basic psychic drama that takes place beyond consciousness, regardless of race or social position. Liberation from categorical thought destroys historical determinism and reveals that such colonial relations as hunter-hunted, or conqueror-conquered are meaningless as records of human relationships and man's past. It is only by destroying its images of such fixed relationships that society will begin to understand the processes of human life.

Harris has tried to reveal the essential forces that underlie social behaviour, to reimagine other cultures and other eras in ways that will show their distinctive vision, bring them into living relationship with the present, and make the particulars of experience part of a transcendent world of processes. Thus the novels include spirits, the reappearance of the dead, the transformations of facts into their opposites, and a prose style often built upon such disjunctive devices as oxymorons and paradoxes, with the result that logically impossible events are recounted in an often bewildering manner.

If Wilson Harris has any direct forebear it is T. S. Eliot with his meditations on time and tradition, and his fragmentation of narrative into a mosaic of dissociated images and symbols expressive of the chaos of modern culture and of the individual mind attempting to piece together an encompassing vision out of personal disorder. While the allusions, techniques, symbols and even occasional phrases are similar, Harris differs from Eliot in trying to create a personal New World myth of process whereas the American poet sought to lose himself in an impersonal tradition, salvaged from the ruins of the Old World. Harris refers to fossils not as records but as gateways to an imaginative participation in the culture and events of the past. It is only through such an extension of the imagination that rigidly fixed cultural and racial boundaries, with their social superiorities and animosities, can be destroyed, and the many peoples of the New World can renew their contact with each other, recognising that their shared history involves more basic experiences than are accepted by such stereotypes as coloniser, slave, or exterminated Indian.

Perhaps the most remarkable illustration of this attempt to fragment rationalist concepts and retrace history to the origins of man is Harris's first novel, *Palace of the Peacock* (1960), where normal expectations and assumptions are continually twisted inside out and outside in, until a new creation symbolically takes the place of the original genesis. Here dream and reality are interchangeable, life is seen as death and death as life, the narrator and the main character in his story exchange places and often fuse into one person as time becomes confused. While it is possible to follow the main thread of the story, it is impossible to state in linear, rational sequence exactly what does take place. The novel is an *Inferno* in which the journey towards the renewal of memory, and thus purgatory, involves a river voyage into the interior of Guyana and its history by a dead, incestuous crew which on the seventh day of de-creation will be shipwrecked at the source of the river and again die. Their death, however, results in the gaining of the Palace of the Peacock, a kind of apocalyptic rebirth into divine harmony.

Palace of the Peacock begins and ends with the narrator's vision. The voyage that he describes is his own journey back through history within his mind. The events in the novel contribute towards the author's creation of a unified sacramental world from the fragments and violence of the Guyanese landscape and past. Separateness has been overcome:

> I felt the faces before me begin to fade and part company from me and from themselves as if our need of one another was now fulfilled, and our distance from each other was the distance of a sacrament, the sacrament and embrace we knew in one muse and one undying soul. Each of us now held at last in his arms what he had been for ever seeking and what he had eternally possessed.[8]

To speak of *Palace of the Peacock* as a therapeutic dream—a Guyanese equivalent of the medieval high vision of the heavenly rose—risks oversimplification and neglect of the narrative, but properly shifts concern from explication of the often irrational to the source or creator of the fragmented structure, the narrator who early tells us 'I dreamt I awoke with one dead seeing eye and one living closed eye.' Representative of the coloniser and colonised, he desires 'to govern or be governed, rule or be ruled'. As he dreams of Donne, the colonising leader of the crew of the ship, we learn 'His wild exploits had governed my imagination from childhood.' As Donne is a projection of the desires of the dreaming narrator and yet his opposite in brutal activity, they are interchangeable contraries within the human psyche: 'He was myself standing outside of me while I stood inside of him.' Although 'the map of the savannahs was a dream' and the names of Brazil and Guiana colonial conventions, the narrator can 'not help cherishing' his 'symbolic map' which he dreams he possesses, His dream or vision progresses from simple desires of exploration and conquest to a deeper, more spiritual possession. The voyage to the interior is through 'the wild inverse stream of beginning to live again'.

It is somewhat ironic that the two West Indian writers, Harris and Brathwaite, who are most favoured by intellectuals committed to optimistic views of the Caribbean situation should be concerned with the muse of inspiration. While his theory that the West Indian novel can express and help strengthen the links between individuals of various races has an attractive liberal sound, what Harris does is perhaps closer to the romantic claim that the writer is a priest of the imagination than to the radical intellectual's demand that art have a progressive political purpose. The radicalism of the novels is to make the reader experience the mind's awakening to others and otherness.

The Whole Armour (1962) and *The Secret Ladder* (1963) further illustrate the imagination making peace with the past by destroying our normal temporal categories of character, place, status and society. *The Whole Armour* begins with Abram aware that he is dying from a pain in his chest. He is a 'bewildered man who wanted to rediscover an innocence at all costs'. Abram is representative of an aspect of the Guyanese past. 'No one knew his true name—or from whence he had come.'[9] Soon we are introduced to Magda, a whore of mixed African and Chinese descent. She wishes Abram to hide Cristo, her son who is wanted by the police for supposed murder. When Abram hesitates Magda attempts to destroy his sense of selfhood and property; by sleeping with Magda Abram has become part of her world whether or not he wishes to be: 'Cristo belong to you as well as me. He could be your real son. I want you to forget yourself and feel this power of belonging. Is there anything stronger than mating and borning in this world until you lose you dying self?' Race, however, still makes Abram hold back: 'Even if you knew me and had me wrapped in you arms a hundred lightning year ago you still wouldn't *believe* Cristo is you flying seed and son; he too *black* and you too *white*.'

The Whole Armour uses an obvious analogy to the relationship of the Old Testament Israelites to the Christians. The similarities of name—Abram, Magda, Cristo—imply roles. Cristo 'was paying for a crime he had not committed'; Abram says 'Nobody innocent'. The relationship of law to sacrifice and the promised land is, however, set in Guyana; 'Cristo felt, a region of absurd displacement and primitive boredom, the ground of dreams, long-dead ghosts and still-living sailors, ancient masters and mariners and new slaves'.

The four novels in the *Guiana Quartet* roughly form a chronological sequence from the days of conquest (*Palace of the Peacock*), the period of slavery and Indian indenture (*The Far Journey of Oudin*, 1961), the establishment of a frontier society and law (*The Whole Armour*) and the imposition of a modern state on the land (*The Secret Ladder*). As the setting approaches modern times and notions of reality, with linked cause and effect, it becomes more necessary to show the primitive truths of experience that are hidden to the modern compartmentalised mind. The attack on what we might call scientific thought is also a freeing of the imagination from the boundaries imposed by colonisation and Europe on the New World. Thus the role of Cristo in *The Whole Armour* both has analogies to the role of Christ in the Christian scheme of redemption and is different as is fitting to a New World context. Underlying the novel is an awareness of basic myths of death and renewal: Abram is killed by a tiger; Cristo is made by Magda to disguise himself in Abram's garment, then he kills the tiger and wears his skin. In his tiger skin he returns to the village and initiates a chain of events that change the lives of important characters within the story. Sharon, formerly a frigid 'snow-maiden', becomes Cristo's lover in the jungle. Cristo is hunted as the tiger and by the law as murderer. His death or sacrifice is part of the tragedy of renewal in a world of process. Such sacrifice is necessary: 'Cristo would be free in the end, it seemed to state, in an armour superior to the elements of self-division and coercion. Magda fell on her knees and prayed. There was nothing else to do.'

The Whole Armour, like *Yurokon* in *The Sleepers of Roraima* (1970), has as its theme a moment when sacrifice is necessary to social and cultural transformation. The Caribs of the later story are absorbed into European culture and their sacrificial myths find new but different expression within Christianity. Cristo takes on the guilt for Abram's death and is killed by the law, but in doing so he and others obtain a wholeness previously impossible in racially, religiously divided Guyana. Cristo says, 'We're reborn into the oldest native and into our oldest nature, while they're still Guiana's first aliens and arrivals.' The purpose of the *Guiana Quartet* is made explicit:

> And we have to start all over again where they began to explore. We've got to pick up the seeds again where they left off. It's no use worshipping the rottenest tacouba and tree-trunk in the historic topsoil. There's a whole world of

> branches and sensation we've missed, and we've got to start again from the roots up even if they look like nothing. Blood, sap, flesh, veins, arteries, lungs, heart, the heartland, Sharon. *We're the first potential parents who can contain the ancestral house.*

Sharon is associated in the novel with the bride in the Song of Songs, a collection of biblical lyrics supposedly written for the wedding of the Queen of Sheba with Solomon, which older biblical commentators interpreted variously as the love of the soul and God, or the Church and Christ. The Song of Songs is both explicitly erotic and has been read as having mystical meaning—the erotic passages, for example, as pertaining to the spiritual blessings felt by the soul in contemplation. That Harris is aware of such interpretations is shown by the quotation from St John of the Cross prefacing Book Three of *The Whole Armour*. Sharon, courted by many suitors and engaged to another, has always only desired Cristo, although her place in society has kept her from encouraging the black son of a whore. But once Sharon feels the ecstasy of love, her divided self becomes whole. She is now free from the self-division and hopeless complexity of the past, from the sense of inferiority which shaped her former vision of reality. In Cristo she finds consummation and Guyana: 'Her fingers travelled across the map of Cristo's skin, stroking the veins in every ancestor's body.'

Since the events are meant to be understood as showing the mythic and ritualistic within the possibilities of Guyana, the story is set against seasonal patterns. As in primitive myths, or in Eliot's *Wasteland*, a drought is symbolic of spiritual deadness, of an infertile land and culture awaiting renewal:

> The inhabitants of the region had not properly wakened to the slaying of the dragon of drought by the spidery feet of the rain which left their trail in every thread and green shoot on the land. The stern winter of hardship had yielded to the spring of fertility but the roots and branches of transformation descended and arose only in the starred eye of love.

The Whole Armour can be understood in relation to the colonial experience, the building of a nation, the rediscovery of the tragic sense, or even as a novel of freedom and responsibility. Harris's technique lends itself to such multiplicity of meaning.

The Secret Ladder concerns Fenwick's seven-day survey of the Canje River for the government as part of a plan to build dams and produce electricity for the coastal industries. Fenwick, with his rational European outlook, has similarities to Donne, the conqueror of the interior in *Palace*. But whereas Donne's voyage was through native Indian territory in search of an Eldorado, Fenwick's survey brings him into conflict with the descendants of escaped African slaves who have lived freely in the country's interior and who, correctly, regard the surveying mission as leading to the eventual confiscation of their land by the government. The confrontation which develops between Fenwick and Poseidon, a god-like leader of the blacks, is tragic in bringing death to the culture of the Africans, but it also forces all the surveying crew into new relationships with the blacks of the interior during which centuries of assumptions are destroyed.

The theme of modern man's enclosure within fixed categories is stated early through one of those explanatory sentences that guide the reader through the unfamiliar territory of the novels. 'Fenwick pulled himself up. Sometimes he felt he had no logical freedom of his own.'[10] The Canje itself is similar to one of the monumental landscapes in Dante's *Divine Comedy* in being a physical representation of a stage of psychological or spiritual progress. The quest is backward, through the depths of darkness, before there can be renewal. Fenwick must meet and experience the past before he can be purged, made innocent and restored to freedom.

Poseidon, 'the oldest inhabitant of the Canje', is the grandson of a runaway African slave. Myths have developed around him and it is said that he is one hundred years old, that his grandfather's spirit possesses him and even that he had lived on the Canje before the first slaves reached Guyana. He has become 'the black king of history whose sovereignty over the past was a fluid crown of possession and dispossession'. While Poseidon is representative of the African brought to the New World, and particularly of those in the Caribbean and South America who escaped to the interior where they continued to practise survivals of their original culture, his name is of a Greek god of the waters—both appropriate to his habitation along the island waterways and allowing Harris to transcend by mixing cultural legends. Poseidon is more than representative of black history: he is a god of the primitive past who has survived into the modern era. Equally important is what Poseidon represents to Fenwick and his surveying crew. To Jordan, the most hard, political and materialistic of the crew, Poseidon is a dangerous but childish savage to be mastered and exploited. To Bryant, a young black, Poseidon is his ancestor, a part of black racial history. Fenwick is a mixture of those who inhabit Guyana. His father is of African descent. His mother, although half French, half English, had skin 'like a fair East Indian's'; and it was rumoured that she 'possessed a fraction of Amerindian blood, as well, and that her grandmother was as Arawak as her husband's grandfather had been uncompromisingly African'.

Fenwick feels that in Poseidon's threat to obstruct the surveying project he is facing part of his own history. The exclusion and exploitation of the African must be faced by modern Guyana before a new society can emerge without the burden of the past: 'If I do not—if my generation do not—leviathan will swallow us all. It isn't a question of fear—it's a question of going in unashamed to come out of the womb again.' Emancipation should have liberated the African from the effects of slavery and made him a new man. Instead history went radically wrong; Fenwick and Guyana can have no settled authority until they can understand how liberation was frustrated and until the African is spiritually as well as legally emancipated. Fenwick's liberalism is undermined by the events that follow. The 'Canje River was invaluable to the absent East Indian rice farmer and the European sugar planter' who need its water. But to build a flood reservoir resurrects the past in the form of Poseidon who sees the project as taking away his land and liberty. Fenwick argues that Poseidon's primitive condition 'is no freedom', but Bryant claims: 'The old man is no slave. . . . He freer than you and me.' The more Fenwick speaks of the necessity of coming to terms with science and authority the less confident he sounds. 'Yes, I confess I owe allegiance to him because of his condition. . . . But surely that does not mean I must reduce myself to his trapped condition, become even less human than he.'

It is exactly such engagement that is necessary before the crew can be freed from the past. The surveying mission has come almost to a halt as a result of Fenwick's indecisiveness; disorder begins to appear within the crew which parallels the chaos of the seventh day during their journey towards de-creation. Then Fenwick is suddenly shocked to learn that 'Poseidon was dead. . . God was dead. . . . This was the dreadful annunciation. The oldest cage of impotency, they knew, had been splintered.' Bryant accidentally killed Poseidon in a defensive gesture during a moment of mutually misunderstood intentions: 'Poseidon stumbled and fell, in his race, of unequal body and spirit, on the cruel knuckles of the one who loved him best, the grandson he had begotten in the dreadful apotheosis of history.'

The killing of Poseidon by Bryant is a result of the necessary engagement of those of African descent with their past. It is also the death of an ancient god and his instruments 'of tradition and law'. Such de-creation is, however, necessary since 'tradition and law' can no longer contain the modern African, or modern man. The past must die, be uncreated, if man is to be reborn free and innocent. As the novel ends Fenwick is dreaming what might be described as an interpretation of the novel: 'It seemed that an inquisition of dead gods and heroes had ended, an inquiry into the dramatic role of conscience in time and being.' Was the novel a dream, an imagining, similar to *Palace*, but this time of Fenwick's rather than the narrator's?

In *Tradition, the Writer and Society* (1967) Harris has said: 'Man's survival is a continual tension and release of energy that approaches self-destruction, but is aware of self-discovery.'[11] Harris's novels not only celebrate such a process, but are based upon the assumption that it is only the recognition of and participation in such tensions that can free the West Indies from the deadening determinism of history.

7 West Indies II: Walcott, Brathwaite and authenticity

Although verses were written in the West Indies during the eighteenth and nineteenth centuries, they might be considered minor English poetry, mainly of interest in revealing stereotyped colonial attitudes towards the tropics and its races. While there were poets who thought of themselves as Guyanese during the last century, the first significant literary circle developed in Jamaica.[1] Thomas MacDermot's patriotic verses and Claude McKay's dialect poems, *Constab Ballads* and *Songs of Jamaica* (1912), were followed during the 1920s by writers now of only historical interest; there was no equivalent achievement in poetry to that of such novelists as H. G. de Lisser and Jean Rhys. It was not until Vivian Virtue's *Wings of the Morning* (1938) that there was a poet of real competence; but the subject-matter and style were within the older aesthetic tradition. Poets had learned how to describe the local scenery, but it was only during the forties that the landscape was used as a symbol of personal feelings. Protest poetry also became common during the forties. It was a decade of good but minor writers who had learned how to use some of the freedom of modern poetry, in contrast to traditional forms of verse, to suggest a West Indian voice and attitude. Kenneth Ramchand has suggested that along with social concerns the use of dialect was one of the ways in which 'the speaking voice got smuggled into West Indian poetry'. The first really significant poet was Martin Carter of Guyana who, in *Poems of Resistance from British Guiana* (1954),[2] combined a radical modern style with protest and who appears to be speaking in a West Indian voice simultaneously of 'man's orphaned condition in the universe' and of the unemployed, uneducated and disenfranchised.[3] Carter was actively involved with Guyanese nationalist politics and with *Kyk-over-al*, the literary and cultural journal in which the local middle class examined what they felt to be their divided and confused heritage.

Derek Walcott's father, a civil servant, wrote verse and was extremely well read; the mother was a school teacher and amateur actress. There was a 'circle of self-civilizing courteous people'[4] and a thriving Arts Guild on his island, St Lucia. Dunstan St Omer, a dynamic St Lucian painter, taught the importance of using local subjects; George Campbell's self-published *First Poems* (1945) with their praise of the Negro were influential at the time; and after Walcott published his own *25 Poems* (1949) he began to receive local attention. He was soon in contact with Frank Colleymore, the Barbadian editor of *Bim*, and his poems were reviewed by the English poet Roy Fuller on the B.B.C. *Caribbean Voices*. He received a Rockefeller Fellowship to study drama in the United States during 1958, and eventually formed his own drama group in Trinidad.

The same middle class of civil servants, teachers and professionals that gave birth to the West Indian writers of the fifties also produced their alienation. Many of the writers went into exile cursing provincial colonial society as backward, isolated and uncreative. While learning to master the various styles of English verse and make them respond to his own personality and West Indian voice, Walcott stayed at home and used his personal dilemma as material for his poetry. A light brown-skinned mulatto with a love of English literature, alien to the poor, black Catholic peasantry of St Lucia, Walcott in his early poems is often concerned with his isolation within his community. As he was later to write in 'The Divided Child' poems of *Another Life* (1973), 'The dream/of reason had produced its monster:/a prodigy of the wrong age and colour.'[5] The examination of the drama of his own life against that of his community and region has been one of Walcott's main themes. His individual experience has become part, if not necessarily typical, of what it means to be West Indian.

Walcott's second volume, *Epitaph for the Young: XII Cantos* (1948, published in Barbados), is in an experimental modern style. The epic-like twelve divisions of *Epitaph*, the parallels and contrasts of a West Indian life with the classical past, are indebted to James Joyce's *Ulysses*. There are echoes of T. S. Eliot and Dylan Thomas. The emphasis on late adolescence and early manhood, in which maturation is seen as a condition of feverish dying, had been made popular by Thomas. While immature in both theme and craft, *Epitaph* is an attempt to move beyond the fragments of lyric poetry to a larger structure shaped around the inner life of the author. The speaker's voyage through life is that of a modern Ulysses, a West Indian who, no matter how much he makes use of European myth, is conscious of problems of ethnic identity and colour: 'The black boy at the piano'; 'oddments/Of an alien culture'; 'A tradition is not made, it evolves'; and 'A civilization of tennis and country club'. 'Club' is a pun as is 'idle/idol' in: 'We string the gold hair of an idle lute.' Alongside the concern with problems of young love in a multiracial society, and the attempt to master the idiom of European elite culture, an ironic awareness of falsity emerges: 'A classical alas,/For naked pickanninies, pygmies, pigs and poverty.'[6] The burden of Walcott's poetry will be to explore his dual inheritance, especially in the various forms it is found within the New World.

Poems (1952, published in Jamaica) shows a concern with the racial, economic and cultural problems of the region. 'Montego Bay—Travelogue II' contrasts the rich white American tourists with the poor black fishermen and waiters. 'The Sunny Caribbean' makes similar contrasts:

> Senile, sterile exiles to this poor man's Riviera,
> Are fixtures in a technicoloured scape,
> Behind them, like summer brews,
> The hunger march, the city fire, the rape,
> Of those whom poverty beats black with abuse.[7]

While Walcott's early verse reveals a consciousness of racial and social problems, the Jamaica poems are most striking for rhymed verse forms and witty puns that were fashionable in American and British literary circles during the 1940s and '50s.

The distance between such early attitudes of irony and protest and the more fully thought out positions later identified with Walcott can be seen in his *Selected Poems* (1964). The now famous 'A Far Cry from Africa' treats of the Mau Mau uprising in terms that mock the usual justifications for and criticisms of colonialism. The ironies are those of compassion in the face of abstractions: 'What is that to the white child hacked in bed?/To savages, expendable as Jews?'[8] Although the poem attacks 'the drunken officer of British rule' and the 'statistics' that 'justify' colonial policy, the second stanza introduces a more encompassing theme, using religious imagery, in which all forms of violence are seen as part of man's long cruelty towards, and wish to dominate, others. In contrast to the animals, 'upright man/Seeks his divinity by inflicting pain'. Coloniser and colonised are both savage. Walcott asks how he can choose, 'who am poisoned with the blood of both';

> Between this Africa and the English tongue I love?
> Betray them both, or give back what they give?
> How can I face such slaughter and be cool?
> How can I turn from Africa and live?

The poem is remarkable for its complexity of emotions. The elaborately rhymed stanzas and regular five-stress lines give formal order to what are essentially confused, irreconcilably opposed feelings: identification with black Africa, disgust with the killing of both white and black innocents, distrust of motives, love of the English language, and dislike of those who remain emotionally uninvolved.

Many of the poems of this period treat of the author's divided heritage in paradoxical celebrations—of compassion towards the dead slave owner, the dead conqueror, or in 'The Train' towards his English grandfather. A recognition of a shared humanity, and more particularly of a common heritage of poetry, changes accusations of guilt to feelings of compassion. 'Ruins of a Great House' with its 'the abuse/Of ignorance by bible and by sword', and 'rage' at the 'thought/Some slave is rotting in this manorial lake' concludes with 'All in compassion ends/So differently from what the heart arranged'. As Walcott meditates upon the past it becomes impossible to keep feelings arranged in polemical alignments. Implicit in his concern with the common humanity of all races is the multi-racial situation of the region, especially the East Caribbean where many bloodstocks may be mixed in one family. There is, however, an abstract quality to the poetry of this period, as if Walcott were rather thinking about than feeling his subject-matter. The poem 'Bronze' begins by rejecting the classical art of Europe, 'Those mottled marbles I admired,/Bone-coloured'; instead he admires a bronzed statue, 'art of a savage race,/Marble, bronze, ebonwood, white, creole, black'. The fusion of races involves a mixture of guilty pasts, but from such a mixture rebirth is possible. The West Indian will be a new Adam, a Robinson Crusoe making his own civilisation from various cultural roots, but creating something new, unique to the region.

Along with Walcott's attempt to translate his divided heritage into a new Caribbean creole culture, there is an increasing use of the varieties of West Indian speech. The 'Tales of the Islands' in *Selected Poems* include such contrasting social dictions as 'it was quite ironic', 'Great stuff, old boy; sacrifice, moments of truth', 'Poopa, da' was a fête!', 'They catch his wife with two tests up the beach', 'And wouldn't let a comma in edgewise', and 'But that was long before this jump and jive'. The various registers reflect the kinds of language found in the islands, ranging from standard English to French patois, and their accompanying social and class value. The increase in linguistic range helps emphasise the brown creolised view of the New World as different from both Britain and Africa.

Chapter V of 'Tales of the Islands' mocks a fête in which 'savage rites' were performed 'for the approval of some anthropologist'. The comic ironies multiply; one of the priests 'was himself a student/Of black customs'. Although the dancers have the 'natural grace/Remembered from the dark past whence we come', the ritual sacrifice of the lamb seems 'more like a bloody picnic', an excuse to drink white rum and fight. In the next chapter we see the same fête from inside the community: 'Free rum free whisky . . . and everywhere you turn was people eating'. But suddenly we are reminded:

And it was round this part once that the heart
Of a young child was torn from it alive
By two practitioners of native art.

Walcott's ironies have shifted from mockery of the disapproving whites and the 'Black writer chap, one of them Oxbridge guys' to a disturbing reminder of what 'savage rites' lie behind the fête.

Walcott's vision of a Caribbean culture has its roots in the social and political ideals of the Federation period. The Federation of the West Indies was an attempt at brown middle-class government.[9] An interregional civil service, dominated by the local professional classes, would have taken over from the British. It was at this time that English Caribbean authors began thinking of themselves as West Indian. No longer British, unable to identify with the local black sub-cultures, the middle class found its political expression in the Federation. The London production of Walcott's play *Henri Christophe* (1952) was regarded as a sign of the new, developing regional culture.

But 'Laventville', one of Walcott's best-known poems, expresses frustration at the confusions, feelings of displacement and cultural ironies that are part of being middle-class West Indian. The violent, overcrowded slums of the impoverished black, the church-going brown Trinidadian elite with their mimicry of English ways, the elaborate social structure and class divisions, the contrasts of poverty and wealth, are instances of a profound historical failure. The culture of Africa was lost, but, as a result of slavery, the promise of the New World was never fulfilled. A new society is still waiting to be born: 'We left/somewhere a life we never found.'[10] The contrast between the Sunday church-goers and the surrounding poverty is not merely social criticism, or an attack on the West Indian middle-class establishment; it illustrates the irrelevance of such ways in a society where religion is part of 'apish habits' and not the 'customs and gods' of a living culture.

Walcott knows that protest in itself cannot give birth to a vital West Indian society. Many of his poems attack the politicians and intellectuals who have turned protest into demagogy and who mistake expressions of anger for art. The complex rhymes, stanzas and subtle patterns of repetition, allusion and contrast in 'Laventville' show that the best engaged writing results from a commitment to literary craft. But instead of the inherited forms of the early poems, Walcott's style has become much plainer and closer to his own speech patterns. The Crusoe poems say that mastering the art of expression is part of the process of cultural birth:

> his journals
> assume a household use,
> We learn to shape from them, where nothing was
> the language of a race.[11]

Walcott's poems in *The Castaway* (1965) use the myth of Crusoe to suggest that the New World is a new beginning, a new Eden. Both white and black have been shipwrecked and while those of African descent suffer an amnesia of their racial past, it is from such forgetfulness that a new culture began. Walcott sees himself in the line of such poets of the Americas as Whitman, Neruda and St John Perse. Art will give form and self-awareness to this new society. But in 'Crusoe's Island' Walcott admits the limitations of art replacing belief. The statement in the third stanza—'I labour at my art./My father, God, is dead'—is followed by reflections on man's need for 'human love'. The most art 'has revealed/Is what a crippled Vulcan/Beat on Achilles' shield'. Watching 'Friday's progeny,/The brood of Crusoe's slave' returning from church, he feels

> And nothing I can learn
> From art or loneliness
> Can bless them as the bell's
> Transfiguring tongue can bless.

Walcott has become increasingly conscious of the life of the St Lucian community which he has left. Where others have sought their roots in Africa, or have identified with the black urban slum dweller, Walcott sees the poor, French-influenced, Catholic black community of St Lucia as his home.

'What the Twilight Says: An Overture', which prefaces *Dream on Monkey Mountain and Other Plays* (1970), is partly an analysis of West Indian culture from the period preceding independence until the Black Power movement of the late 1960s:

> My generation had looked at life with black skins and blue eyes, but only our own painful, strenuous looking, the learning of looking, could find meaning in the life around us, only our own strenuous hearing, the hearing of our hearing, could make sense of the sounds we made.

What is needed is the acceptance of being West Indian:

> so that mongrel as I am, something prickles in me when I see the word Ashanti as with the word Warwickshire, both separately intimating my grandfathers' roots, both baptising this neither proud nor ashamed bastard, this hybrid, this West Indian.[12]

In contrast the governments of the islands promoted a folk art which has become sterile and artificial. The folk culture of the past cannot be resurrected. The Black Power intellectuals mimic foreign revolutions in urging the people 'to acquire pride which meant abandoning their individual dignity'; even the fury of the intellectual was 'artificially generated' by an imitation of foreign 'metropolitan anger'. Thus Walcott angrily attacks politicians and intellectuals in *The Gulf* (1969) and *Sea Grapes* (1971):

> Why are the eyes of the beautiful
> and unmarked children
> in the uniforms of the country
> bewildered and shy,
> why do they widen in terror
> of the pride drummed into their minds?[13]

Walcott's plays range from attempting to give classical form to folk society to examining the psychology of black radicalism in the Caribbean. *The Sea at Dauphin* (1954) is a tragedy that combines celebration of folk life with protest. It is influenced by the dramas of the Irish Renaissance, especially John Synge's *Riders to the Sea*, in its ritualistic style, its mixture of folk speech and formal poetry and its elevation of the peasantry to tragic dignity. *The Sea at Dauphin* is Walcott's attempt to give St Lucian life the qualities of Greek drama: there is a small cast; the death of the old man takes place off-stage and is narrated by others; the speeches are sometimes in verse; dialect and French Creole are interwoven with English, and the life of the poor is set within a cosmic context. The sea and the island appear as elemental divine forces against which man is pitted to survive. Afa, the bravest of the fishermen, is a Captain Ahab, an old man of the sea who seeks by challenging God: 'God is a white man. The sky is his blue eye,/His spit on Dauphin people is the sea.' If the play expresses man's incomprehension of the human condition, it also suggests that the condition of the islanders is the result of a world made by the white man. Although the play mocks the priest's message of accepting one's condition, there is a religious vision: 'The sea/It have compassion in the end.'

The techniques of West Indian oral literature and folk-tale are successfully adapted to the stage in *Ti-Jean and His Brothers* (1958). The story is framed by a prologue involving speaking animals and insects, and the subsequent play is supposed to be narrated by a frog. These are both creatures of the folk imagination and descendants from the Greek comic theatre. The plot is based on the common folk-tale motif of three brothers who, faced by a problem, make choices that exemplify their essential character. The family is starving 'While the planter is eating/From plates painted golden'. As they debate what to do, outside their house a 'BOLOM *or Foetus*' announces that the Devil is 'dying to be human'. If anyone can make the Devil feel 'anger,/Rage or human weakness' he will 'never more know hunger/But fulfilment, wealth, peace'. But those who fail will be eaten by the Devil. Gros Jean, the eldest brother, who represents brute strength, tries and is eaten.

Mi-Jean, the second brother, who represents intellect, also fails. Ti-Jean, the youngest brother, who believes that 'whatever God made, we must consider blessed', uses the help of the animal creatures whom he treats as equals to drive the devil into a rage by trickery, foolish behaviour and lack of fear.

The play has several kinds of significance which are conveyed rather through juxtaposition than by straightforward development. There are the colonial and racial themes when the Devil assumes, along with his disguise as a wise old man, the mask of a white planter, adopting the speech habits of white colonial and capitalist society attitudes towards black peasantry. The play suggests that neither brute resistance (Gros Jean) nor intellectual positions (Mi-Jean) can defeat colonialism and neo-colonialism. It is necessary to have Ti-Jean's closeness to the peasantry, his faith in God's goodness, his reluctance to accept older wisdom. The significance of the Devil is psychological. All of God's creation is good. The two older brothers fail because of the evil within themselves; they create the devil that is an authority to be fought against and destroyed. Ti-Jean wins because he does not respect the old categories. He drinks the Devil's wine, sets fire to his house, eats his goat and is without worries. It is this psychological liberation that brings about the birth of the Bolom, representative of the new West Indies that have remained stillborn as a result of the rigidly defensive psychology of those similar to the two older brothers. Neo-colonialism is a state of mind that results from thinking in terms of history, the colonial period, past injustices, humiliations, national dignity, and other inherited concepts. The rebellious hero of Walcott's play refuses to become entangled in attitudes inherited from the colonial situation. He is an unfallen Adam who can act directly and in a straightforward fashion because he has faith. It is faith that gives dignity to the peasant and ex-slave, that creates a new world from the old and that avoids the self-torturing, self-defeating anguish of the black and Third World intellectual.

Dream on Monkey Mountain (1967) is printed with an explanation that the 'play is a dream, one that exists as much in the given minds of the principal characters as in that of the writer'. Through the use of dream and fantasy, time and space are treated freely and poetically. Voodoo, song, dance and masquerade contribute both to the sense of an African heritage and help to fulfil demands that Trinidadian arts make use of local props and atmosphere. If the surface characteristics of the play are consciously West Indian, it should be realised that the masquerading, changes of identity, rapid dissolutions of scene and fantasy world owe as much to the example of Jean Genet and conventions of the modern western theatre as they do to a search for authenticity. Walcott remains a cosmopolitan while contributing to the search for a regional theatre.

The play forms part of the West Indian debate about African sources of folk society and the availability of Africa as a replacement for European culture. The treatment of ritualistic possession and its failure shows Walcott's belief that a spiritual return to Africa can only be a dream for West Indians.

Dream begins with a prologue, a 'conteur' chanting in dialect and a chorus replying. The technique, although found in western art forms, is now usually associated with the call and response of African music. Makak, a sixty-year-old peasant, is in the police station for damaging a local bar while drunk. He is questioned by Corporal Lestrade, who represents the black middle classes with their contempt for the peasantry. The drunken Makak claims to be the direct descendant of African kings, a healer and the saviour of his race. He claims that in a vision, when 'my feet grow roots', a blonde white woman told him about his past and hidden powers. He is an epitome of the confused desires and hopes that have shaped the black West Indian peasant—fantasies of blonde white women, dreams of returning to Africa, desires to find one's origins in the African kingdoms of the past, and a mixture of Christian faith with peasant superstition.

The core of the play consists of dreams Makak has while drunk. They are not, however, simple fantasies, as he progressively gains in knowledge. In the last dream he finds himself forced by others to be king of an African tribe who demand that he behead the white 'Venus, the Virgin, the Sleeping Beauty' of his vision. As soon as he does this he claims he is 'free' and wakes up from his sleep, announces his real name, Felix Hobain, and, released from jail, returns home singing:

'Other men will come, other prophets will come, and they will be stoned, and mocked, and betrayed, but now this old hermit is going back home, back to the beginning, to the green beginning of this world.' Makak only remembers his real name—a non-African name—when he has been confronted by the death of the blonde woman who gave him his vision. European culture and the disdain of whites have alienated him from his true self, and led to the compensatory fantasy of Africa. It is only by freeing himself from such Manichean dichotomies that he can realise that he is a new man, a West Indian, whose origins are in the mountain village of his island. It is in this 'green beginning' that his own culture and identity has its origins. It is to this he must return.

Part of the power of Walcott's long autobiographical poem, *Another Life* (1973), results from the setting of the author's life within his community, the sensitivity with which his childhood is shown, and the way the verse universalises the particularities of St Lucian society without sentimentalising or claiming a false dignity. Dialect and patois sit comfortably alongside Latin, rhyming prayers in French, and a variety of complex verse forms and rhythms which seem necessary to the range of experiences being expressed. Since the nineteenth century the confessional autobiography has replaced the epic; the author's spiritual development and relationship to his culture have taken the role formerly given to the warrior or exploring hero. Autobiography is particularly relevant to those in an emerging nation or rapidly changing society and has resulted in some of the best West Indian and African literature. Walcott's examination of the divided consciousness of the mulatto in a mixed community—the evocations of childhood, the stages of maturation, middle-class life, family, individuals in the community, school, the priest, local merchants, friendships, early loves—recreates a world of which the narrator is a product and in which he is still involved. By using the confessional mode which Robert Lowell made popular, Walcott has produced a classic of West Indian literature which celebrates the local landscape, the many races, mixed culture and languages of the islands.

While Edward Kamau Brathwaite of Barbados has identified himself with what he considers to be the second, or contemporary period of West Indian post-independence writing—a period of protest, of political radicalisation, Black Power, and the search for an African heritage—he began publishing traditional English poetry in *Bim* and other journals during the 1950s. Many of these earlier poems are fragmentary and treat of the moments, problems and sources of inspiration.[14] In the later works, of which the trilogy *The Arrivants* (1973) is the best known, such inspiration is found in the communal history, and its African sources, of the black West Indian. The poems record how Brathwaite found inspiration from his personal experience of exile, life in Africa and return to the islands. In an essay, 'Timehri', he says that like other middle-class blacks of his generation he went to England thinking of himself as British, only to learn that he was a foreigner. As disillusioned with the provinciality of West Indian society as Naipaul, Lamming or other writers who chose exile, he took a job in Ghana where he discovered a culture in which there is a profound relationship of the individual and of the spiritual world to the community:

> I was a West Indian, roofless man of the world. I could go, belong, everywhere on the world-wide globe. I ended up in a village in Ghana. It was my beginning.
>
> Slowly, slowly, ever so slowly; obscurely, slowly but surely, during the eight years that I lived there, I was coming to an awareness and understanding of community, of cultural wholeness, of the place of the individual within the tribe, in society. Slowly, slowly ever so slowly I came to a sense of identification of myself with these people, my living diviners. I came to connect my history with theirs, the bridge of my mind now linking Atlantic and ancestor, homeland and heartland. When I turned to leave, I was no longer a lonely individual talent; there was something wider, more subtle, more tentative: the self without ego, without I, without arrogance. And I came home to find that I had not really left. That it was still Africa; Africa in the Caribbean.

Brathwaite's work, as a historian, pamphleteer and poet, has been to 'transcend' the colonial sense of rootlessness and isolation:

> In the Caribbean, whether it be African or Amerindian, the recognition of an ancestral relationship with the folk or aboriginal culture involves the artist and participant in a journey into the past and hinterland which is at the same time a movement of possession into present and future. Through this movement of possession we become ourselves, truly our own creators, discovering word for object, image for the Word.[15]

Brathwaite mentions two events during the late sixties as influencing 'the growth and direction of the West Indian imagination'. The first was the visit of Stokely Carmichael, the Trinidadian-born American Black Power leader, to London. The second, also in London, was the founding in 1966 of the Caribbean Artists Movement, which brought together writers painters and intellectuals 'exiled' in England. As a result of conferences, readings, exhibitions and publications, 'a relationship between artist and audience had become possible'. The Beacon Bookshop and New Beacon Publications in London became one centre for this movement and the journal *Savacou*, printed in Jamaica, provided a regular voice for the new wave of often more radical West Indian opinion which was concerned with defining an 'authentic' Caribbean culture.

The Arrivants trilogy is essentially a record of the stages of Brathwaite's life from feelings of exile, through the years in Africa, to the discovery of his African heritage in the New World and the resulting sense of community. It is a creation of a mythology for the black West Indian to replace earlier images of the self created by white prejudice, colonialism and European history. *Rights of Passage* (1967), the first book of the trilogy, is a *Wasteland* based on the various roles and postures ('Uncle Tom', 'Spider', 'the Negro') of the descendants of Africans taken to the New World. It is partly a lament for a lost world: 'We kept/our state on golden stools—remember?'[16] It begins with an evocation of the past: 'Drum skin whip/lash' and examines the life of the black man in the Americas and Europe.

The second part of the trilogy, *Masks* (1968), celebrates the life Brathwaite found in Africa, particularly among the Akan in Ghana. Africa is a land of history remembered, music, dance, ancestors, customs and especially religion. The poem 'Making of the Drum' concerns the sacrifices that sacramentalise ordinary objects in African life. 'The Barrel of the Drum' is a catechism praising the holiness of the wood from which the drum will be made. 'The Two Curved Sticks of the Drummer', 'Gourds and Rattles', 'The Gong-Gong' are among the various musical objects given a religious significance. The 'Path-finder' poems treat of African heroes and places of the past. 'Limits' recalls the movements of the West African tribes from their supposed home in Egypt, across the Sudan, until they settle on the coast, where the voyage to the New World and slavery will begin. 'The Return' treats of Brathwaite himself in Africa:

> you who have come
> back a stranger
> after three hundred years
>
> welcome
>
> here is a stool for
> you; sit; do
> you remember?

Africa, however, is home and not home: 'Whose/brother, now, am I?' The new tribal elders of modern Africa are 'tarnished with . . . love of/profit'. Brathwaite laments: 'Will/your wood lips speak/so we see?', and prays: 'Make me a black/mask that . . . smiles no pretence.' The second part of the trilogy ends with the poet's awareness that he is 'an orphan' who will leave Africa, 'exiled from here', carrying a vision: 'Walking that dark/path again, you/must help me.'

Returning to the West Indies, Brathwaite sought to rediscover the sacramental in survivals of African religion among the folk in contrast to middle-class European culture. He sought community in what he calls the creolisation of the West Indies, by which he means the coming together of the various races and cultures of the region into one people. If this appears to resemble Walcott's claim for a new West Indian identity, or Harris's vision of an American society and culture in continual process, Brathwaite's perspective is different in being shaped by those of African descent and their heritage. Creolisation to him means the formation of a regional personality based on acquiring the black culture of the Caribbean, especially that of the folk with their retention of African customs. While the survival of such customs is a still disputed subject, Brathwaite has tried to show in his scholarship as a historian that West Indian peasant culture is primarily African in origin.

The poems in *Islands* (1969), the last third of the trilogy, reject the imitation of European culture in the West Indies and treat of restoration, the recognition of African roots which will contribute towards the making of a new authenticity in the New World. The 'New World' poems begin with another invocation:

> Nairobi's male elephants uncurl
> their trumpets to heaven
> Toot-Toot takes it up
> in Havana
> in Harlem.

While invocations are conventional to the epic mode, Brathwaite's poems often refer to music, which is his symbol for 'black' creative inspiration. Jazz is used as an analogy for poetic art; various allusions to jazz musicians, jazz dances and jazz styles offer an impression of the artist in the fallen world, symbolised by New York, creating an angry blues of the New World: 'With my blue note, my cracked note, full flatten–/ed fifth, my ten bebop fingers, my black bottom'd strut'. The racial amnesia Walcott celebrates as the beginning of the West Indies is for Brathwaite a tragedy: 'A dark skin is a chain but it cannot recall the name/of its tribe.' Within the New World there are signs of older African gods, although now not remembered. The poet searching his memories, the land and others, finds signs and hears voices. Ananse, the trickster god,

> he stumps up the stares
> of our windows, he stares, stares
> he squats on the tips
>
> of our language
> black burr of conundrums
> eye corner of ghosts, ancient his-
> tories.

Legba, another African god found in Caribbean worship, is seen in 'a lame old man on a crutch' who comes 'to church' and 'fought in the last war'.

'The Limbo' sequence, based on a dance derived from exercises the slaves performed in the crowded ships of the middle passage, consists of laments concerning dispossession: 'I can travel no farther.' Only music (poetry) helps: 'sun coming up/and the drummers are praising me/. . . and the music is saving me'. The 'Rebellion' poems concern the difficulty of writing ('For the Word is peace/and is absent from our streets') and the need for anger ('Goin' to burn burn now'); they are followed by poems about possession. Brathwaite has written:

> The basic point about African gods and the Caribbean gods that derive from them is that they can 'possess' and be possessed by the ordinary, believing, participating, individual worshipper. Possession, which is the climax of the service—in form a dance-drama—is induced by the drums or by rhythmic hand-clapping and chanting. The celebrant's body acts as a kind of lightning conductor for the god. . . . In the Caribbean, these African-derived religions are looked upon as the province only of the underprivileged and deprived masses of the population.[17]

In these poems Brathwaite makes use of the two significances of the word 'possession'. Those who undergo possession will possess, whether the object to be possessed is poetry, the past, property or the future. After possession comes renewal in the form of a new 'Beginning' (Section V): 'The Word becomes/ again a god and walks among us.' Possession links together the desire for spiritual repossession with finding a source for poetic inspiration. While he is drawing upon the African belief that gods descend upon the possessed during rituals, Brathwaite is aware of various traditions that view the artist as a priest-like medium for the muse. The poetic becomes religious, and *The Arrivants*, like Soyinka's long poem *Idanre*, becomes a modern tribal epic.

Just as Brathwaite's themes concern the descendants of the Africans in the New World, so he has created a 'black' style carrying suggestions of Africa, the West Indian poor and the American Negro. The style is made up of unusual rhythms, inventive stanzaic forms, odd placements of rhymes, many puns and other forms of word play associated with black speech. References and allusions to New World black culture, the use of African words and various black dialects, and the parody of expressions associated with 'bondage' contribute to the idiom of 'black consciousness'. There are many stresses, internal rhymes, alliterations and other effects creating both a sense of spontaneous speech and a sometimes misleading impression of rebellion against standard English usage. The impression is misleading because many of the techniques have become part of the accepted modern repertoire and can be found in earlier twentieth-century English poets and in Aimé Césaire's *Cahier d'un retour au pays natal*. Moreover, the kind of complex effects found in some stanzas might be described as a back-handed affirmation of the conventions of English verse in contrast to the free, undisciplined, rhymeless style normally associated with recent 'revolutionary' verse.

The following are basically English pentameters broken so as to rhyme the first half of the line with its conclusion: 'But he must do/what fate had forced him to'; and 'at birth his blood/was bent upon a flood'. The repetitive stresses that begin 'Negus' are a device common to T. S. Eliot's middle period:

> It
> it
> it
> it is not.

The rhymes and rhythms of 'Caliban 2' are based on Caliban's own celebration of his new master in *The Tempest*:

> And
> Ban
> Ban
> Cal-
> iban
> like to play
> pan.

The rhythms imitative of sound in 'Folkways 2' belong to a by now long tradition of Harlem and Negritude writing in which syncopation is associated with the black experience. The inclusion of slogans and phrases from popular songs has been part of modern poetry since at least the 1920s. The African words in the 'Libation' sequence follow the use of African expressions in the Cuban Negrito and Francophonic Negritude poets.

If Brathwaite's trilogy first gives the impression of utilising the surrealist disjunctive techniques that in Césaire and Senghor express liberation from the bounds of European rationality, the sequence is more linear. Brathwaite's concern is to link past and present into a timeless vision that will be the culture the poet expresses as he attempts to understand his own relationship to a traditional world which, in the materialistic chaos of modern society, has been lost. While Brathwaite's verse has been popular as the expression of a second phase, post-independence radicalism and as an expression of folk culture, its real lineage is in such poems as T. S. Eliot's

Wasteland, *Ash Wednesday* and *Four Quartets*. Brathwaite's desire to establish a cultural tradition grounded in communal ritual and his concern with individual moments of escaping from the fragmented, chaotic present into an experience of oneness, in which the artist becomes the voice of a culture and its beliefs, show that he has profoundly understood Eliot. Brathwaite is an example of a poet in an emergent literature finding within the European *avant-garde* techniques and attitudes which can be adapted to express the cultural concerns of a new nation or the Third World. The style of European alienation has become that of colonial liberation.

Mother Poem (1977), the first book of Brathwaite's new sequence, focuses on his native island, Barbados. The narrative is similar to many Renaissance and eighteenth-century long poems that follow the topology of a landscape as a unifying structure. While *Mother Poem* shares features with *The Arrivants*, it is different in its greater concentration on social and racial protest: 'her husband out there on the plantation/her children locked up into their cell'.[18] The poems offer an impression of Barbados ruled by middle-class civil servants and merchants with the black man doing the labour, or serving white masters in menial capacities: 'Trash, windmill, crack, bubble o vat in de fac'try/load pun me head, load in de cart, de mill spinnin spinnin spinnin.' Religion, training, schooling and other characteristics of middle-class upbringing are seen as means of keeping those of African descent in an inferior position. For those kept down by society it is not possible to advance to the ownership of property. For the black, three hundred years of the New World have been a failure.

Mother Poem makes more use of dialect than *The Arrivants*. Although it is written in standard English, approximately half of the verses make use of various dialect features. Partly this is to create an appropriate voice for the speakers, but more often the function appears to be identification with the poor. Sometimes verses are reminiscent of the social-protest poetry of the 1930s: 'Not a cent/not a bline bloody cent/not even a dollar a year for de rock he was wrackin/not even a placket to help pay de rent.' The protest style of *Mother Poem* is less interesting than the earlier poetry. Public poetry, except during the Augustan period, has usually been less successful in English than private verse, and where it has been successful it has had the resources of a developed body of social myth from which to draw its imagery and with which to make imaginative linkages; Brathwaite uses the less rich resources of the tradition of black American protest. It is an interesting tradition and has produced good minor poets, but it does not provide a writer with the resources that Brathwaite in *The Arrivants* could find in T. S. Eliot's vision or in Césaire's surrealist-influenced *Cahier*.

That Brathwaite has been consciously reshaping his style closer to protest poetry can be seen from his essay 'The Love Axe/1: (Developing a Caribbean Aesthetic 1962–1974)', with its call for 'connections and continuity with what we can now call the folk or alternative tradition in our part of the world'. He claims that 'the first major event was unquestionably the revolution in Cuba under Fidel Castro' which defeated 'Western mercantilism'. Whereas the western intellectual tradition 'warped itself in the colonies',[19] becoming debased through its attempt to justify 'slavery and racism', a new revolutionary, anti-colonialist tradition developed out of various West Indian historians, local Marxist politicians, Black Power, underground and student leaders, to the West Indian protest movements of the late sixties and early seventies. Within the context of contemporary political and cultural events, Brathwaite has harnessed his search for an organic cultural tradition to the radicalism and black consciousness that were the West Indian equivalent of neo-nationalism during recent years.

Although Walcott and Brathwaite hold contrasting cultural ideals, they both express the conflicts of a middle-class generation that came to maturity around the time of self-government, and both have drawn upon the style and techniques of modern literature to write autobiographically of their developing consciousness of themselves as shaped by their society. Despite the differences of position—which might be explained by temperament, politics, travel, and that Brathwaite teaches in predominantly black Jamaica while Walcott's theatre is in multiracial Trinidad—both poets have tried to find in an aspect of local society the materials from which to build a vital culture. Walcott's transformation of foreign models and Brathwaite's claim to speak for the folk are the two poles between which a national art moves according to the temperament of its practitioners and the intellectual fashions of the time.

8 New Zealand: Frank Sargeson and colloquial realism

Despite the later settlement of New Zealand (beginning in the 1840s) than that of the West Indies, Canada or Australia, its literature shows similar traits of development. The early novels were essentially attempts at recording the experience of the pioneers, in which fact and fiction were uneasily blended.[1] George Chamier's *Philosopher Dick* (1891) is often considered the first attempt at serious New Zealand writing; it deflates the idealism of pioneer rhetoric. Its main character, who emigrates from England, disgusted with its greed and triviality, finds life in New Zealand barely above the level of brute existence and is depressed by the lack of civilisation and moral order. Such awareness of the discrepancy between colonial hopes and reality is a necessary step towards a literature that goes beyond the documentary and the exotic treatment of a new land to the interpretation of a society. The 1890s witnessed the same burst of nationalism noticeable throughout the Empire, and the turn of the century showed the usual reformist, progressive writing of the period. Such novels as Edith Searle Grossman's *Angela, a Messenger* (1890) and *The Heart of the Bush* (1910), William Satchell's *The Toll of the Bush* (1905) and Jane Mander's *The Story of a New Zealand River* (1920) show a deepening understanding of the difference between English and local life, the harshness of pioneer settlements, or express a woman's awakening to love and her individuality, but the only significant writer was Katherine Mansfield, who, having recorded in her diary 'Go anywhere. Don't stay here' (1908), left for Europe.

It was in the 1920s with R. A. K. Mason's more modern poetry and in the '30s with the realistic and protest novels of John Lee, Robin Hyde and John Mulgan that New Zealand literature moved beyond ballads, amateur poetry and an obsession with pioneers and settlers. The depression of the 1930s disrupted and caused a re-examination of older social patterns. Writers turned towards the poor, the down-and-out, the local version of the proletariat. In the 1930s, under the editorship of Mason, the *Phoenix* became a journal of Marxist thought and criticism; involvement with politics and economics meant a shift from English values to local issues. Mason and A. R. D. Fairburn argued for a New Zealand art that would give form and consciousness to the life of the country. In this new climate poetry was becoming more concrete, more explicitly referential to New Zealand life. Focus on local society meant an increased awareness of its faults, limitations and provinciality.

In a colonial situation where English middle-class social values are inappropriate, the first really believable characters in fiction are usually the eccentrics and outcasts. It was Frank Sargeson who made such types representative of an authentic New Zealand. Sargeson's grandparents emigrated to New Zealand in the 1870s. His father was a shopkeeper who studied to be a public accountant and later became a town clerk. His mother when young worked briefly as a teacher and one of his grandmothers was an artist. Sargeson himself studied law, qualified as a solicitor and worked in a law office until 1927 when he left for England and Europe where he travelled, read widely and tried to write an autobiographical novel. Increasingly aware that England was not 'home' and that there he was an alien, Sargeson returned to the New Zealand from which he had previously fled because of its puritanism, conformity and lack of culture. He worked briefly in a government department, but after a mental collapse he decided to give up any attempt to live a conventional, respectable life. Although it would mean a break with his family, he decided to be a writer and began studying the problems in adapting the craft of fiction to the circumstances of local life. While for a short time during the 1930s Sargeson belonged to the Communist Party, he quickly rebelled against its discipline. Sargeson follows a pattern often noticeable in Commonwealth writers: rebellion against a stodgy middle-class background, expatriation, discovery abroad that one is not British, return to the native land both as a critic of its colonial bourgeoisie and with a new awareness of it as home.

During the 1930s and '40s Sargeson worked towards creating a fictional style appropriate for his country. The result was a small body of sketches and short stories, in which language, subject, attitude, characters and form capture representative qualities of New Zealand life. Drawing upon the depression concern with the down-and-out, the out-of-work, the poor, he wrote realistically of the attitudes and world of the social underdog, the disappointed immigrant, the drifters, wanderers and rootless. While the stories imply sympathy and compassion, the tone is flat, objective and tinged with irony in comparison to the idealising of the poor often found in 'protest' writing. The stories often indirectly attack the middle class and capitalism by quietly bringing into prominence callousness, exploitation and social conformity.

Sargeson showed how realism could be used to portray colonial culture. He looked directly at the society around him, refused to idealise it, and attempted to describe it accurately. The social disorder resulting from an underpopulated, underprivileged settler society was reflected in the episodic lives of his fictional characters and in the anecdotal nature of his stories. He captured the then often remarked upon isolated, improvised quality of local life, especially among the labourers, in the small towns and on the farms. It is a society in which men are equal but without communal bonds, an atomised society in which the 'mate', a companion of the same sex, temporarily becomes what equivalent there is of family. To create a representative, seemingly authentic quality, Sargeson often pared the short story form to dramatic monologues or dialogues of three hundred to five hundred words, narrated seemingly objectively in a colloquial but toneless voice by someone outside the middle class. As in the European tradition of realism, the suppression of the author as narrator requires that values be implied by irony, symbols and other means of 'placing' characters and events. The language of the stories is idiomatic, the vocabulary has many local words, and the rhythms of speech and sentence patterns give the impression of typical New Zealand talk.

The following quotations from 'They Gave Her a Rise' will indicate the usual tone, shape and manner of Sargeson's short stories:

> When the explosion happened I couldn't go and see where it was. I'd been working on the wharves, and a case had dropped on my foot. It put me on crutches for a fortnight.
>
> But it was some explosion. Mrs Bowman and I were in the kitchen and the crockery rattled, and the dust came down off the light shade. Sally Bowman was working out at the ammunition factory, and Mrs Bowman never said anything but you could see she thought that's where it might have happened. Of course people were talking out in the street and the news came pretty quick.
>
> It was out at the ammunition factory. And they said some of the hands had been blown to smithereens.
>
> Mrs Bowman broke down.
>
> She's dead, she said, I know she's dead.
>
> The next thing was Sally was brought home in a car, one of those big limousines too. The joker driving had been going home from golf and he'd volunteered. He had to help Sally out of the car and up the steps because she was just a jelly. Her hat was on crooked and she couldn't stop crying. Of course the neighbours all came round but I told them to shove off and come back later on.
>
> Oh, indeed, young lady, Mrs Bowman said. So that's the way you're going to talk. Not going back! Will you tell me where our money's coming from if you're not? Huh! You'd sooner see your mother scrubbing floors, wouldn't you?
>
> Listen mum, Sally said. Listen . . .

> Well, I left them to it. I went over next door to talk to the people, and you could hear Sally and her mother squabbling from there.
>
> Of course Sally wasn't off for long. And they gave her a rise.[2]

Several stories treat of immigration, the contrast between expectations and reality, and the problem of cultural conflict as felt by the poor. In 'The Making of a New Zealander': 'Nick and I were sitting on the hillside and Nick was saying he was a New Zealander, but he knew he wasn't a New Zealander.' In 'Big Ben':

> But maybe it was something deeper than that. Maybe Ben began to feel that living in New Zealand he'd always be sort of living on a desert island. Perhaps even his experience of gardening had told him he'd never really get the hang of colonial life. It was O.K. for the kids, he certainly knew that, but what about his wife? He certainly must have had a pretty good idea what it was like for her. After all, he could go out working alongside his mates but his wife hadn't a friend. She hardly ever spoke to anyone outside the house except when she was buying the mutton flap and suchlike.

Sargeson's stories are similar to V. S. Naipaul's early fiction in recording, where there was no literary tradition upon which to build, the nature and quality of a society undergoing change, and where colonial myths were not relevant to actual life.

The models for Sargeson's art are recognisable, if subtly transformed to fit New Zealand: Mark Twain, Sherwood Anderson, Ernest Hemingway, James Joyce, and perhaps the Australian Henry Lawson. Each of these writers worked within the realist tradition of fiction and each was concerned with matters of the narrator's voice, objectivity, and implied ironies, especially towards middle-class and conventional values. The colloquial voice, laconic dialogue, and apparent naiveté of Sargeson's narrators are within the tradition of Twain, while the extreme understatement and economy show study of Hemingway and Joyce. Like many other Commonwealth writers, Sargeson has availed himself of the lessons learned by American and Irish authors concerning the techniques by which a local society can be treated seriously in literature without falling into idealisation or condescension.

While Sargeson is one of the best writers of short stories within the new national literatures, there are obvious limitations to the conventions and techniques he has found useful to describe New Zealand life—naive narrators and extreme reliance on colloquial speech and social underdogs. Such writing is at first liberating from the English novel of manners or novel of ideas but suffers from many of the same handicaps as local colour sketches, folk tales and frontier stories. It cannot respond to the texture of settled society, record subtleties of manners and sensibility, examine the intricacies of public power or the complexities of human desire. It is essentially sentimental in its assumption of natural goodness and innocence among the poor. And it is notoriously difficult to create sustained fictional narrative from such anecdotal methods and material. Those who argue that the lack of settled societies in the new nations results in more successful short-story writers than novelists are rather accepting the perspective of a literary method than accurately observing their local cultures which often are complex.

The limitations for a writer who sees society from the perspective of its wanderers, outcasts and impoverished are shown by Sargeson's difficulty in expanding his fiction to larger forms. The episode, anecdote and sketch cannot be fused into a sustained long narrative. (Even the picaresque novel usually traces a single life, makes use of social contrasts, and is constructed around a journey.) 'That Summer' (1943) is an attempt at capturing within the apparently casual joining up of two 'mates' an analogous relationship to that more often associated with an intense, shattering, doomed love affair between a man and a woman. It would be unnecessary to comment upon the homosexual foundation of the story, as Sargeson has elsewhere written about his friendships, were it not so often implied that women, marriage and domesticity are dangerous traps for the kind of person the author admires, and if such male relationships were not often conspicuous in other new English literatures. Exploration, the frontier, pioneer society, and a life of wandering on the road create a culture for men which women threaten. The responsibilities of marriage, children, steady jobs, mortgages and staying in one place no more appeal to Sargeson's heroes than they would to Walt Whitman, Twain's Huckleberry Finn, Melville's Ismael, or J.F. Cooper's Deerslayer. The frontier and vagabond themes found in some new national literatures reflect anti-bourgeois attitudes and a rebellion against a local middle-class society which, along with its other sins of gentility, hypocrisy and injustice, the author usually sees as a relic of European colonialism. (By contrast, in the African or Indian novel romantic love sometimes is idealised as liberating, in opposition to traditional arranged marriages.)

The first two paragraphs of 'That Summer' are an example of the style Sargeson developed for notating the speech, outlook and environment of the New Zealand worker.

> It was a good farm job I had that winter, but I've always suffered from itchy feet so I never thought I'd stick it for long. All the same I stayed until the shearing, and I quit after we'd carted the wool out to the station, just a few bales at a time. It was just beginning December and I had a good lot of chips saved up, so I thought I'd have a spell in town which I hadn't had for a good long time, and maybe I'd strike a town job before my chips ran out.
>
> The old bloke I was working for tried hard to get me to stay but there was nothing doing. I liked him all right and the tucker was good, but him and his missis were always rowing, and there was just the three of us stuck away there with hardly any company to speak of. I had to sleep on an old sofa in the kitchen because it was only a slab where they lived in with two rooms, and I got a bit sick of hearing them fighting every night when they'd gone to bed. The old bloke told me he'd had money enough to build a decent house long ago, but his missis said if he did she'd be there for keeps. So she wouldn't let him, but they'd gone on living there just the same.

The sentences are loaded with idioms, colloquialism, slang and the clichés of lower-class speech: 'The old bloke/I was working for/tried hard/to get me to stay/but/there was nothing doing.' The harshness of his life ('old sofa', 'only a slab') and isolation ('hardly any company') are quickly touched upon as is the married state of the employers ('fighting every night'). In many of Sargeson's stories the narrator is uncomfortably present at a scene of domestic disharmony. The use of many linking or connective words ('but', 'and', 'so') contributes to the feeling of rootlessness, while the emphasis on 'I' in relationship to a context of 'they', 'him', 'his' and 'she' creates a perspective of casual relationships in which people are present without belonging to a community.

Although it is during the depression, and jobs are almost unobtainable, Billy, the narrator, quits his employment, goes to town, tries to 'pick up with a girl' and rents a room in a boarding house where the husband and wife 'squabble'. He meets, treats to dinner, goes to the movies, and gets drunk with a casual acquaintance named Sam. He is free with the little money he has. Besides paying for Sam, he drops coins around a tree where his landlord's child can find them, and shrugs it off when another casual acquaintance, Ted, robs him of his remaining money: 'What's money anyhow, I thought.' Bill survives on odd jobs, trickery, petty thievery and betting on races. He becomes mates with Terry, another of the unemployed, with whom he shares a room. Unlike the quarrelling husbands and wives of Sargeson's stories, Bill and Terry seem to get along through some unspoken man-to-man code. They undergo various adventures in trying to survive, the point of which illustrates 'A man wants a mate that won't let him down, he said.' Bill is seduced by Maggie, who tells people that he raped her. After being imprisoned, awaiting trial, he is freed when Maggie is frightened by Terry into withdrawing her complaint. Outside prison, Bill finds Terry has been put in hospital because of his bad lungs and is unable to walk. He manages to sneak him from the hospital and takes him back to his room in the boarding house where he cares for him until he dies.

The penultimate paragraph of the story stands in sharp

contrast to the various quarrelling and anguished relationships portrayed between men and women, and is an excellent example of Sargeson's craftsmanship:

> I'd look at him lying there.
>
> Terry, I'd say.
>
> What is it boy? he'd say.
>
> Nothing, I'd say.
>
> And then I'd say, Terry.
>
> And instead of answering he'd just have a sort of faint grin on his face.
>
> Terry, I'd say.
>
> But I never could get any further than just saying Terry. I wanted to say something but I didn't know what it was, and I couldn't say it.
>
> Terry, I'd say.
>
> And he'd sort of grin. And sometimes I'd take his hand and hold it tight, and he'd let it stay in my hand, and there'd be the faint grin on his face.
>
> Terry, I'd say.
>
> I'm all right boy, he'd say.
>
> And sometimes I couldn't stand it, I'd have to just rush off and leave him there.
>
> And one night when I came back again I looked at him and knew it was the finish.
>
> Terry, I said, and he didn't answer.
>
> Terry, I said, and I said I was going to get the priest.
>
> Cheers boy, is what I think he said, and I rushed off without even saying goodbye.

The repetitions, the dependence on the notation of inarticulateness, and the intrinsic sentimentalism reveal the limitations of Sargeson's method and sensibility. This is good writing, but it is also the romanticising of the dumb ox beyond the extremes sometimes found in Hemingway's fiction.

It is paradoxical that in a supposedly puritan, conformist, conventional society Sargeson's homosexual stories should be seen as the quintessence of New Zealandism. A possible explanation might be seen in the transformation he made of a cultural ideal. Nationalism often identifies authenticity with rural areas and the poor—the land and the people. In contrast high culture is seen as foreign, metropolitan, cosmopolitan, snobbish, elitist, a form of imperialism. The writer rebelling against his middle-class background usually either heads towards London, Paris or New York, with their international and metropolitan values, or identifies himself with the land and the people. Sargeson, like Mark Twain or Synge, creates a folk tradition from those on the fringes of society.

But the imitation of the 'people' does not offer sufficient material and technical interest to make an artistic tradition. If it is necessary to liberate a new national literature from foreign dominance, and necessary to learn how to use local voices and subject-matter for art, it is also necessary to go beyond the sketch, the short story, the life of the poor, the affection among mates, to larger literary forms and more complex material. A New Zealand literature primarily concerned with the wandering labourers of 'That Summer' would be as false to reality as a Nigerian literature that kept singing the glories of the tribal past. Sargeson was aware that his own art had to progress beyond the short story to the novel and from focus on the outsider to a more personal exploration of problems of individual and national identity. While 'That Summer' is an attempt at such progress, it is an interesting dead-end. Sargeson had to move on to the novel itself. His later narratives include some of his best and worst work, but in either case the increase in length, range of subject-matter and style shows his awareness that he must go beyond the anecdotal realism of the short stories.

Of the later works the most significant is *I Saw in My Dream*, a novel concerning a young man's rebellion against his middle-class conformist family and his subsequent discovery of himself while working on a farm. The novel might well be described as a New Zealand *Portrait of the Artist as a Young Man*, especially as Sargeson had, many years before when in London, attempted such a Joycean fictionalised autobiography and given it up realising that he was not yet an artist and had not yet experienced enough. The project had, however, always remained in his mind as necessary to his development as a writer. First, however, he had to create the representative New Zealand style of his short stories. Looked at from this perspective, it could be said that the ironic, realistic stories are his *Dubliners* (or V. S. Naipaul's *Miguel Street*) and *Dream* is his *Portrait.* Autobiographical fiction about growing up and becoming different from one's family is especially appropriate to the new national literatures where either education to or rebellion against colonial middle-class values is a central experience of writers in a rapidly changing society. Another influence is Bunyan's *Pilgrim's Progress.* Reacting against the puritanism of his family and New Zealand, Sargeson saw in Bunyan a parable for all those who must escape conventional society, with its death to the spirit, and become pilgrims in search of salvation. He correctly saw that Bunyan's story is a spiritual autobiography, a metaphor of a psychological quest, and of relevance to all those who feel they must flee the city of destruction for some promised land. Here, as in many other nationalist writers, the holy city is the land itself and its inhabitants are those who live close to it.

I Saw in My Dream has a three-part structure. The first part begins with memories, similar to *Portrait*, of Henry's early childhood:

> WHO LOVES YOU?
> Mummy and daddy.
> Who else?
> Auntie Clara.
> And who else?
> Gentle Jesus.
> And who else?
> Our Father which art in heaven . . .
> And when that was over mother said,
> *Goodnight, sweet repose,*
> *All the bed, and all the clothes,*
> and she kissed you and took away the candle, and you were left in the dark, warm in the hollow of the bed, *snug as a bug in a rug.*[3]

The phrase 'snug as a bug in a rug' introduces a motif repeated throughout the book of enclosure, protection, caves, balls and prisons, which is associated with the inhibitions of puritanism and middle-class values. The use of italics occurs throughout the book, usually to indicate interior monologue, stream of consciousness or as counterpoint between psychological description and the external reality. In attempting to move beyond irony and realism, Sargeson made use of the modern experimental novel with its symbolism, disruption of normal time sequence, associative and recurring patterns and other poetic and impressionistic means of penetrating beyond the surface of life to psychological truths.

The events and stages of Henry's childhood and young manhood include: warmth from his mother, awareness of family, first school morning, guilt at forbidden adventures including sexual initiation with a girl cousin, followed by acceptance among the men and a job in a law office during the depression. At the office he is shocked by his employer spending most of each day drinking in a pub; Henry is usually left alone with a fifteen-year-old secretary who flirts with the older men working outside the office. Henry is shocked at her behaviour but attracted. Despite or because of her lack of education, manners and breeding, he becomes obsessed. After she tells him that she intends to go out some night with 'a rough specimen', Henry locks her into the office store room, supposedly to keep her out of trouble. Exactly what happens afterwards is not clear, but he is left with a fear of the girl. His confusion is indicated by such italicised passages as '*And he hadn't done anything, he hadn't. But say SHE said he had. Say yes say she went out with that man or jockeys and blamed him instead.*' The theme of enclosure is repeated again at the tennis club when he meets Marge who wants to leave New Zealand for Australia and America. She is a socialist, has no intention of marrying and thinks church-going is a joke. When Marge goes to 'the ladies' place' someone fastens the catch on the door and she is locked in for half an hour. 'Now, whoever would do a childish thing like that? Somebody was asking for it anyhow. But who do you reckon it could have been?' It was Henry, of course. His shocked response to Marge is shown by his confusion towards what he has done.

Shortly afterwards, Henry handles a legal case against a labourer who owes '£9–15–9, plus costs'. The man is out of work, has a wife in hospital and six children, and is trying to earn money as a potato farmer. Henry asks him when he can pay off the debt. The man becomes aggressive: 'Birds that sat on their backsides all the year round could always manage to get themselves kept in plenty of good tucker, but . . . didn't Henry think it could be the other way round sometimes, just for a change?' Immediately after the man leaves, a detective enters the office and Henry faints. During his convalescence he recalls scenes from his childhood of fear, conformity, running home from school, the seduction by his cousin, and his puritan upbringing: '*Father always said nobody should be allowed to go in swimming without a bathing suit that covered them from neck to knee.*' His mother urges him to return to work, but he undergoes a crisis: 'I don't know a thing, he said.'

Sargeson has modified the realistic method of his earlier stories for a larger, more thematic, associative way of writing fiction. The flatly stated, objectively presented events are counterpointed by memories and emotions revealed in the italicised passages. Puritanism, conventionality, enclosure and middle-class comfort are contrasted to sexual desire, individuality, freedom, the working class and economic insecurity. The life Henry lives is oppressive, contrary to his inner emotions, and causes his breakdown. That he collapses when a detective appears at the office shows Henry can no longer bear his feelings of guilt, guilt expressed by his compulsive enclosure of two uninhibited women. After a cleansing dive into the river that concludes Part I, which symbolically washes away his inhibited, colonial, middle-class behaviour, he is reborn not to a new identity but to an awareness that he must define himself in relationship to his environment. The search is personal but can be seen as representative of the nation. Part I ends with Henry lying naked on a grassy river bank. He must begin again.

In Part II Henry uses the name Dave while working on a farm in the hills. The change of name corresponds to his awareness of the problem of his own identity. The opening paragraph parallels yet contrasts to the first paragraph of Part I:

> Now and then he would go off to sleep, but mostly the cold kept him awake. And lying tightly curled up in the chilly bed, feeling the ache and cramp in his legs, he kept on telling himself he'd have to get up and look for some extra covering. Yet hour after hour he went on lying there without moving, wanting to stretch out his legs to ease them, yet knowing how freezing cold it would be for his feet down at the bottom of the bed—*why am I oh why am I here in the cold and the dark? Cold bed rolling over to the sun, cold embryo waiting to be born. Why am I waiamihea.*

In Part II the detail and texture of the story are more filled in, the episodes longer, and there is more continuity. If the fragmentary style of Part I implied a dazed, inhibited, enclosed, sketchy, unresponding relationship to life, the more novelistic feel of Part II shows a growth in awareness, of others and of reality. Form reflects content; genre imitates psychology. In Part II Dave puts up with discomfort, has friends, is more relaxed and in touch with nature, and is open to experience. The landscape itself is a new world awaiting fulfilment:

> And now the world outside, through the gap between the boards, was empty and yet somehow waiting. Only the bush, all lit by the sun up the east side of the spur now, with birds coming out high up near the skyline to circle, black against the blue, before going in again, made you feel it had a life of its own. Everything else seemed somehow to be empty and waiting now that the dogs had gone, and the boss and the missis and Johnny. The grass, green now even where there were shadows, but wet with the melted frost that the sun was catching, was waiting.

The hill is not Eden. It is a change from the constrictions of puritan suburbia. It is a chance to begin again, a chance to discover one's authentic self. But it is also lonely, isolated and dangerous. It is New Zealand itself from which the middle class flees into the constriction and snobbery of colonial suburbs. Two motifs are of particular importance in this quest: the presence of the Maoris, and Cedric's escape from being imprisoned by his family.

The Maoris' presence reminds Dave of the newness of his own race on the islands. The Maorised title of the house, Waiamihea, shows the superficial adoption of the English to a foreign land and culture: the house title is actually 'Why am I here?'. The seemingly instinctive and mysterious ways of the Maoris contrast to those of the Europeans, and are more suitable for the landscape, but the Maoris have been dominated and pushed to the outer fringes of colonial society. The Maoris represent to Dave the physical, sensual and natural which his family has repressed. This cannot be his own identity, but he must accept it as part of himself and the land.

The mysterious Cedric Macgregor, who is spoken about but never actually appears in the novel, found his freedom through the Maoris. Raised in the hills 'with only those dirty Maoris down the road for nearest neighbours' he stays away from school and spends his time with the Maoris and their women. Cedric is 'wild', a 'child of nature', contrary to a well-brought-up middle-class child, the opposite of Henry in Part I. The Macgregors decide Cedric is out of his mind and convert a cave into a prison where they intend to keep him. Johnny, who supervises the construction of the prison, is an instance of those who having themselves been imprisoned try to imprison others; this parallels Henry's locking the office girl in the store room to keep her out of trouble. Apparently with the aid of the Maoris, Cedric flees. The Macgregors pretend he is living a conventional life in the city, but he has disappeared. A careful reading of the novel would show that Cedric's actions often parallel those of Dave and Henry. Henry's nude swimming at the conclusion of Part I is echoed by Cedric's with Elaine. Henry, we later learn, swam with Marge. The Macgregors' attempted imprisonment of Cedric should probably be understood as similar to family pressures to force Henry into a law office. Cedric's mysterious escape cannot, however, be Dave's freedom: '*it's all right for Cedric. Cedric's Cedric . . . Cedric never had a Henry to forget . . . I've been Henry, now I'm Dave. But I'm only TRYING to be Dave.*' The rural hills and farms are not the end of Dave's journey. They also could be a trap, a false home. In a passage which anticipates by two decades the return to primitiveness in Margaret Atwood's Canadian novel, *Surfacing*, Dave imagines:

The escape idea would be all right if there was anywhere to escape to. Is it a question of place? Because if it is, Ron's wrong. If I had him with me now he'd admit it. Because, look! A dream comes true. Every bit of it is there and better than I ever dreamed of. The happy land, where there is neither rain nor snow. Nor any cold wind. Running water shall be my viol, the wild strawberry my violet. Or asphodel. And when I tire of the eternal noonday I shall go to my bed of moss behind the hanging vine. You bookish bastard. But I know what I must first do. Strip. Because I must take with me nothing. Not a thing. Nothing to eat or drink. Neither food, nor seed, nor spade, nor shoe nor sock, nor anything to wear. All that's behind me now and forgotten. And no book. Particularly no book. And you ought to burn your clothes. Or bury them.

As in *Surfacing*, primitiveness cannot be the journey's end. It is another comforting delusion of being 'as snug as a bug in a rug'. Nature is also violent and dangerous. The land slip that follows a flood kills the Macgregors and their dogs. But the trees remain.[4]

It is because Henry has lived as Dave that he can, in the brief concluding Part III of the novel, think of marrying Marge, think of travelling around the world, or assume he can 'do something special . . . something nobody else can do except me'. The final 'yes, yes' of the novel is an affirmation of life, creativity, the individuality and selfhood Henry lacked. It is Sargeson autobiographically celebrating his decision to become a writer.

I Saw in My Dream is a remarkable book. It is a blend of symbolist experimental techniques with a kind of realism common to regional literature; but it is from the dialectic between *avant-garde* and nationalist currents that the best works of the new literature have resulted. Unfortunately Sargeson did not have the skill to create another *Portrait of the Artist*. The realism and mental associations in *I Saw in My Dream* are imperfectly integrated; the italicised passages are often crude attempts at symbolism; and Part III, the conclusion, is unconvincing. *I Saw in My Dream* was a necessary attempt at liberation from the limitations of a local realism, but Sargeson's skills remained principally those of his early stories.

His later attempt, in *Memoirs of a Peon* (1965), to write a sophisticated satire on both the New Zealand middle-class establishment and on those who pretended to rebel against it fails because the style lacks the subtlety to be convincing. Influenced by his reading of European literature, especially Casanova, the narrator describes his sexual and social conquests in an imported literary fashion. The comedy results from the discrepancy between the literary models and both the unromantic reality of New Zealand life and the narrator's own lack of energy and ambition. The experiment of *I Saw in My Dream* had, however, broadened Sargeson's palette; several good novellas followed which, while avoiding *avant-garde* symbolism, are more extended and cover a greater social and emotional canvas than the short stories.

It seems probable that *I Saw in my Dream* has had an influence on subsequent New Zealand creative writing. In particular Janet Frame's novels follow in their mixture of realism and poetry, objective detail and imaginative association, linear narrative and fragmentation, autobiography and fiction, nostalgia for a rural or primitive order, and understanding that fixed patterns of life are not possible in the modern world.[5] While her writing (to be discussed in Chapter 12) is appropriate to our age—with its investigation of patterns, structures, codes and private languages in literature—she seems indebted to Sargeson's experiments and to his awareness that alienation from established society and the desire for a natural order are in themselves insufficient answers to the problems of living.

9 Australia: Richardson to A. D. Hope and the middle class

Australia was settled after the American War of Independence when England needed a new colony to which to transport criminals. The origins of Australia have haunted its literature whereas penal transportation to the older colonies is a neglected subject in American writing. While Americans see themselves as the heirs of the Puritans who supposedly fled the tyranny of the Old for the paradise of the New World, Australian literature has treated its new world ambiguously. If Henry Savery's *Quintus Servinton* (1830–1) was an idealised autobiography of a transported criminal, and Henry Kingsley's *Recollections of Geoffrey Hamlyn* (1859) shows transplanted Englishmen living English country lives on the stations, other novels, such as Marcus Clarke's *For the Term of His Natural Life* (1874), concerned the innocent or near innocent criminal unjustly transported from England to the horrors of a barren, dangerous colony—a tradition still carried on during this century by Eleanor Dark and Thomas Keneally. In the nineteenth-century Australian novel it is often difficult to decide whether the country is worse than the brutalities of the colonial government and society. The early diaries, journals and other documents, however, give a more balanced picture of the land. The literary tradition which portrays the early settlement as horrible probably results from later attitudes and is based on a selection of historical facts. The early distinction between prisoner and government contributed towards treating the outlaw and those outside society as authentically Australian.

The literary treatment of the gentry and the middle class as British or European was strengthened in Australia by the fact that social divisions remained more obvious and sharper than in, say, Canada. Immigration to Australia was more working-class than in the other colonies, and a local middle class developed less rapidly. The social establishment appeared to consist of British-born officials, those connected with the government, or those wealthy enough to keep up English social ties. The identification of labourers and outcasts with Australia in contrast to the pro-English elite was strengthened by a tradition of radicalism originating in the late nineteenth century when large-scale immigration took place during an era of socialist ideology and unionisation. From 1860 to 1900 the population grew from one to three million. Between the working-class dream of a new start in the colonies and the socialist ideas of the period, a radical nationalist ideology emerged which has persisted until the present.

The radical nationalist tradition began in the 1880s and '90s. At a time when Melbourne, with a population of over a million, had become one of the supreme examples of a Victorian city and when the country had begun to be urbanised, such writers as Henry Lawson and 'Banjo' Paterson revived the 'bush' ballads of previous generations in which European folk songs had been accommodated to local conditions. The new literary ballads were part of a movement in which the short stories of Lawson and the novels of Joseph Furphy attempted to create an authentic Australian voice —democratic, somewhat inarticulate, uneducated, tough, stoic, realistic and outside established society—in contrast to the English gentlemen who were the heroes of novels by Henry Kingsley and Rolf Boldrewood. Often a casual labourer, sarcastic towards refinement, laconic in speech, the Australian in this new literature is a descendant of the early convict, and of the later bushman and the squatter; he is a 'mate' with a sense of working-class solidarity which is part of his patriotism in contrast to the polished manners and social injustices of Europe. This Australian version of Walt Whitmanism was given prominence by the Sydney *Bulletin*, a radical nationalist journal with a preference for ballads and for short stories about workers and life in the bush. *The Bulletin* was republican, in favour of federation, strongly nationalistic, and set the tone which was adopted by those who looked back on the 1890s as a national ideal which was later lost.

David Walker's *Dream and Disillusion*[1] traces the subsequent history of the radical nationalist search for a cultural identity. Such writers and intellectuals as Vance Palmer, Louis Esson, Frank Wilmot and Frederick Sinclaire created a legend of the 1890s in contrast both to the existing urban, middle-class Australia and to Europe. Their nationalism was an ideal, often at odds with actual Australian life before and after the First World War, and which, therefore, had to be set in the past and the future. The Australian radical nationalists should be seen as part of an international reaction on the part of intellectuals and writers against middle-class, urban, industrialised society. Their socialism developed from the intellectual climate of Shaw, Chesterton and Wells; their desire for simplicity was a development of a late nineteenth-century European disillusionment with the complexity of modern life. The First World War and the debate over conscription in Australia further heightened tensions between those with imperial loyalties and those who hoped for a new nation freed from the injustices and associations of Europe.

While the legend of the 1890s and radical nationalist history has been accepted by few major Australian writers—Judith Wright being the one significant exception—even writers with no sympathy towards cultural nationalism have echoed the attack on suburbia, criticised its mass conformist society and implied that an essential Australia can be found in the desert and outback. Patrick White's *Voss*, the novels of Randolph Stow, A. D. Hope's early poem 'Australia' and the first volume of Judith Wright's poetry have in common the rejection of the middle class, which is seen as foreign, and, in varying degrees, the implication that whatever is uniquely Australian will be found outside the cities. Probably the most common theme of Australian literature is the lack of intensity, passion and spiritual consciousness in middle-class life.

Henry Handel Richardson (Ethel Florence Lindesay Richardson) wrote *Maurice Guest* (1908), the first novel by an Australian to achieve an international reputation. She went to Europe to study music and did not return except for a brief visit to do research towards a novel about the life of her father. Her novels were for a long time ignored by Australians. Her literary tradition was that of nineteenth-century European realism. Like Flaubert, Ibsen and others, she carefully removed any trace of the author from the work, presented characters without comment, aimed at psychological depth, worked at accuracy, dramatised rather than narrated, and allowed subtle implied ironies to 'place' her characters. *Maurice Guest* takes place in central Europe of the late nineteenth century when Nietzsche's doctrines of the superman going beyond good and evil were still known only to the young intellectuals and artists who confused doctrines of will with romantic notions of genius and love. Its theme is obsessive, amoral devotion to art and love contrasted to the provincial, bourgeois mediocrity of those who conform to social convention. Maurice's life ends in suicide after a disastrous pursuit of Louise, a free spirit with no conventional morality who loves Schilsky, a musical genius. *Maurice Guest* is a novel of ironies, and the final irony is that Louise and Schilsky may be as lacking in genius as poor Maurice. The novel could be seen as a comedy of provincial manners masquerading as an international tragedy. There is no evidence in the book of genius except that the young claim to recognise it and, of course, the story is told from their point of view.

Maurice Guest was once famous, even notorious for its objective record of amorality, suggestions of sexual perversion and other contraventions of English social mores. While it is possible to criticise its clichéed dialogue and sometimes stiff naturalistic description, it is a great novel. But in what sense is it Australian beyond the surprise that Louise, the archetypal European *femme fatale*, is from Australia? Richardson belongs to the same internationalism that included Jean Rhys, Claude McKay and Katherine Mansfield, who left the colonies for the opportunities and cultural interests of life abroad, but who felt alien in European society. If the young provincial Englishman

Maurice is seen as a substitute for a representative colonial, *Maurice Guest* will be found similar to the novels of Jean Rhys which show the deepening humiliation and demoralisation of an outsider by more forceful, self-centred Europeans. Seen in this way, Maurice is the Australian in Europe. However, Louise is also an outsider. Maurice and Louise are opposite sides of the same coin: Maurice is the provincial bourgeois, ill at ease among those whose passions govern their behaviour; Louise is the rebel, dissatisfied with conventional life.

Brian Kiernan claims that 'The importance of *Maurice Guest* in the canon of Australian novels is that it points up most acutely the Romantic theme of the outsider versus the bourgeoisie', which he finds in the best Australian fiction.[2] He claims that the talented individual's sense of isolation from society was anticipated by Joseph Furphy and is common to the novels of Christina Stead, Patrick White and Thomas Keneally, where instead of communality the author shows a radical dissatisfaction with Australian life. Kiernan admits that the feeling of life in society being insufficient is common to both American and European literature, where it is traceable to the Romanticism of the nineteenth century. I suggest that the radical nationalist tradition is another branch of the same plant.

Richardson's major Australian novel, *The Fortunes of Richard Mahony* was published in three volumes: *Australia Felix* (1917), *The Way Home* (1925) and *Ultima Thule* (1929). Based on the life of her father, it tells the story of another outsider, an Irish emigrant who is neither at home in Australia nor in Europe when he returns. As in the novels of Martin Boyd, it is remarkable how often the characters travel around the world on trips or in futile attempts to settle. Mahony's life of unease is portrayed realistically against the society and history of his time. He is both a victim of a colonial society and of his desire to be superior. He has romantic longings for greatness and individuality but few of the necessary talents to be more than a highly successful colonial doctor. If provincial Australian society offers no outlets for his aspirations, it does provide the wealth and connections that allow him to expect more than he might have obtained if he had remained in the Old World. On his travels to Europe he is often struck by its ignorance, lack of energy, pinching of pennies and distrust of outsiders. But the Australian economy which provides surprising opportunities for an immigrant is also subject to rapid fluctuations. Mahony, who is careless with his investments, goes from riches to poverty and ends life insanely seeking transcendental spiritual truths.

Richardson has portrayed a type and an era. Mahony is a financially better off, better educated version of the restless, uprooted Australians found in the literature of the 1890s. He has a similar feeling of the purposelessness of existence to Furphy's Tom Collins. Heir of the Enlightenment, of Romanticism, of Victorian loss of faith, of Old World culture and New World opportunities and aspirations, Mahony is in permanent exile. As so often in the new national English literatures, the very characteristics that make for a local significance are also those that refer to the modern condition. Mahony, the immigrant with European cultural and social aspirations which can be satisfied neither in Australia nor in Europe, may represent the divided mind of the colonial bourgeoisie, but he is also an instance of modern man wanting more from life than is possible. Significantly he is not an artist, lover, or anyone with claims to genius. At various times in his life he thinks of pursuing new experimental interests, but they are usually dropped in the course of what, beyond his restlessness, is an ordinary medical career.

It is part of Richardson's objectivity that the irony of Mahony's ordinariness is not clear until we are well into the narrative. Unlike *Maurice Guest* where selection and economy compress presentation and irony together, in *The Fortunes* the first volume is given mostly to exposition from Mahony's point of view and it is probably not until the second volume that we become uneasily aware that the hero may have an inflated sense of himself as well as being psychologically prone to depression, dissatisfaction, and irrational delusions. Similarly his wife, Mary, is first seen through what is essentially her husband's perspective as making expensive and annoying demands to fulfil social appearances; by the last volume she is seen as a solid rock of common sense and practicality who uses her social contacts to help the family survive. Richardson's irony is supported by parody. Many passages in *Maurice Guest* parody clichés from the nineteenth-century romantic novel and from the international comedy of manners.

Martin Boyd's *Lucinda Brayford* (1946) has something of the same epic sweep as *Fortunes*. It follows generations in the lives of several families, tracing their rise and fall. The opening of *Lucinda Brayford* is similar to earlier Australian novels in its improbabilities, coincidences, general artificiality and atmosphere of parody; its predecessors seem more the eighteenth-century novels of Fielding, Smollett and Sterne than the nineteenth-century realism of Austen and Eliot. It is almost as if the novelist could not take seriously the existence of an earlier Australian society. Marcus Clarke's *For the Term of His Natural Life*, *The Fortunes of Richard Malony* and *Lucinda Brayford*, even Patrick White's *Voss* and *The Aunt's Story*, all begin with high stylisation in what for the period in which they were written is a mode approaching parody, as if to suggest that older Australian lives can only be seen in terms of eighteenth-century exaggeration and irony. Once the novels start, however, the narrative becomes realistic.

After Lucinda Vane's family rises in the Australian social world, she eventually marries into the English aristocracy and becomes Lucinda Brayford. In England she finds an aristocracy of taste, sense, refinement and elegance as well as breeding: 'No one whom she had known in Melbourne would have talked of a "gutter millionaire", nor of life being made more passionate by art.' The Brayfords view Russian ballet and Nijinsky's dancing with the eye of experts; they paint, have a deep appreciation of art and music. Lucinda is shown to have a natural nobility of behaviour even superior to that of the Brayfords. Her husband, Hugo, resigns his commission in the army, gambles himself heavily into debt, uses Lucinda's money and carries on an affair. Throughout the novel she behaves with a true aristocracy of spirit; she has elegance, taste, wit, and just the right balance of moral alertness, pleasure and responsibility. Unlike James's Isabel Archer, Lucinda is free of American puritanism and repression; she is a product of both the Australian and English upper classes; she has the money and aspirations of the former, and the taste and good sense, without the vices, of the latter. Her life is set against the decline of the aristocracy in the decades following the First World War and during the Second World War. Unprincipled commercial interests become dominant in the government and enter the House of Lords. The novel ends during the Second World War with the destruction of the aristocracy and the civilisation for which it stands.

Martin Boyd belonged to a distinguished English family which had established a branch in Australia. In his novels Europe is the centre of culture because its long history of aristocracy has provided the conditions in which art can develop and be appreciated. By contrast, Australia is a land where the newness of its inhabitants, the struggle to survive and the appearance of sudden wealth have produced a contempt for tradition and fine living. Good taste is looked upon as effeminate and art is only valued as investment or a display of wealth. The status of art is representative of the quality of life. The Brayfords' taste, common sense, tolerance and wit are the product of centuries of breeding. Boyd's view is conservative. Culture depends on tradition, breeding and leisure. The middle classes are too concerned with wealth and practical achievement to create a high culture. Lucinda's life is a work of art, but she does not work at it; she responds to situations with the tact that is part of civilisation and culture.

While the values of *Lucinda Brayford* might be described as the aesthetics of culture, such a nostalgia for an aristocratic tradition has in our century usually led to Rome. Boyd's neglected novel, *Nuns in Jeopardy* (1940), is an elegant reply to those who, trusting in the goodness of man, believe that Eden can be restored in a new land outside the past injustices of civilised society and without taking into account man's imperfect nature. Without religion, authority, tradition, hierarchy, breeding and responsibility, any society is doomed. The novel is a witty illustration of the effects of original sin and as such may be seen as Boyd's most profound response to the arguments offered by what I have described as the radical national tradition of Australian thought.

Patrick White's dislike of Australian materialism and suburban life is well known. Australia has become an extension of European class society and evaluates life by adjustment, success and simplistic pleasures. In contrast to this White offers in *Voss* (1957) an Australian hero who is a half-mad visionary, unconcerned with material success, whose dreams end in failure and yet who might be said to have created an Australian national identity of a more profound and authentic kind than those who have found success in the settled urban areas. Voss's doomed exploration is to the inland deserts, among the Aborigines, at whose hands he and his companions will die.

The basic symbolic contrasts are made early in the book when Voss is introduced visiting the well-settled house in which he meets Laura Trevelyan, who will be the Laura or Beatrice of his travels. Although themselves recent settlers, Laura's family and acquaintances have all the social comforts and class consciousness of Europe. Their world is cluttered with dresses, furniture, talk of good marriages, and petty snobberies. To them Voss is an eccentric German who does not obey the rules of society. His belief in self-pride, pure will and rejection of Christian humanity makes him representative of the Nietzschean streak that entered Australian intellectual thought in the late nineteenth century and that has remained a lasting part of the nation's intellectual heritage. The novel shows that such pride is self-destructive, but that men can be redeemed by suffering.

One of the questions raised early in the novel is whether the recently arrived German explorer can become part of a country in which the English settlers are still lost and without roots. Laura claims, 'He is obsessed by this country', but not afraid of it. She is told, 'I would not like to ride very far into it . . . and meet a lot of blacks, and deserts, and rocks, and skeletons, they say, of men that have died'. Laura admits, 'It will be some time, I expect, before I am able to grasp anything so foreign and incomprehensible. It is not my country, although I have lived in it'. But when someone says 'It is not that German's', Laura replies, 'It is his by right of vision'. Mr Bonner puts the view of the settler, of the new suburbs:

> Here we are talking about our Colony as if it did not exist until now . . . Or as if it has now begun to exist as something quite different. I do not understand what all this talk is about. We are not children. We have only to consider the progress we have made. Look at our homes and public edifices. Look at the devotion of our administrators, and the solid achievement of those men who are settling the land. Why, in this very room, look at the remains of the good dinner we have just eaten. I do not see what there is to be afraid of.[3]

Mr Bonner's opinion is sharply in contrast to the visionary dreams of Voss in which Australia, because it is still uncharted, is seen as a land in which to explore and expand one's soul through will, action and suffering. Its possibilities are spiritual rather than material.

Since Voss lacks the petty snobberies of the settlers, including racial prejudices, he has no fears of the native 'blacks'. He tries to treat them as equals in brotherhood—we are perhaps reminded of this theme in Cooper, Twain, Melville and other American writers—but is disappointed by their rejection of his handshake, expressive of an equality of souls. And the expedition fails. Voss loses most of his men and material. Exhausted, sick, without supplies, he and the few remaining explorers are captured by an inland tribe and killed. Before his death Voss learns humility and admits that he has been defeated, that he can no longer help or even lead his men. By conventional terms he has been a failure, but within the terms of the novel, which are the creation of a national spiritual identity through will and suffering, he has become part of the myth of the authentic Australia: 'Well, you see, if you live and suffer long enough in a place, you do not leave it altogether. Your spirit is still there.'

Voss's history is part of the attempt of Australians to come to terms with their strange land. Topp, the music master, 'out of his hatred for the sour colonial soil upon which he had been deposited many years before, had developed a perverse love, which he had never yet succeeded in expressing, and which, for that reason, nobody had suspected'. Laura tells him: 'Some of you . . . will express what we others have experienced by living.' The conversation drifts to the topic of Australian mediocrity:

> Topp has dared to raise a subject that has often occupied my mind: our inherent mediocrity as a people. I am confident that the mediocrity of which he speaks is not a final and irrevocable state; rather is it a creative source of endless variety and subtlety. The blowfly on its bed of offal is but a variation of the rainbow. Common forms are continually breaking into brilliant shapes. If we will explore them.

Australia is a land of mediocrity, but if it is explored, if its seemingly sordid history of convicts, failed explorers and alienated artists is examined, there is a source for a true understanding of the nation. Laura, for example, would appear to be, if seen by conventional social values, an overly intellectual woman who has had an illegitimate child by an unknown father and settled for a lower-middle-class life as a school teacher. But, in contrast to such conventional attitudes, Voss is spiritually the child's father (although in fact Laura has taken on another woman's child as her own), and Laura spiritually accompanies Voss on his travels to the desert, sharing his suffering and even contemplating sacrifice of her child in the hope of saving him from death. In her own way, she is as mystical, visionary and heroic as Voss. It is from such sufferings, White would seem to say, that the true Australia can be apprehended.

White, however, is a more subtle and profound writer than I have so far indicated. More than one critic has commented on the way Voss is made to seem rigid, proud and impractical. Laura, similarly, is held at a distance and shown to be uninterested in the truth concerning Voss's expedition and death. The author seems to imply that Australian legends are to be distrusted. There is an overall ironic quality about the novel, an archness in the telling which both magnifies and subtly undermines. 'The German was shivering with the cold that blew in from the immense darkness, and which was palpitating with little points of light. So, in the light of his own conquest, he expanded, until he possessed the whole firmament.' While Voss is a hero, around whom a national legend is shaping, it is possible to see the legend as a romanticisation of an egotistical Nietzschean attempt to rise above the human condition by a frail young German. Laura's spiritual communication with Voss is similarly open to question. *Voss* is both a rejection of suburbia and another example of Australian literature following a late Romantic mode of irony in which the hero and what he represents is looked upon wryly while apparently being celebrated. '"They cannot kill me," said Voss. "It is not possible." Although his cheek was twitching, like a man's.'

The Aunt's Story (1948) and *The Tree of Man* (1955), like *Voss*, are examples of White investing unpromising local material with high spiritual dignity. The main character in both books is a misfit, an eccentric, a loner, a mystic. The novels attempt to map out other sources of Australianness beyond the usual contrasts of democracy versus gentility or bush versus city. In a country with a provincial bourgeoisie and in which people are mainly concerned with getting what they want, the intelligent and sensitive person feels extreme alienation and leads a secret life. In *The Aunt's Story* Theodora's distance from others, her lack of close relationships, would seem to suggest that society is unworthy of her. Her father's library filled with classical authors and stories of Ethiopia and Greece has nourished her imagination and sensibility at the cost of her rejecting the actual advantages, such as marriage to a rich, intelligent man, that are locally possible. With the death of her mother, Theodora, now financially free to travel, visits Europe, only to find that its supposed fineness no longer exists. The Russian Revolution and Hitler have destroyed the old order; its supposed aristocracy consists largely of impecunious impostors whose pretentiousness alternates with crude manners and feelings.

But Theodora's involvement in Europe is in any case largely imaginary; the fragmented style and discontinuous narrative reveal both her state of mind and the society that surrounds her. There is no society of the superior kind she desires. The higher reality she seeks can only be inward, the reality of a mystic or a saint. Her final insanity is a victory and celebrated by the novel as the self-realisation she has sought. That she finds peace among the poor in a barren section of California suggests that her spiritual journey can only end, as does that of Voss, in the deserts beyond society. But, as in *Voss*, we may question whether its conclusion is ironic. Is Theodora's insanity really a triumph?

Characteristics of White's novels include an emphasis on suffering, mysticism, the use of myth, and a poetic style. In a democratic immigrant culture dedicated to a rising standard of living which does not provide the artist with the status found in older hierarchical European societies, the instinct is to turn inward. Where efficiency and material accomplishment are the main social values and where the crude often succeed, failure becomes spiritual success. The lack of a usable high society (since in a colony society is seldom seriously involved with contemporary art) means that the author will not, as in Europe, write of man in society; rather the emphasis will be on the self, especially the spiritual realisation of the individual, often in opposition to convention. And as American literature often uses and parodies romance, so Australian literature with its nineteenth-century heroes often parodies the romantic.

Many of White's novels make use of Greek legend, biblical stories, or other bodies of symbolism and myth. In *The Aunt's Story* the parallels are to the *Odyssey*[4] and are probably influenced by the example of James Joyce's *Ulysses*. White does not use an elaborate framework of parallels; he depends on an allusive body of poetic symbols so that at various points in the novel the reader recalls similarities to the Odyssey story. Such myth-influenced literature was part of the modernist literary movement and its function, as in Joyce's *Ulysses*, was both to give classical order to the fragmented modern world and to show eternal similarities between past and present behaviour. The technique, or some variation of it, subsequently became common to serious literature and, while less fashionable at present, has remained a method often employed by some of the better writers in new nations—Walcott, Soyinka, R. K. Narayan, Wilson Harris. Its advantage to the Commonwealth writer is that it universalises and externalises the local, giving significance and value to what might otherwise seem provincial. It gets around the problem of local versus metropolitan subject-matter and values by seeing local particulars as examples of the universal. At the same time it holds local material at a distance; the same symbolism which elevates also can be seen as ironic. To do this requires a prose style unlike the local realism advocated by nationalist critics. White, like Soyinka and Harris, uses a poetic style, involving unusual syntax and recurring images to convey the sensitivity, will and inner vision of his main characters.

The elevation of local material to high cultural significance is often noticeable during a period of nationalism, although the writer may not be part of such movements. The desire for a high culture, not found locally, often leads to a celebration of regional history or local eccentricities as noble, heroic or tragic. Henry James commented upon similar tendencies in Nathaniel Hawthorne's fiction; in a society with little texture, short traditions, few dark nooks and fewer firm social distinctions based on manners, morals and mores, the writer, feeling that society is not a usable literary subject, turns towards romance. While simple romantic novels and poetry may occur early in a literary tradition, when the exotic is sufficient, high cultural romance occurs later, when nationalist ideas are in the air. Such nostalgia is noticeable in Australia in the early poetry of Judith Wright alongside the novels of Patrick White and Randolph Stow.

Wright's first volume of poems, *The Moving Image* (1946), is filled with nostalgia for a lost Australian past of innocence, forests, dreamers, pioneers, explorers and other versions of the pastoral:

> Where your valley grows wide in the plains
> they have felled the trees, wild river.
> Your course they have checked, and altered
> your sweet Alcaic metre.

> Not the grey kangaroo, deer-eyed, timorous,
> will come to your pools at dawn;
> but their tamed and humbled herds
> will muddy the watering places.
> Passing their roads and cities
> you will not escape unsoiled.[5]

One nationalistic movement which influenced Australian writers of the 1940s, the Jindyworobaks, was marked by the use of Aboriginal material in contrast to urban and European culture. Wright's justly famous 'Bora Ring' recognises the impossibility of resurrecting such tribal culture in the modern world:

> The song is gone; the dance
> is secret with the dancers in the earth,
> the ritual useless, and the tribal story
> lost in an alien tale.

Her poems are filled with signs of a provincial rural society 'listening to the radio', where 'blind-drunk sprees' and 'the freak who could never settle' are heroic gestures. The 'Soldier's Farm' is 'This ploughland vapoured with the dust of dreams'. Wright's attitudes are often pity, feelings of loss, desire for the overwhelming and a sensitive closeness to nature as a substitute for the humdrum poverty of daily life. 'Country Town' romantically contrasts the harsh life of the early settlers with contemporary Australia: 'This is no longer the landscape that they knew,/the sad green enemy country of their exile.' Like Derek Walcott in 'Laventville', Wright rejects the comfortable, uninteresting society: 'What is it we have lost and left behind?/Where do the roads lead? It is not where we expected.' In 'Nigger's Leap, New England' the lost, primitive past is felt to have been more vital: 'Never from earth again the coolamon/or thin black children dancing'. The often anthologised 'Bullocky' celebrates a 'mad apocalyptic dream' of the early settlers, laments for the lost visions of the past, and attempts to feel a link between it and the present.

While Wright has long since developed beyond themes of nostalgia to poems of mysticism, love, family life, self-observation and, recently, social involvement, there remains a tendency towards meditating upon nature, the past and solitude, towards projecting emblematic significances on the world, towards creating a self-identity rather from sensitivity than engagement with others. The final stanza of 'Shadow', at the end of her *Collected Poems*, is characteristic:

> World's image grows, and chaos
> is mastered and lies still
> in the resolving sentence
> that's spoken once for all.
> Now I accept you, shadow,
> I change you; we are one.
> I must enclose a darkness
> since I contain the Sun.

Judith Wright's contrasting the Australian past with the present is a rare instance of a poet early finding a strategy to handle national material. Whereas the novel, with its bias towards realism, may thrive on representative local lives, the tensions of colonial society, dialect, and subjects associated with cultural conflict, poets have often found such material an unsuitable basis for a tradition. The best poetry in the new national literatures has usually begun within the international modernist tradition before gradually accommodating the kinds of material found in the novel. If new national literature contains within itself a dialectic between international and national traditions, a major poet is more likely to begin with the international or metropolitan tradition than with the local.

A. D. Hope began publishing during the cultural nationalism which Judith Wright's early poems reflect. Hope and his friend James McAuley, however, campaigned to redirect Australian verse into the mainstream of the English and European tradition. This meant rejecting both provinciality and the imitation of London fashions. As critics they recommended the study and imitation of the classics, a consciousness of *genre*, the mastery of stanzaic forms and an almost eighteenth-century concern with public address, craftsmanship and awareness of a European tradition.

Whereas it is usual to say that the new literatures begin in imitation, develop into assertive nationalism and mature into an independent national tradition, Hope claims that the early stage is of isolation from the parent stock, which is followed by a provincialism as the effects of isolation continue. Maturity is reached when, as a result of increased communication and cultural development, writers of sufficient ability appear that the national literature can be reintegrated to the parent tradition. Where others see independent national literary traditions, Hope sees regional varieties of a European tradition of which English literature is itself a part. There is much to be said in favour of Hope's analysis of the development of new national literatures, especially as it implies that various stages are dependent on such matters as the state of international communications, the access to travel, and the political and economic importance of the colony or new nation within the network of English-speaking culture.

While his pronouncements and attitudes are cosmopolitan, Hope has been one of the most influential critics of Australian literature. He has looked carefully at what others have superficially examined and seen a greater complexity which has had the effect of raising the value of the literary text in critical estimation. His essay on Furphy's *Such is Life* was perhaps the first to note the difference between the narrator and the author, showing that what appears colloquial ramblings was in fact a complex work of art.[6] Hope shifted criticism of Henry Handel Richardson from a biographical approach to an understanding of her themes and the presence of Nietzschean ideas in her work. His essay on Martin Boyd is still among the best critical appreciations. It might be said that recent criticism of the major Australian authors in part derives from Hope's quiet but controversial revision of what often had been less sophisticated explication.

His poetry begins with many of the same assumptions about contemporary Australia expressed by the radical nationalists. Suburbia, Americanisation, the middle classes, conventionality, domesticity and the lack of passion and creativity are among his satiric themes. His early poem 'Australia' (1939) may appear a criticism of local life, but the kinds of dissatisfaction, the exasperation with the educated chatter of Europe, and the wish that from the Australian deserts a new prophet (and culture) may emerge, is consistent with the ideas of Palmer. Hope has had little sympathy with the supposed wasteland mentality of T. S. Eliot; his own work has been marked by a vitality and emphasis on heroic passion that seems a direct development from earlier Australian vitalism with its roots in Nietzschean will, nineteenth-century optimism and romantic notions of the outsider. Indeed, his poems are sometimes similar to the novels of Richardson and White in portraying the heroic while treating it with irony.

The early poems in *The Wandering Islands* (1955) contrast emotions and desires with the actualities of life. 'The End of a Journey' (1930) compares Ulysses's memories of his adventures with the final domesticity of 'An old man sleeping with his housekeeper'. After 'Calypso singing in her haunted cave,/The bed of Circe, Hector in his grave', 'the petty kingdom he called home' is the 'delusive song' which tempted him to shipwreck. Many of the poems treat of sexual obsessions: 'the landscape of erotic dreams'. Alongside poems on the psychology of lust there are satires on contemporary culture. In 'The Explorers' (1939) Hope ridicules 'All those nice young girls, so properly brought up', who, having preserved their virginity until marriage, can feel safe:

> The little brick cottage, the ration of lawn in front
> And a kiss at the gate and a pair of trousers walking daily
> to the office.[7]

'Standardization' (1938) mocks the 'fatuous, flatulent, Sunday-paper prose' and the 'green aesthete' who complains at mass production. Nature

> does not tire of the pattern of a rose.
> Her oldest tricks still catch us with surprise.
> She cannot recall how long ago she chose
> The streamlined hulls of fish, the snail's long eyes,
>
> Love, which still pours into its ancient mould
> The lashing seed that grows to a man again,

From whom by the same processes unfold
Unending generations of living men.

The ironies of the poem are not a defence of mass culture; rather they satirise modern slackness of thought which fails to see that all life consists of recurring natural patterns:

And beauty standing motionless before
Her mirror sees behind her, mile on mile,
A long queue in an unknown corridor,
Anonymous faces plastered with her smile.

Hope's major poems create a modern myth which shows that all great belief is a poeticising and giving pattern to instinctual, primitive natural forces. The poems are a celebration of heroic desires, especially of obsessive lust and will, in contrast to the drab conventionalities of modern urban society.

'Easter Hymn' (1940) begins 'Make no mistake, there will be no forgiveness;/No voice can harm you and no hand will save'. The poem is not, however, an attack on capitalism or an expression of Christian existentialism. It offers a secular world in which the past is repeated and ideals conflict with realities: 'The City of God is built like other cities . . . You will be glad of Pilate's casting vote.' 'The Wandering Islands' (1943) is perhaps the most striking presentation of Hope's feelings of isolation in a purposeless world where only sex can momentarily overcome solitude. 'You cannot build bridges between the wandering islands;/The Mind has no neighbours.' 'They rush together, their promontories lock', 'But all that one mind ever knows of another' 'was in that instant'. As in 'Easter Hymn' there is no hope of resolution to the human condition: 'The Rescue will not take place.'

Seeing no spiritual, social or cultural purpose in the universe, Hope is not consistent in attitude on minor matters from poem to poem. He is often content to allow the genre or model imitated decide what is being said. In such poems he is a maker, a craftsman, part of a tradition of poets, and not a seer. But there are other poems which attempt to create a perspective which will link past to present, myth to our reality, and tradition to the individual. These poems are celebrations of will and desire seen as expressions of the basic vitality of life; they are celebrations of poetry and creativity as a restatement of universal urges and needs, the same libidinous and egotistical forces which built the masterpieces of culture, created empires and exhausted slaves.

The somewhat obscure 'An Epistle from Holofernes' (1946) is Hope's first attempt to explain the relationship of will to passion. 'Myths formed the rituals by which ancient men/Groped towards the dayspring and were born again.' Myth now must have 'other uses'. It proves 'The heart's conjectures and approves its terms/Against the servile speech of compromise.' Myth defines 'Our figure and motion in the Great Design', cancels 'the accidents of name and place'. The poem must 're-create the fables and revive/In men the energies by which they live'. But myth also is dangerous as its followers can starve themselves of flesh and blood: '*verbum caro factum* is our part'. If the fruit of knowledge is 'Our prayers translated to a brutal hiss', it also begins the process of redemption. It is this process which 'Renews the heart' and turns 'fables into living fact':

> If in heroic couplets, then, I seem
> To cut the ground from an heroic theme,
> It is not that I mock at love, or you,
> But, living two lives, know both of them are true.

In 'Pyramis or The House of Ascent' (1948), Hope sees similarities between poets and 'Those terrible souls, the Pharaohs' who force 'a nation piling stones/Under the lash in fear, in sweat, in haste' to build personal monuments against the indifference of the world. Great works of literature are 'other pyramids', 'incredible monuments of art', and their builders men of 'Intemperate will and incorruptible pride' who 'put aside/Consideration, dared, and stood alone'. 'William Butler Yeats' (1948) praises the Irish poet for having 'been afraid neither of lust nor hate' and for his *Vision*, 'the eternal moments. . . . That we had grown to be'.

'Soledades of the Sun and the Moon' (1957) is similar to

Robert Graves's 'To Juan At the Winter Solstice' in attempting to bring into relationship all myth as a universal pattern. But whereas Graves makes all legends into one. Hope sees in natural process the source of life, myth, and poetry:

> Accept the incantation of this verse;
> Read its plain words; divine the secret message
> By which the dance itself reveals a notion
> That moves our universe.
>
> In the star rising or the lost leaf falling
> The life of poetry, this enchanted motion,
> Perpetually recurs.
> Take, then, this homage of our craft and calling!

The best of the later poems, such as 'An Epistle: Edward Sackville to Venetia Digby' (1959), 'Vivaldi, Bird and Angel' (1969) or 'The Countess of Pembroke's Dream' (1970) are attempts to recreate the Renaissance myth of the Great Chain of Being in our age of science, rationalism and scepticism. Sexual desires and original sin are seen as part of the universal process, as a 'mutual ecstasy of consenting love'. 'All voices of the universal frame/Join in and swell that great polyphony.'[8] Art imitates what in other ages would be called the divine order.

While Hope's poetry belongs within a wider frame of references than nationalism or new national literatures, his evaluation of Australian society is not significantly different from that of the radical nationalists. 'Australia' in his best known poem is a place 'where second-hand Europeans pullulate/Timidly on the edge of alien shores'. Unlike the nationalists, however, he turned from the supposedly mediocre, devitalised urban middle class not towards a simplistic vision of an organic rural community but towards desire, will, pride and cultural history as means of creating a universal myth of natural process: 'The mending of a lost primordial link' during an 'age of plastics and alloys.'[9]

10 India: R. K. Narayan and tradition

Indian creative literature in English began in the early nineteenth century when several colleges were established, which promoted English language and literature; their teachers included the first writers who used the colonial language to praise, in borrowed images, their homeland. After the British government took over the administration of India from the East India Company (1835), British rule became consolidated during the century. As India since the break-up of the Mughal Empire had lacked any central government, there was good reason for many of the intellectuals to welcome a new era when the continent might recover from its political chaos and cultural barrenness; consequently English was associated with progress, rationality and the Enlightenment. The serious study of ancient Hindu culture was essentially a development of European scholars, passed on to the Indians along with English. By the third quarter of the century there were Indian writers of talent and ability who were accepted in London. Toru Dutt's poetry was praised by Edmund Gosse and her novel *Le Journal de Mademoiselle d'Arvers* (1879) was praised as French by the French—perhaps their highest award available to a foreigner. While some of the poets and prose writers predictably followed the then fashionable aestheticism, others began using Indian subject-matter, legends, and translating the ancient epics. With the coming of a western-educated Indian elite, modern Indian nationalism began. The first political-cultural associations soon gave birth to the Indian National Congress in 1885. The cultural revival produced Tagore who, although he seldom wrote in English, was, through his own translations, part of international English-speaking culture early in this century.[1]

The 1920s witnessed the development of a political nationalist movement determined to achieve independence. Gandhi's leadership of the movement united the masses behind the westernised elite by combining aspects of traditional Hindu values with modern ideas. Thus Gandhi urged a return to the use of handspun cloth—symbolically important as a rejection of European industrialisation—while urging the abolition of the caste system and untouchability—which would bring the lowest classes into democratic politics.

During the mid-1930s the first good modern Indian novels in English appeared: Mulk Raj Anand's *Untouchable* (1935) and *Coolie* (1936), Raja Rao's *Kanthapura* (1938), and R. K. Narayan's *Swami and Friends* (1935) and *The Bachelor of Arts* (1937) introduced what have become the three major Indian novelists. Indian poetry, however, was entangled in a mixture of Victorian rhetoric, local mysticism and epic ambition. It was not until the late 1940s, at the time of national independence, that a consciously modern Indian poetry in English developed; and it was not until the 1960s that a sufficient body of worthwhile verse had appeared that it became possible to speak seriously of individual writers of talent.

As happened elsewhere during periods of nationalism, language usage reflected politics. While the nationalists urged a return to Hindu, Anand and Rao experimented with modifying English diction, syntax and idiom to create an Indian prose. Anand translated the dialogue of his early novels from his mother tongue. He used slang, swear words, abuse, and other forms of vernacular speech especially common among the poor. Influenced by Marx, Engels, Tolstoy, William Morris and Ruskin, Anand is a writer of the political left. *Untouchable* concerns the plight of those lower castes of Indian society that Gandhi called the 'men of God'; *Coolie*, with its contrast of countryside and city, is an attack on capitalism and on existing Indian society. Munoo, the victim of society in *Coolie*, suffers equally at the hands of rich Indians and the British. Indeed, he is also mistreated by poor Indians. In later works, such as *The*

Private Life of an Indian Prince (1953), Anand has attempted to remain a critic of the ruling class.[2]

Raja Rao has used the confrontation of India and Europe to create experimental, poetical novels. In the foreword to *Kanthapura*, he claims to have used Indian techniques of narration and an Indian prose style. The narrative method is leisurely and digressive, having the appearance of oral literature. Use is made of mythology. The language is both Indianised and made to express the social caste of the speaker. Narration is given an epic, Sanskritic effect by repetition, by length of sentences, by accumulation of detail, use of sound, and other techniques that change English into an Indian English. Rao wants a style which moves quickly and yet captures the supposed interminableness of Indian life. There are dislocations of syntax, literal translation into English, and similes drawn from local life. The relationship of the novel to the nationalist movement can be indicated by K. R. S. Iyengar's comment: 'The theme of *Kanthapura* may be summed up as "Gandhi and our Village".' Whereas Anand's early novels are within the social-realist protest tradition, Rao's work aims more at capturing a spiritual India, an India whose essential culture is different from western materialism and rationalism. He is aware that the educated elite often feel separate from traditional communal life, and that their cultural nationalism is sometimes merely the wish to govern.[3]

Rao's *The Serpent and the Rope* (1960) is both a study in the psychological maladjustments brought about by the meeting of two cultures and a record of a Brahmin's search for spiritual perfection. Ramaswamy, the main character, is associated with Rama, the hero of the *Ramayana*. Rama is by western standards an unheroic hero, as he is more concerned with the spirit than such supposedly masculine characteristics as sexual dominance and aggressiveness; he is passive and refined. In attempting to solve the tensions of cultural conflict, Ramaswamy seeks the Absolute India as an ideal, the Eternal Being in contrast to particulars. But, as *The Serpent and the Rope* is a novel within an Indian philosophical tradition, the Absolute is the self. Because the truth for Ramaswamy is metaphysical, the novel has little action. Events take place but only as passing phenomena. As we begin to understand Ramaswamy's mind we also become aware of his irritability, contradictions, and failures of character. If the narrator's vision forces on us an Indian sense of reality, the novel makes us aware that the narrator is himself painfully proclaiming a Truth that he does not possess. It is this complexity that prevents *The Serpent and the Rope*, despite its lack of drama, from becoming a lifeless expression of a philosophical idea.

In contrast to the commitments that shape the novels of Anand and Rao, R. K. Narayan appears a natural story-teller, unbothered by problems of political reform, cultural conflict, or questions of national and self identity. Often, however, the novels record the comedy that results from people acting in situations of social and cultural change when old ideals do not fit new situations, or when cultural myths seem both strangely appropriate and inappropriate. There is thus both the human comedy of people acting at cross-purposes and the cultural comedy that results from wry incongruities and discrepancies. But the references to myths and cultural ideals are neither satiric nor ennobling; the novels treat Indian philosophy and legends ambiguously, leaving the implication that traditional wisdom is still true, although its truth is revealed more through absurdities than the strict application of traditional formulas to modern life.[4] Narayan's method, although lighter in touch, more comical and tentative, has similarities to a technique, sometimes found in Roman Catholic novelists, of seeing possibilities of the divine in unexpected places and personages. This sense of incongruity contributes towards a tolerance of sometimes disagreeable social behaviour.

Narayan is of the Brahmin caste, the same priestly caste to which V. S. Naipaul belongs. The family came from the province of Madras to Mysore. His father attended Madras University before becoming headmaster of the government school in Mysore. Narayan himself rebelled against the Christian teachers at the Christian Missionary School in Madras:

> I was thinking the other day why it is that I can't write a novel without Krishna, Ganesa, Hanuman, astrologers,

> pundits, temples, and devadasis, or temple prostitutes . . . Do you suppose I have been trying to settle my score with the old boy? Um! In any case, that has turned out to be my India.[5]

After graduating from Mysore University he found teaching unsuitable and decided against such usual Indian middle-class careers as the civil service and journalism. Instead he wished to become a writer, a profession which then did not exist in India as there was no local or foreign market for Indian novels. Although a vegetarian and follower of Indian spiritual practices, Narayan chose his own wife rather than follow the traditional custom of having an arranged marriage. When an astrologer warned his intended wife's family against the marriage, Narayan paid a second astrologer to cast a more favourable horoscope.

Narayan's novels usually treat of those stranded between tradition and contemporary life. He does not write of peasants or urban workers; rather he shows the townsman who still thinks in older ways but who inhabits the modern world. George Woodcock has perceptively said:

> For if there is one characteristic which Narayan's characters almost without exception share, it is mediocrity. Eccentrically colorful as it may strike one on first introduction, Malgudi is a city of the petty and the unfulfilled . . . The sickness from which all the citizens of Malgudi suffer, and which their mediocrity reflects, is the mid-twentieth-century alienation of the Indian middle class. Their traditional codes and hierarchies have become fragmented and private, so that no man can any longer fulfil himself in a traditional way except by holy withdrawal; yet the material success on the western model to which the Malgudians aspire belongs to an alien world which they rarely understand, so that here too their lives are diminished and unfulfilled.
>
> When the inhabitants of Malgudi do seek to break out of their encircling mediocrity, they fail because their ambitions overleap their capacities.[6]

Whereas other writers might use such a social situation for themes of cultural or political conflict, Narayan sees Indian life as 'farcical' and perhaps more governed by fate and the tricks of destiny than will or character. It is the quiet ambiguity and inconclusiveness of his stories that make them seem innocent, impish and elusive. His art is similar to his vision of Indian life; he uses a natural Indian English, without the deliberateness of style found in Rao and Anand. He aims more at portraying the strange comic ways of the world than at any thematic or cultural significance.

The complexities of Narayan's fiction result from the neutral tone, the use of narrators who are themselves participants, and the ambiguous relationship of traditional myths and values to the events of the novels. In *The Printer of Malgudi* (1949), published originally under the title *Mr Sampath*, myth is recalled by being used as the plot for a film while the actual events that take place both in the film and in the novel are contrary to the myth. Myth is thus set against its inversion or parody. Throughout the novel we are aware both of the difference between present-day India and its mystic past and of how the two continue alongside each other, rather intertwined than in a state of tension:

> 'They are initiating a new religion, and that camera decked with flowers is their new god, who must be propitiated.' To him it seemed no different from the propitiation of the harvest god in the field. To Somu and all these people, God, at the present moment, was a being who might give them profits or ruin them with a loss; with all their immense commitments they felt they ought to be particularly careful not to displease Him. As he was a champion of this religious sect, there was nothing odd in De Mello's submissiveness before it. Srinivas wished he had his *Banner*. What an article he could write under the heading 'The God in the Lens'.[7]

Just as the film producers change the myth into modern cinema entertainment, with songs and dances, so the events of the novel parody the original myth.[8] The actor playing the god Shiva demands more money and is fired. The young man whom we expect to fall in love with the actress becomes insane as a result of her affair with the printer, a married man, and destroys the film set. The actress leaves the printer, being quickly tired of her role as an irresistible woman; she prefers to take care of her child by her former husband and returns home to lead a new life.

The relationship between Narayan's use of myth, the reality of Indian life, and his art of parody is expressed in Srinivas's confusion:

> By externalizing emotion, by superimposing feeling in the shape of images, he hoped to express very clearly the substance of this episode: of love and its purification, of austerity and peace. But now they wanted to introduce a dance sequence. Srinivas found himself helpless in this world.

While Narayan cultivates a pose of being helpless before the energy and violence of life, behind the pose is an acceptance of the eternal, non-changing India that goes on regardless of seeming deviations:

> Dynasties rose and fell. Palaces and mansions appeared and disappeared. The entire country went down under the fire and sword of the invader, and was washed clean when Sarayu overflowed its bounds. But it always had its rebirth and growth. And throughout the centuries, Srinivas felt, this group was always there: Ravi with his madness, his well-wishers with their panaceas and their apparatus of cure. Half the madness was his own doing, his lack of self-knowledge, his treachery to his own instincts as an artist, which had made him a battle-ground. Sooner or later he shook off his madness and realized his true identity—though not in one birth, at least in a series of them.

> The recent vision had given him a view in which it seemed to him all the same whether they thwacked Ravi with a cane or whether they left him alone, whether he was mad or sane—all that seemed unimportant and not worth bothering about. The whole of eternity stretched ahead of one; there was plenty of time to shake off all follies. Madness or sanity, suffering or happiness seemed all the same . . . It didn't make the slightest difference in the long run—in the rush of eternity nothing mattered.

The omnipresence of the past, never pure, always expressing itself in parodies of ideals, is the basis of Narayan's vision; he accepts his society, regardless of its faults. If Narayan seems passive and accommodating, the Indian sensibility has always placed a high regard on inactivity and accepting the flow of life: indeed, doing so is a classical Hindu virtue.

Narayan has been criticised for not having the social concerns of Anand or explicitly examining cultural conflict as does Rao. Such disapproval ignores what makes Narayan a major novelist. The absurd question of whether Raju, the main character in *The Guide* (1958), is a saint or a charlatan is relevant. *The Guide* is more than the story of a single life; it can be understood, although Narayan never says this, as representative of the confusions of modern Indian life and especially of the difficulty in separating the true from the false in Indian spirituality.

The novel is told in the form of a double narrative which juxtaposes past and present. It begins with Raju, freed from jail, uncertain where to go, finding temporary shelter in a deserted shrine. He is interrupted by a rather simple-minded peasant who assumes that he is a holy man and seeks his advice. Having no wisdom to offer, Raju acts aloof. The problem eventually resolves itself and Raju having unaccountably gained credit becomes, against his will, the spiritual leader of the village. Although he laughs at his absurd role he acquiesces in it. By making, when the mood strikes him, delphic pronouncements, he is brought food and clothing.

Interspersed with the present are memories of Raju's past,

presented in a chronological order. He was the son of a poor man whose business was an uncovered street stall. When the railroad came to Malgudi, Raju opened a refreshment stand which soon expanded to selling second-hand journals and books. He begins guiding tourists to see the local sights, about which he has no knowledge and for which he invents false histories—sometimes changing the dates by two thousand years! From his railway station stand, the tips and kickbacks from local hotels and taxidrivers he rises above poverty and becomes well known. While acting as a guide he meets Rosie, the beautiful wife of a scholar obsessed with Indian history. The daughter of a caste of snake dancers who are traditionally prostitutes, she has somehow become educated and married a rich man. Raju sees her shimmering to the music of a snake charmer and learns that she wants to devote herself to classical Indian dance, which her scholar husband, ironically, regards a disgraceful career. Neglected by her husband she is seduced by Raju. When the husband learns that Rosie and Raju have become lovers, he leaves her penniless and she moves in with Raju and his mother. Devoting all his time to her dancing studies, Raju loses his business, goes into debt, loses his house and, after a bitter quarrel over Rosie, is rejected by his mother, who leaves to live with relatives. Bright, active, Raju is less a character than someone who is shaped by those outside himself.

Rosie's career now begins. She rapidly becomes a famous dancer, earning fantastic sums of money which Raju spends on a large new house, hangers-on, gambling and creating the impression of a successful entrepreneur. Rosie begins to feel guilty at having betrayed her husband, who unexpectedly sends Raju a copy of his studies in India history and sends her a legal document she must sign to regain some jewellery. Raju, jealous and puzzled by the husband's motives, does not tell Rosie about the book and forges her signature to the document. The husband recognises the forgery and has Raju arrested. Despite the help of a famous lawyer he is sent to prison for two years.

In prison his character changes once more. He grows vegetables, becomes a leader of men, and is happy. After years of intense activity he is content to drift, and when released from jail he longs to return to it and has no aim in life. The narration of the past now catches up with the present. There is a terrible drought bringing disease and starvation on the region. His attempt to stop the villagers fighting is misunderstood by a half-wit who reports that Raju will fast for twelve days to bring rain. Unwilling to lose face, and hoping somehow to cheat, he begins his fast which soon, in our age of mass communication, becomes an international event, accompanied by government doctors and filmed by an American company. He becomes delirious and the doctors warn that he should end his fast or die. In the last scene of the novel, on the twelfth day, he struggles to the river and announces that he can feel rain coming.

The conclusion is left open to the reader's imagination. Have the rains in fact come or is Raju suffering delirium? Will he die and are these his last moments? Has he become a holy man who has given his life to save others, or is he still a drifter and fraud without any purpose in life? Was Raju's drifting a road to loss of identity similar to the higher stages of Indian spiritual life? Is the comedy—and it is an extremely humorous novel—the result of a misunderstanding by which such a disreputable character is treated as a holy man, or does the author's detached amusement suggest that indeed this rogue has inexplicably become gifted with divine powers? There are no answers to these puzzles hidden in the text awaiting a close reading. Nor are there any clues of the author's attitude to be gained from his other writings, which both show unlikely people becoming seers and suggest that Indian culture is so chaotic that rational understanding is an absurd joke.

Because Narayan's characters seem to accept their emotions, actions and fate without reflection, their psychology is different from the studies in will, introspection and identity found in western literature. Narayan's characters have obsessions, desires, hatred, or fall into passivity, but they never deeply examine the causes of their emotions or try to will their feelings towards an effective purpose. Raju becomes a guide without any thought of establishing a career, he becomes involved with Rosie without any thought of the future, he sends his mother money but does not bother to pay off the mortgage of his house so that she can live in it, he watches Rosie fall out of love without asking why she is changing, he hides the book and forges her signature on mistrustful impulses, he begins his fast through a misunderstanding. For a period he is rich and one of the best-known men in India; as soon as he is arrested he becomes impoverished, loses all his friends and is forgotten by everyone.

Similar rapid transformations of identity or inconsistent action can be witnessed in the other characters. Rosie's husband leaves the trial without a word to Raju or Rosie, and even Rosie totally forgets Raju to begin her career again with obsessive fanaticism, as if she had not been weary of it before the trial. Having in the past never concerned herself with the commercial side of her career, she suddenly turns into an efficient manager who builds a business empire. We are not only shown an India where haphazard chance (or destiny?) rules, we are introduced to people who seem uninterested in cause and effect or in shaping reality. Raju only knows what happens, not why it happens. He can only submit to his emotions or respond to the actions of others; he cannot analyse, evaluate and order his life. He never examines his own emotions.

While his characters' lack of psychological understanding might seem a weakness in a novel, Narayan has presented alternative kinds of material to give his book a rich feeling of reality. Instead of the realities of introspection and society, there is the alternative reality of how life appears to those who live without analysis and observation. In its own way Narayan's book is as rich with life as a nineteenth-century novel; but it is a different life from the social detail and moral observation found in the work of Jane Austen or Charles Dickens. As an illustration of the kinds of feelings portrayed, it would be useful to examine the six pages that are given to Raju's emotions when he receives the letter offering Rosie the jewellery. There is unthinking jealousy, cunning, suspicion, fantasy and hysteria, not rational thought. Indeed it is difficult not to assume Narayan is being ironic and that all of Raju's suspicions of the husband are projections of his own unexamined motives. It is possible that Raju is a fraud who will sell the jewellery for his own profit, but it is doubtful he so sees himself.

Narayan brilliantly portrays a representative Indian who lives from moment to moment without thought of the future and without the ability to analyse and therefore understand his own behaviour or destiny. But if the portrait is comic rather than satiric, it is not solely because Narayan is amused by, rather than disapproving towards, such characters. Raju is treated sympathetically after his imprisonment; his fast, although partly a matter of vanity, is more the fault of the village and his own agreeableness than cunning. Raju confesses his past history to a village leader who treats it indifferently, perhaps seeing humility as part of holiness. And then, of course, there is the disturbingly ambiguous, somewhat sad conclusion when Raju may indeed have died to save the villagers from the drought. If Narayan is a sceptical, sophisticated insider laughing at the foibles of Indian self-deception, he also allows for the possibility that such apparently purposeless lives may be divinely influenced. In doing so he salvages what might be treated as a harsh criticism of Indian culture by implying that for all we know the irrationality may indeed have spiritual authenticity. The comedy may be a divine comedy. Perhaps Rosie is even a reincarnation of the serpent goddess?

The American edition of *Waiting for the Mahatma* (1955) has a glossary of Indian words. Significantly, the first term is *Ahimsa*, defined as: 'Kindness. Non-violence. A Hindu ethical ideal.'[9] It is the basis of Gandhi's doctrine of non-violence and also the ideal that seems to direct the action of many of Narayan's central characters. In *The Man-Eater of Malgudi* (1961), the two main characters, Nataraj, a printer, and Vasu, a game hunter and taxidermist, represent respectively the two Hindu principles of inactivity and activity. Throughout the novel these principles are expressed thematically in terms of such opposites as passivity and aggression, non-violence and violence, embarrassment and self-assertion, morality and immorality, or religious obedience and disobedience. Vasu imposes himself on Nataraj, takes over part of his printing shop without paying rent, uses the upper floor of the house to skin, preserve and stuff animals, takes out a legal injunction to prevent Nataraj from ejecting him, fills the place with prostitutes, takes to stealing money from a public fund Nataraj is heading, and plans to kill a temple elephant that is being used in a village ceremony. Humiliated, continually bothered, threatened, on the verge of collapse, Nataraj cannot take any action against Vasu, and recalls Gandhi's preaching of non-violence. At the book's conclusion the situation is resolved when Vasu in a fit of temper accidentally kills himself. Non-violence wins over violence, passivity and obedience defeat activity and self-assertion.

The Man-Eater of Malgudi often parodies Indian customs. There is the poet who writes an epic life of God Krishna in monosyllabic verse with such classic lines as 'Girls with girls did dance in trance'. Most of the activity in the village seems close to farce. While characters discuss large national issues, nothing is done. Such simple commercial activities as printing three-coloured labels for bottles of soda water, a speech or some cards are always delayed and left unfinished. Against the foreground of such a comic India, there are reminders of another India:

> Aggressive words only generate more aggressive words. Mahatma Gandhi had enjoined on us absolute non-violence in thought and speech, if for no better reason than at least to short-circuit violent speech.[10]

The India of non-violence is, within the novel, also the India of non-achievement, in contrast to the American, scientific, get-rich-quick attitudes of Vasu. If it is an India of inefficiency, it is also an India of manners, customs, ceremonies and tradition.

While Vasu represents progress and westernisation, he also is associated with a demon of Hindu mythology:

> 'He fits all the definitions of a *rakshasa*,' persisted Sastri, and he went on to define the make up of a *rakshasa*, or a demoniac creature who possessed enormous strength,

> strange powers, and genius, but recognized no sort of restraints of man or God. He said, 'Every *rakshasa* gets swollen with his ego. He thinks he is invincible, beyond every law. But sooner or later something or other will destroy him.'

During a discussion of Hindu mythology there is a foreshadowing of Vasu's fate:

> Then there was Bhasmasura, who acquired a special boon that everything he touched should be scorched, while nothing could ever destroy him. He made humanity suffer. God Vishnu incarnated as a dancer of great beauty, named Mohini; the *asura* became infatuated with her and she promised to yield to him only if he imitated all the gestures and movements of her own dancing. So a dance began: the demon was an accomplished one; at one point of the dance Mohini placed her palms on her own head, and the demon followed this gesture in complete forgetfulness and was reduced to ashes that very second, his blighting touch becoming active on his own head. Every man can think that he is great and will live forever, but no one can guess from which quarter his doom will come.

At the end of the novel, after we learn that Vasu killed himself by misusing his tremendous strength to strike a mosquito on his forehead, we are reminded of this story:

> 'Because,' said Sastri puckishly, 'he had to conserve all that might for his own destruction. Every demon appears in the world with a special boon of indestructibility. Yet the universe has survived all the *rakshasas* that were ever born. Every demon carries within him, unknown to himself, a tiny seed of self-destruction, and goes up in thin air at a most unexpected moment. Otherwise what is to happen to humanity?' He narrated again for my benefit the story of Bhasmasura, the unconquerable, who scorched everything he touched and finally reduced himself to ashes by placing his fingers on his own head.

There are various possible interpretations of *The Man-Eater of Malgudi*. We could see it as a reaffirmation of traditional Hindu teaching, or we could suspect Narayan of writing the story with a sceptical twinkle in his eye.

Narayan's calmness, humour and acceptance seem an alternative to, almost a comment upon, the commitments and cultural themes in other pre-independence writers. V. S. Naipaul is possibly correct in seeing in Narayan's humour a passivity or tolerance that will become increasingly difficult as India modernises. Narayan's charming *The Painter of Signs* (1977) tells of the failed love of a rather spoiled provincial Brahmin intellectual for a westernised, casteless, modern Indian woman who preaches birth control and who breaks all the pieties to which he still adheres despite his claim to be a rationalist. The story is a retelling in modern guise of an old legend concerning King Santhanu and his goddess wife. Raman, the sign painter, in accepting whatever Daisy wants, performs in modern India the same unhappy role as Santhanu with his goddess, but whereas the goddess kills her own children, Daisy in her modern incarnation, preaches population control. Since Raman is sceptical of Indian traditions, except as they offer him creature comforts, his failed marriage is doubly ironic.

Narayan usually writes about the semi-westernised middle class, those who hold modern ideas and practise modern styles of living but who in times of stress are emotionally tied to traditional culture. His provincial heroes often find themselves in conflict with a representative of extreme westernisation or a representative of traditional values, or, more ironically, someone who although appearing modern is an incarnation of a Hindu devil or goddess. By treating the presence of myth, spiritualism and traditional values in the modern world, Narayan has given Indian culture a modern validity without resorting to polemics and assertion. As his stories are often narrated by the main characters, he has portrayed representative Indians living in the transition between old and new. His loosely constructed, quietly ironic stories, with their unasserted presence of traditional Hindu values and myths, are in their own way as much a reflection of a concern with national culture as the fiction of Frank Sargeson or Chinua Achebe. Whereas the main Indian poets of the first half of this century wrote mystic visions of the past, Narayan has implied that spiritual realities may exist, although in rather unexpected and humorous forms, in modern life.

A renewed concern with myth has been part of western culture since the Romantics. To such modernists as Joyce and Eliot myth was a means of imposing order, timeless patterns and the truths of the past on the seeming chaos of the modern world. Myth has been of especial importance to writers in the new nations, where it is often used to connect the present with its cultural roots and the local with universal. Rao, Anand and other Indian novelists have invoked myth, usually by explicit association of characters as types of cultural symbols or legends. Narayan's treatment is more ambiguous, ironic and thus more convincing:

> Our normal view is limited to a physical perception in a condition restricted in time, like the flashing of a torchlight on a spot, the rest of the area being in darkness. If one could have a total view of oneself and others, one would see all in their full stature, through all the stages of evolution and growth, ranging from childhood to old age, in this life, the next one, and the previous ones.[11]

Narayan's quiet affirmation of an eternal India might be contrasted with the focus on individual crisis found in the younger generation of writers. Anita Desai's *Bye-Bye, Blackbird* (1971) offers a complex sense of alienation, human separateness and crisis of identity in the portrait of Sarah Sean, an English woman married to an Indian. Sarah feels withdrawn from both English and Indian life; she feels her life consists of frauds, charades and roles, that she is really nobody. Bharati Mukherjee's *Wife* (1975) is another instance of recent Indian fiction about the alienation, confusion and violence felt by some middle-class Indian women towards the roles they have been taught to play in life and the effects of Americanisation on their image of themselves. The novel ends with the wife killing her husband. Indian novels of the 1970s have a different cultural perspective from those of the older, more established writers.

A similar transformation has taken place in Indian poetry which until independence was dominated by long mystical epics combining the most unreadable qualities of those who imitate Tennyson and Milton with the diffuseness of Indian spiritualism. In the late 1940s a small group of writers, led by P. Lal, initiated a modern movement. Influenced by T. S. Eliot, they insisted on a natural voice, realism and contemporary verse technique. Nissim Ezekiel was the first poet of stature to emerge from the new wave; his verse—minimalist, hard-edged, clear, professionally crafted—was the opposite of the soft, blurred rambling of the older Indian poets. Detached, ironic, satiric, concerned with the author's own sensibility and private history, its spiritual focus is on moral conduct, not vision, myth or destiny.

Whereas pre-independence Indian poetry tried to accommodate English to sonorous philosophical verse discourses and epics expressive of Indian spirituality, the new poetry, with its insistence on individuality, preciseness and firm technique, created a means of expressing the modern mind. Pritish Nandy's selected poems in *Riding the Midnight River* (1975) are striking in having created a vision which is both highly personal, an expression of the modern psyche, and consciously of post-independence India. The poems, while sometimes tender, have a violence which reflects the external world, a world of poverty, massacres, wars and persecution. Often Nandy's narrator appears as prisoner, criminal, victim, or suffers from feelings of being hunted. But he too is also a hunter. Since Nandy's language is unemotional, unmetaphoric, he creates a range of metaphoric significance by using contrast, disjointed syntax, oblique references and obscurity. Structural unity is achieved by repetition of phrases and images within the short lyric poems and within the book as a whole. The dislocation of narrative and language creates a focus on the self as the central consciousness within a threatening, alien world. Memories, both personal and of India, haunt his verse, with each poem being not so much a reconciliation as a confrontation. The rhythms, the rhymes, the use of English, the images are of our time. The more profoundly Nandy explores violence within himself and shapes it into well-crafted stanzas, the more his poems convey the tensions of urban life.

Kamala Das's confessional verse is another development of interest. Although the poetry is sometimes rhythmically slack and monotonous, the realistic notation of the immediacies of her private life, the openness about personal matters and the prosaic tonality represent a further stage in the movement of Indian literature away from protest, nationalism, myth and spiritualism towards recording direct involvement of individuals with the modern world.

11 Canada: Robertson Davies and identity

Are the novels of the Northern Irishman Brian Moore written during his residence in the country Canadian? Are the novels of Malcolm Lowry, an expatriate Englishman, Canadian? The inhabitants of the Maritime provinces and Nova Scotia during the eighteenth and early nineteenth centuries were a variant of the New England Yankees. English-speaking Canada hardly existed until after the American Revolution when loyalists from New York moved north. Newfoundland, first settled in the seventeenth century, did not join Canada until 1949. The threat of Quebec separation is always a danger. What is Canada? It is a continuing problem and one reason that the national search for identity is analogous to that of the Third World.

Canada had the usual early literature of exploring, pioneer settlements, refined English ladies roughing it in the backwoods while being scandalised by local manners, collections of folk tales, imitation eighteenth and nineteenth-century English poetry written on Canadian landscapes, stories of immigrant life, local colour sketches and historical romances. With Confederation (1867) there was an outburst of nationalism which produced some good nature poetry, now of little interest to non-Canadians, although the vague lyrical transcendentalism of Bliss Carman formerly had its foreign admirers. Up to the beginning of this century fiction usually concentrated on describing local colour, landscape, or other simple bucolic virtues. The emphasis on small-town life, still noticeable in Canadian literature, produced Stephen Leacock's nostalgic comedies, *Sunshine Sketches of a Little Town* (1912). That Leacock's Ontario had in fact radically changed is shown by another significant prose writer of the period, Sara Jeannette Duncan, best known for *The Imperialist* (1904). The two authors might be considered the polarities between which the best Canadian writing has often moved. Leacock, influenced by Dickens and Twain, wrote in the North American humourist tradition which pricked the pretences of the sophisticated and the genteel. Using the persona of an innocent, he wrote humorous vignettes of provincial life. Duncan, who after marrying mostly lived abroad, wrote cosmopolitan novels making use of the distinctions between Canadians, Americans and English. She had a strong eye for what we would now call the structure of society, how the various English-speaking groups formed close-knit communities according to religion and ethnic stock, and how this influenced personal relations and politics. Herself a defender of a closely linked Empire, she could see that England's economic conditions made such unity dubious and that the colonies were justified in being suspicious of such ideals. The young imperialist of her novel's title warns Canadians of the need for closer ties throughout the Empire to meet the challenge of American economic expansion. Turning to politics he loses an election and seeing no future for himself in Canada he, ironically, moves to the United States. A minor Henry James, but with her feet more firmly planted in economic and political realities, Duncan should be better known.

The main Canadian novelists of the first half of the century are G. Frederick Philip Grove, Mazo de la Roche, Morley Callaghan and Hugh MacLennan. Grove brought nineteenth-century European naturalism to North America; whereas others wrote idylls, his books about the prairies shifted regional literature from romance to realism. The titles are indicative: *Settlers of the Marsh* (1925), *Our Daily Bread* (1928), *The Yoke of Life* (1930). Grove, like the Australian Katharine Prichard, bridges an older socialism of the 1890s and the protest writing of the 1930s by portraying the poor immigrants, settlers and farmers struggling with hostile nature. Inevitably the younger generation rebel against the hardships required by pioneer life. Mazo de la Roche is much more romantic in her treatment of rural Ontario than is Grove with the prairies. The *Jalna* series, beginning in 1927, is an instance of the family sage covering several generations often found in the colonies. Although the idea is influenced by Galsworthy, there is the colonial relevance of establishing a history, a sense of a romantic past also noticeable in the Kaywana trilogy of the West Indian novelist, Edgar Mittelholzer.

With Callaghan, at one time part of the Paris literary scene during the 1920s, and a contributor to such *avant-garde* journals as *transition* and Ezra Pound's *Exile*, the Canadian novel moved towards urban realism. His early writing is objective, spare and understated in the Hemingway–Anderson manner. He is also similar to Sargeson in being an excellent short story writer who sometimes appears less at ease with the novel form, where he has increasingly found the need to use symbolism to convey a complex Catholic humanism. Although his novels are set in Canada, they are not concerned with nationalist themes; his concerns, like those of his generation, are universal. But Callaghan's *The Loved and the Lost* (1951) is a landmark of Canadian fiction in portraying Montreal as a real city which, like New York or Paris in the work of other writers, epitomises man's spiritual dilemma.

Canadian writing, except for those nationalists associated with the Confederation, offers little sense of a unified country before the Second World War. The literature was regional rather than national and reflected the political and social geography of the country itself, a string of cities and provinces stretching from the Atlantic to the Pacific, with no cultural unity such as that created by the American Melting Pot or British tradition. The communications network necessary in such circumstances for a sense of national identity began in the 1930s with the establishment of the Canadian Radio Broadcasting Commission (1932) and the National Film Board (1939). The nationalism of the 1940s led to the structures of cultural support which began in the 1950s with the Massey Report (1951) on how to create a distinct national identity, the creation of a National Library (1953), and the establishment of a Canada Council (1957). The introduction of jet airline travel in 1960 also made communication easier over large distances.

Hugh MacLennan is a rather unimaginative and old-fashioned novelist, but his *Barometer Rising* (1941) gave clear expression to the new nationalism that was developing during the war years and that had been implicit in some of the protest writers of the 1930s such as Dorothy Livesay and Leo Kennedy. The end of colonialism is clearly expressed through the symbolic allegory of the novel's plot. Canada is seen as in bondage to serve England during wars and as neglected during peace. MacLennan graduated from Dalhouse University, studied at Oxford and later did his doctorate at Princeton. It was while studying in other countries that he became aware of the differences between Canadians and other nationalities. MacLennan's subsequent novels analyse the French–English conflict (*The Two Solitudes*, 1945), the difference between Canada and the United States (*The Precipice*, 1948), and the rise of national consciousness during the Second World War (*The Watch That Ends the Night*, 1959).[1]

Canadian fiction follows approximately the same development as other new nations since the late nineteenth century: it goes from local humour through an early internationalism, historical romances, stories of provincial and settler life, realism, and a new nationalism in the early 1940s. In the decades after 1920 Canadian poetry also made the necessary journey from the Maple Leaf style to modernism. The development is somewhat less clear as, with the exception of E. J. Pratt, the better poets did not publish books of verse until after the Second World War. The tone is cosmopolitan but sometimes still imitative of T. S. Eliot as writers emancipated themselves from the amateurism and romanticism of the earlier poets. E. J. Pratt's heroic narratives with their celebration of vitality, defiance, will and competence in a menacing world, begin in an earlier modernism but, like the long poems of Kenneth Slessor and R. D. FitzGerald in Australia, are more radical in vision than technique. The adoption of a modern style was, however, a necessary step before such writers as Earle Birney, Irving Layton, James Reaney, P. K. Page and Eli Mandel could find their own voice. In the 1950s the Canadian novel begins to 'take off' with Robertson Davies, Mordecai Richler, Mavis

Gallant, Sheila Watson and Margaret Laurence. Richler's best novels have portrayed the tensions of growing up in Canada's urban immigrant communities, especially in relation to becoming an individual. His view of Canada is largely satiric and dismissive of nationalism and national culture. Having been born into the Jewish immigrant community in Montreal, Richler's cosmopolitanism and scepticism have similarities to V. S. Naipaul's. Davies is a more complex case and is perhaps the first major novelist Canada has produced.

Robertson Davies's *Tempest-Tost* (1951) concerns the behaviour, manners and morals of an amateur theatre group in a provincial Ontario city. The group has chosen to perform Shakespeare's *Tempest*, which in such a cultural backwater is thought of as somewhat daring; 'pastoral' has not been produced previously by a local theatre group. Ironically, the play is relevant to the behaviour of the cast, as off stage the interaction of the actors has a parody resemblance to the main characters of the drama. A dull, pedantic university professor is the novel's Prospero; his daughter is an unloved Miranda, and the play's Ferdinand attempts to seduce the girl who acts the part of Ariel.[2] While it is not necessary to recognise the similarities between the novel and the play, the analogies serve a triple function. They satirise, bringing out by contrast the narrow vision and weak passions of local life; they give a universal significance to otherwise petty behaviour in a small provincial city; they implicitly suggest that Shakespeare's 'pastoral' is grounded in continuing realities. The social comedy of the novel can, like *The Tempest*, alternatively be seen as a pleasant escape from the hard facts of life or as an embodiment of recurring, fundamental kinds of human behaviour. The author's amusement with the rivalries and snobberies of a provincial city is playful, but the novel is also highly satiric; *Tempest-Tost* reveals the hypocrisy, malice, pride and other evils of provincial Ontario. As in Shakespeare's play, literary convention and stylisation make comedy out of what might otherwise be extremely unpleasant situations and behaviour.

Although *Tempest-Tost* makes use of the reader's literary and social sophistication, it also draws upon a specifically Canadian literary tradition. Indeed *Tempest-Tost* might be seen as a further development of Leacock's treatment of Ontario; amusement, fun and the pastoral sugarcoat social satire and an awareness, which Leacock preferred not to explore, of the darker side of life.[3]

Davies has created from what might be character sketches a complete, self-sufficient little world, with its own social hierarchies. The local university, cathedral and Royal Military College represent the continuation of colonial culture in modern Canada. There is a continuity between manners, behaviour and morals which allows the reader to place and judge each character even though Davies's fictional world is more stylised, lighter in texture, and more obviously reliant upon types than that of the great nineteenth-century novelists. While manners, class and desire are noted, they are both exaggerated and simplified into caricature; the people in *Tempest-Tost* inhabit a community seemingly unthreatened by the radical anxieties of our century. As in many novels of R. K. Narayan, the conflicts of personalities and classes within provincial life appear mere foibles, but the author's tolerance is deceptive. The comedy is only possible because the characters, having been already judged, are sources of amusement.

Davies has said:

> About the period that I was working on the Salterton novels, just after the 1945 war, there were still people living in places like Salterton whose tradition was directly Edwardian, and who saw nothing wrong with that. They weren't even conscious that their ideas were not contemporary. I remember driving with my wife from Peterborough to Cobourg to see a production of Chekhov's *The Cherry Orchard* . . . After the first act I wandered around in the corridors listening to the people talk, and they were talking about the play as if it were a brand-new play—because it *was* a brand-new play to most of them, and yet they were people of some education, of a very considerable amount of tradition . . . Suddenly it broke in upon me: these people don't know that the play is about

> *them*—and yet there it was. I knew who some of them were: they were descendants of people who'd come to this country in the middle of the nineteenth century or earlier . . . they still hadn't grasped the fact that an entirely new Canada had come into being, and that their sort of person was really almost dinosaur-like in its failure to fit into the modern scene. You could see what happened in *The Cherry Orchard* happening around there, because all kinds of places were having to be bought up, and people didn't quite know why, but somehow the money had run out. Canada is full of these people and very rarely do they get written about, but I write about them, and they're *real*.[4]

Although *Tempest-Tost* records in detail part of the social life of provincial Ontario, its perspective towards events and characters is sophisticated and cosmopolitan. It appears to belong to the English nineteenth-century tradition of the novel of social comedy, modified by Canadian humour, emphasis and subject-matter; but it also belongs to the 1950s when wit, judgement, order and tone were key terms of critical praise:

> Tom took it very well. Very well, that is to say, for a gardener. He pointed out that it was not the damage to the lawns that he minded; that could be repaired by a month or so of rolling. It was the way people got their feet into his borders that bothered him. However, he realized that his employer had to lend the garden sometimes, and from what he had heard, the Little Theatre performances did not draw very big crowds, so it might not be too bad.[5]

The narrative causes us to agree with such judgements against the provincial, staid, mean-spirited, conventional and puritanical Canadian as:

> 'Well, I don't agree,' said Solly. 'I think it's the logical outcome of his education and the sort of life he has led . . . He thinks that when his belly is full and his job safe, he's got the world by the tail. He has never found out anything about himself, so how can he ever know anything about

> other people? The condition of a vulgarian is that he never expects anything good or bad that happens to him to be the result of his own personality; he always thinks it's Fate, especially if it's bad. The only people who make any sense in the world are those who know that whatever happens to them has its roots in what they are.

Davies's novels examine what Canadians are and how they became that way. If *Tempest-Tost* makes Chekhovian comedy from the colonial haute bourgeoisie, Davies is aware that the real history of the country is in the small-town Protestants; raised in poverty they have made their cruel puritanism into a national character which lacks vitality and ambition and represses desire. The satire on Hector Mackilwraith, the calculating, reserved schoolmaster, who lives at the YMCA and eats at the Snak Shak, is Davies's first attempt to explore one of the main themes of *Fifth Business* (1970) and the Deptford trilogy—the division of the Canadian soul between its puritan heritage and its hidden romantic aspirations. Beneath the seemingly settled views of the author there exists a radical streak which will come more to the surface in later novels. It is interesting that Margaret Atwood will also see Canadians as lamenting their fate, and urge them to discover what they are.

Tempest-Tost was followed by two further novels of Salterton, *Leaven of Malice* (1954) and *A Mixture of Frailties* (1958). There is a noticeable deepening of moral concern, an awareness of how breeding and environment influence behaviour. In *Leaven of Malice* a false engagement notice is inserted in the Salterton evening newspaper stating that Pearl, the daughter of Professor and Mrs Walter Vambrace, will marry Solomon Bridgetower on 31st November. The announcement brings out the worst in the characters. Professor Vambrance and Mrs Bridgetower are selfishly possessive of their only children, look down socially upon each other's family, and regard the engagement notice as a humiliating plot against their dignity. Since 31st November does not exist as a date, Professor Vambrace threatens to sue the newspaper for defaming his daughter's character. Supposed friends of Mrs Bridgetower insinuate that she will lose face unless her son takes some legal action to protect the family name. A situation thus occurs when both Pearl and Solomon may go to court claiming each has been defamed by the other through the engagement notice. Eventually the two young people are brought together by their parents' attempts to keep them apart; and at the end of the novel they are indeed engaged to be married.

The announcement was inserted by a Mr Bevill Higgin, an immigrant singing teacher who carries with him a sense of being treated unjustly and who appeals to colonial prejudices of the local Canadians. Although Higgin, like Iago, is malicious, cunning, and has an unjustified sense of grievance, he is basically a catalyst for the malice in others. The Dean, who has been accused by those who feel he is too liberal and tolerant, says of malice: 'Who can separate the leaven from the lump when once it has been mixed? But if you learn to know it by its smell, you find it very easily. You find it, for instance, in unfounded charges brought against people that we dislike.'[6] That is an accurate description of the conduct of many characters in the novel; given the leaven of Higgin's malice they have risen to impute ill will and evil to others, demanding that a harmless, poor, but rather unconventional musician be fired from his job as church organist, plotting to remove the editor of the local newspaper and threatening each other with various lawsuits.

Although *Leaven of Malice* ends on a happy note, and therefore technically speaking is a comedy, it has shown the potential for evil that is available in a provincial Ontario city. Davies has kept to the conventions of social comedy, but his Salterton novels recognise the dark side of human nature under the trappings of local eccentricities. Where Duncan showed Ontario as capable of being an important place in the Empire—and which failing to do so still had a significant social, economic and political life—Davies, working less assertively, notes the presence of evil disguised under conventional manners and attitudes. The third novel of the trilogy, *A Mixture of Frailties*, shows Davies's growing concern with how the past influences the future. A dead mother has attempted to dictate to her son through her will, denying him his inheritance until he has produced a son to carry on the family name. Instead the money is used to train an uncultured local gospel singer as a concert artist. The novel indicates that education and experience, especially that gained abroad, are necessary for a fuller life than that found in Canada. The singer only begins to develop as a musician after a love affair with her teacher in Europe.

That Davies was conscious of the weakness of nationalistic literature can be seen by the humorous treatment of the great Canadian novel in *Leaven of Malice*. Henry Rumball, a young reporter, is writing a novel called *The Plain*. Rumball won't review American novels as he is trying to avoid 'outside influences'. His own novel is about the Canadian West. Whereas other novels are 'about man's conquest of the prairie', Rumball's

> is just the opposite. It's the prairie's conquest of man. See? A big concept. A huge panorama. I only hope I can handle it. You remember that film *The Plough that Broke the Plain*? I'm calling my book *The Plain that Broke the Plough*. I open with a tremendous description of the Prairie; vast, elemental, brooding, slumbrous; I reckon on at least fifteen thousand words of that. Then Man comes. Not the Red Man; he understands the prairie; he croons to it. No, this is the White Man; he doesn't understand the prairie; he rips up its belly with a blade; he ravishes it. 'Take it easy,' says the Red Man. 'Aw, drop dead,' says the White Man. You see? There's your conflict. But the real conflict is between the White Man and the prairie. The struggle goes on for three generations, and at last the prairie breaks the White Man. Just throws him off.

While Davies's first three novels are known mostly within Canada, his recent trilogy has been an international success. *Fifth Business* (1970), *The Manticore* (1972) and *World of Wonders* (1975) might be said to extend the Ontario novel to the world scene. The three books trace the history of several Canadian families from the early twentieth century to the present. Davies has broadened the scope of the usual family saga beyond a record of social changes to show the transformation of a representative Canadian from a provincial to involvement with the modern world and to show how fear of uncovering the truth about the Canadian past has prevented self-discovery and liberation.

If Davies's novels began as social satires of provincial Ontario society they progress to unmasking what is hidden beneath surface appearances and then to an implied statement about the need to accept and use the subterranean depths of the soul as part of growth towards wholeness. The particular and universal are explicitly shown to be related, in *The Manticore*, through Jungian archetypes and other myths that reveal the inner spiritual life and true self. Indeed, following on more subtly from *Tempest-Tost*, Davies explores the relationship of illusion and reality, dream and truth. *World of Wonders*, the third book in the Deptford trilogy, suggests that man is half human, half animal; myths are summaries of experience, and a real world of 'wonder' exists below the surface of life, which can be found from the study of history, psychology and magic.

World of Wonders is essentially the biography of Magnus Eisengrim. Magnus's original name was Paul Dempster. The snowball which in *Fifth Business* Percy Boyd Staunton intended for Dunstan Ramsey instead hit Mary Dempster, bringing about Paul's premature birth and her craziness. After his mother was discovered with a tramp, Paul's life became unbearable in their village and he escaped, only to become the captive of a sodomising circus magician. Years of degradation resulted in his evolution into the greatest modern magician and his change of name. He represents a hidden side of the Canadian character, which contrasts to Dunstan's grey, schoolmaster qualities. It is the discovery and acceptance of such opposites that, Davies seems to imply, is necessary for psychic health.

Although Davies's Jungianism and international canvas may seem unrelated to Canadian nationalism, except as a criticism of provincial attitudes, his novels are attempts to explore what makes Canadians tick. The snowball that Boyd Staunton denies having tossed may seem a peculiar incident around which to build the plot of three novels, but his sense of humiliation, vindictiveness and injustice, the craftiness of the narrator, Dunstan Ramsey, and their refusal to admit guilt are similar to the poverty and cruelties of the small town, part of the past which must be uncovered if deep currents in the national character are to be understood. Davies has spoken of Canada as having a northern mysticism behind the tight, puritanical appearance it offers to the world. A concern with myth and Jungian archetypes has for several decades been a feature of Canadian literary culture, as can be seen from the critical theories of Northrop Frye, the poetry and plays of James Reaney and, more recently, the work of Margaret Atwood. The attraction of Jung to Canadian intellectuals is that his theories of archetypal polarities being at the core of the soul, and their suppression being the cause of psychic disturbance, might utilise the presence in Canada of such opposites as the English and French languages, British and American culture, the blandness expected of Canadian behaviour and the harsh realities of life in northern winters, or the divided loyalties sometimes felt by the settlers and immigrants.

World of Wonders raises some of these possibilities in explaining the attraction in the past of an out-of-date Englishness to many Canadians:

> The audiences thought England was wonderful. The Tresize company came from England, and if the truth is to be told it came from a special England many of the people in those audiences cherished—the England they had left when they were young, or the England they had visited when they were young, and in many cases an England they simply imagined and wished were a reality . . . every audience had a core of people who were happy just to be listening to English voices repeating noble sentiments. The notion that everybody wants the latest is a delusion of intellectuals. A lot of people want a warm, safe place where Time hardly moves at all, and to a lot of those Canadians that place was England.[7]

Behind the attraction towards an imaginary, timeless England is the anxiety of being in a land which, despite being long settled, was as isolated and foreign as the New Zealand of Sargeson's stories:

> It was speaking to a core of loneliness and deprivation in these Canadians of which they were only faintly aware. I think it was loneliness, not just for England, because so many of these people on the prairies were not of English origin, but for some faraway and long-lost Europe. The Canadians knew themselves to be strangers in their own land, without being at home anywhere else.

If the anxieties of being 'strangers in their own land' turn people towards blandness and a desire for security, it is only possible to discover the truth and be reborn by accepting the undemocratic, discriminatory, pitiless ways of wonder:

> We have educated ourselves into a world from which wonder and the fear and dread and splendour and freedom of wonder have been banished. Of course wonder is costly. You couldn't incorporate it into a modern state, because it is the antithesis of the anxiously worshipped security which is what a modern state is asked to give. Wonder is marvellous but it is also cruel, cruel, cruel. It is undemocratic, discriminatory, and pitiless.

Magnus claims:

> Everything has its astonishing, wondrous aspect, if you bring a mind to it that's really your own—a mind that hasn't been smeared and blurred with half-understood muck from schools, or the daily papers, or any other ragbag of reach-me-down notions.

The trilogy illustrates this. It begins in rural poverty, petty provincial small-mindedness, and progresses to the international scene and Jungian psychology, and concludes with one of the most amazing fictional biographies in modern literature.

It is significant of the need to give meaning and pattern to colonial and new national cultures that many of the writers from the Commonwealth use myth in their work. Davies's early novels may appear to be social comedies of a settled society, but in fact the tendency of his work is similar to that of Soyinka, Harris, Narayan and Hope, in seeing within myths profound realities which would give significance to the apparent lack of purpose in ordinary life.

Davies has a richer palette available as a writer of fiction than Sargeson's colloquial realism; this has resulted in a fulness and largeness of narrative art. His methods are not necessarily better than Sargeson's, but they are less limited. Putting aside questions of temperament or facility, the advantages Davies has would seem to result from a sense of Canada having a usable social history, a tradition in which provincial Ontario society has been treated as of interest to such writers as Leacock and Duncan, and a mature relationship to the intellectual and literary movements of New York and London. To those who claim that he is writing about the past, his boyhood in post-Victorian Ontario, Davies replies that he is writing about real life, 'people who are still there', and a Canada which has rejected its past, but which has not yet accepted its future.[8] That he has worked in the theatre and himself written plays is evident from the kinds of characters, dialogue and situations found in his novels. It is possible that his involvement with the theatre has contributed to his skill in representing the universal through local society.

Alongside Davies's sophistication and closeness to international culture there are similar anxieties and conflicts to those found throughout the new English literatures. The satire on settled Ontario in the early novels reflects a generational conflict and rejection of an established bourgeoisie during a period of social change when the economy and attitudes are being transformed and modernised. The portrayal of an early, poverty-stricken, rural Ontario in *The Fifth Business* searches the past for the roots of present anxieties. Perhaps the main theme of Davies's trilogy is 'Who am I?' In each of his novels there is the uncovering and recognition of evil behind the apparent blandness of Canadian life. The experiencing of and conflict with evil brings about wondrous transformations which share characteristics with myth. If I understand correctly, Davies is showing that the mean-spirited puritanism and conventionality associated with Canada hide the evil, romance and longings of real lives. The early novels show passions repressed; but it is with the recognition of evil in *A Leaven of Malice* and the need to experience life fully in *A Mixture of Frailties* that he found the perspective which shapes his later trilogy. Although he brings an international perspective to his novels, Davies is conscious of working within what has in recent decades become the tradition of Canadian thought and uses concepts that have since been used by many neo-nationalist writers.

Robert Koretsch, author of *The Words of My Roaring* (1966), says:

> In the United States, the Freudian metaphor has swept the boards, the superego versus the id kind of thing. The id is the good guy trying to free himself, and the superego takes many forms, the government, or the military-industrial complex, or, in recent history, the universities. The good guy is the youth or the frontiersman, the man in the ten-gallon hat . . . I suspect we're more Jungian in some way. We see opposites in necessary balance all the time—maybe that becomes paralysing, I don't know . . . But we're caught in a balance, and not only the French–English one, though that's the supreme political one. The hope–despair balance is fascinating to me, because that's the razor's edge; that's where we live. We become fascinated with problems of equilibrium.[9]

Margaret Atwood claims that her novel *Surfacing* (1972) demonstrates the necessity of overcoming passivity:

> But what I'm really into in that book is the great Canadian victim complex. If you define yourself as innocent then nothing is ever your fault—it is always somebody else doing it to you, and until you stop defining yourself as a victim that will always be true. It will always be some-

> body else's fault, and you will always be the object of that rather than somebody who has any choice or takes responsibility for their life. And that is not only the Canadian stance towards the world, but the usual female one. Look what a mess I am and it's all their fault. And Canadians do that too. Look at poor innocent us, we are morally better than they.[10]

David Godfrey, one of the more strident neo-nationalist writers, author of *Death Goes Better with Coca-Cola* (1968), *The New Ancestors* (1970) and an editor of *Read Canadian* (1972), says that nationalism is a 'defence mechanism against Americanization'.[11] Godfrey's nationalism developed after a period of study in the United States and his return to Canada where he found himself in conflict with the sons of an older Canadian establishment:

> Then I came back and went to school at Trinity and that was somewhat disastrous. That was the old Trinity, and I found myself in a lot of social conflict with kids from private schools whose life style and life expectations were in complete conflict with mine. And I wrote as a kind of escape out of that, and also to compete with them.

His sense of the role of the intellectual in a nationalist movement conforms to accepted sociological opinion:

> Most popular novels, in a sense, arise at the point where some group or sub-group is rising or discovering itself within the society.
>
> You get these people who have a sense of social oppression, and they're a kind of weathervane and they speak for a group that's coming along but isn't quite vocal yet.[12]

Canada in the late 1960s and early '70s went through a phase of radical nationalism. The expansion of American business and political leadership was intensely felt north of the forty-ninth parallel. The American involvement in the Vietnamese war, the sanctuary found in Canada by many Americans opposed to the war, the hiring of many Americans in the new Canadian universities, and the takeover of local business by international companies, were among the reasons why British cultural and political domination appeared to have been exchanged for Yankee-style imperialism.

Other influences on the new nationalism include the rapid urbanisation and expansion of education and job opportunities that were part of the affluence of the period. As rural Canadians moved to the cities and universities in which foreign professors, managers and businesses were visibly present, a similar situation developed to that which had occurred elsewhere during times of social change and modernisation. Consequently Canadian literature became concerned with problems of national rather than regional identity. Whereas before the 1940s Canadian literature offered a sense of the distinctiveness of each province or ethnic group in isolation, writing of the 1960s and '70s treated isolation and solitude as problems to be overcome in the quest for a true national culture. The characteristics of the past that Atwood or Godfrey define as Canadian are also passive qualities which they wish, paradoxically, to replace with the assertion of a national identity. The independence rhetoric of the 1950s and early '60s caught on; there were the usual comparisons made between Canada and Africa, between the French Canadians and black Americans, and between supposed Canadian underdevelopment and that of the Third World—an analogy that puzzled many West Indians who saw Canadian investment as a threat to their land and economy.

The relationship of literature to the second wave of post-war social changes can be seen from Margaret Atwood's comments about the lack of a tradition of the Canadian novel and the imitative style of earlier Canadian poetry:

> I started writing in 1956 roughly, and that was in high school, and we sure weren't getting any Canadian literature in high school then . . . So my early poetry is all fairly strange. It all reads like Wordsworth and Lord Byron. But when I did discover Canadian writing it was a tremendously exciting thing because it meant that people in the

> country were writing and not only that, they were publishing books, then so could I . . . I was talking with P. K. Page a couple of years ago, and she said that when she was writing there wasn't any Canadian tradition, they were all turned on to people like W. H. Auden . . . your models, the people you were learning to write from were all in other countries, and that isn't true of me. I learned to write from people in this country.[13]

Atwood's novel *Surfacing*, the best-known work of the neo-nationalists, has surprising analogies to Frank Sargeson's *I Saw in My Dream*. The narrator, a young woman, withdraws for a time from the problems, comforts and conventionalities of urban life to rural primitive conditions. Her return to northern Quebec brings her in contact with her past, especially as she investigates and imagines the life of her father, who seems to symbolise the various attempts Canadians have made to adjust to their land. The rediscovery of the past, in contrast to modern, Americanised, urban Canada, is the equivalent of a national search for identity and authenticity. As in Sargeson's novel the narrator becomes progressively more involved with the land, the 'natives' (here the Indians, with Sargeson the Maoris), and undergoes a period of primitiveness and derangement, which is a necessary stage towards possible psychic renewal. (The same pattern and symbolism occur in the final section of Davies's *The Manticore*.) Afterwards there is a short affirmation of hope, although the actual signs of it are perhaps more rhetorical than apparent. Many similar themes, details and techniques are noticeable: rejection of family, an unreliable narrator, the doubling or mirroring of the narrator's actions in others, the use of stream of consciousness, and poetic rather than realistic organisation. If Sargeson's novel is the fictional biography of a young man discovering his way towards being an artist in New Zealand, Atwood's novel records a woman stripping her social mask, defences and ideas to discover her essential self. In both cases a story about an individual has been seen by critics as a statement concerning the nation and its search for cultural health in contrast to the sickness of colonialism.

A feature of the new national literatures is that many writers see their own dramas as those of the former colonies. It would be possible without much critical ingenuity to argue that the problems of Atwood's women are equally applicable to Canada and to the modern world. It is such potential multiplicity of allusion that has made literature from the new nations of international interest.

12 Three novels and some conclusions: *Guerrillas, The Adaptable Man, Heat and Dust*

Similar forms, themes and preoccupations developed in each of the new literatures, and the literatures have been as much influenced by international political and cultural developments as by local events. Usually the best writing has occurred where there is a tension within local culture between nationalists and those with a more international outlook. Indeed the new English literature is largely the product of a colonial elite or rising proto-elite under the stress of decolonisation or a nationalist movement or rapid social change. It usually combines the characteristics of nationalist literature—such as the use of local character types, regionalism and linguistic variants—with a craftsmanship, formalism, ambiguity and frame of reference of a metropolitan and international literary tradition. Looked at from the outside, there is surprisingly little difference between the development of literature in older dominions of settlement and in the Third World; the literature of both reflects similar problems of decolonisation, nationhood, cultural conflict, and is often expressed by similar technical means in each decade. Often the problems of assembling a literary tradition are also similar and depend on creating an audience and market through universities, journals and local publishing houses, which, for political reasons, occurred at approximately the same time throughout the Commonwealth in various colonies and new nations.

The same influences that led to the emergence of new national literatures also had a direct impact on the literatures of England and the United States. The forces that led to nationalism after the Second World War were part of a sensibility as much rooted in liberal concepts of democracy, representation and equality as in the independence movements themselves. From the social changes and slogans of the fifties the revolutionary spirit of the sixties and early seventies was born; moreover, the spread of mass communication and the shifting of attention to the drama of the new nations created a continual feed-back between new and older nations. The coming of Labour to power in post-war Britain, the setting up of a welfare state, the educational act that made university scholarships available to those who were qualified for entrance, the shift of power to the labour unions and the retreat from the Empire resulted in a transfer of cultural allegiance from the upper-middle class and from those elite values that had manned the Empire to the lower-middle and working classes. The Angry Young Men, the Movement poets, and the kitchen-sink, 'chips with everything' drama of the fifties was significant of new claims of cultural recognition by those who formerly, if they had become part of the cultural establishment, would have probably accepted the 'high' cultural values of the upper-middle classes.

Along with the shift in cultural values came a redefinition of the tradition of English literature. The attention given the literary criticism of F. R. Leavis, with its emphasis on moral seriousness, the realistic portrayal of life, English lower-middle-class non-conformity, and the notion of a provincial English—in contrast to an international, metropolitan or cosmopolitan—cultural tradition was taken up by many young writers, critics and students as standing for the essential England in contrast to the superficial elite values of the wealthy, the expensive public schools and the London literary establishment. Similarly the 'cosmopolitan' writings of Yeats, Eliot and other 'modernists' were increasingly seen as foreign, non-British, French or American influenced, the opposite of those who understood what English life and literature are really about. The displacement of Henry James and T. S. Eliot as English writers was followed by the creation of an 'authentic' English tradition based on such writers as Arnold Bennett, H. G. Wells, William Empson, Robert Graves and Thomas

Hardy. The novels of John Wain and the poetry of Philip Larkin and Donald Davie concerned provincial life in the Midlands and the north of England.

One of the more significant attitudes of the fifties was the dislike of 'abroad' by the younger writers who in their concern with English life rejected the vast body of English writing about life in India, the West Indies and the Mediterranean as exotic, upper-class one-up-manship. Kingsley Amis's *I Like It Here* (1958) is representative of this mood. Amis's objection to foreign places is analogous to the nationalisms and independence movements that developed after the war. While Indians and Nigerians were replacing the British in former colonies, in England the lower-middle classes were asserting their claims to 'authenticity' and a place in the sun against the traditional values of those who had kept the Empire going and who had formerly represented British culture.

John Osborne's play *Look Back in Anger* (1956)—which along with Amis's first novel, *Lucky Jim* (1953), seemed to create the 'Angry Young Men'—concerns a working-class intellectual who rails against established society and especially against his upper-class wife. Her family represents everything that Jimmy Porter finds wrong with England. They are well bred, assured, Edwardian and—this comes up over and over in the play—associated with the Empire. Alison's father, who was a colonel in India, has mostly lived abroad and only returned to England after the war. If Porter hates the class that made the Empire he also envies it and realises that power has now passed to the Americans.

After the Second World War there were significant social changes within the United States. The presidency of J. F. Kennedy, of Irish Catholic descent, and the new cultural prominence of many Jewish novelists and intellectuals were indications that some former minorities had begun to be integrated and to challenge the older 'WASP' establishment. The 'Beat' writing of the 1950s and early '60s was the first wave of what was to be a revolt against the conformity that had descended over the United States during the early days of the Cold War. To Allen Ginsberg, perhaps the only writer of real talent among the original Beats, English literature meant the iambic pentameter, snobbery, breeding and middle-class gentility; instead Ginsberg took Walt Whitman as his model. Beat attitudes planted some of the seeds of the revolt of the late 1960s and Ginsberg was one of the heroes of the younger generation. The explosion of the late sixties may be explained as a time when the tension between modern liberal, progressive cultural ideals and the reality of social organisation snapped under the stress of rapid change and the war in Vietnam. Just as the First World War brought disillusionment with imperial values, so the war in Vietnam turned a generation of young Americans against involvement in foreign politics.

The rise of American power after the Second World War and the expansion of American influence throughout the world led to what is often known as the Americanisation of society. Essentially such Americanisation is modernisation accompanied by liberalisation, egalitarianism and the effects of increased production, advertising and consumption within a mobile mass society. Americanisation thus undermined traditional social and cultural structures. It created in their place a potentially volatile mass society, with middle-class social and economic expectations, taught that individual dissent and unrest is a form of progress. While the rapid international diffusion of such attitudes was the result of American leadership during the Cold War, the same revolutionary mood that had developed abroad was brought back to the United States through its involvement overseas. The spread and efficiency of modern communications, especially television, resulted in empathy and identification with foreign lands and situations. The coming of independence to Africa, for example, contributed to the rise of black American radicalism. The rhetoric and ideology that had created the new nations made the ideal of the new nations a model for ethnic and other groups within more developed older nations. While the crisis within the United States during the 1960s and '70s can be variously explained, and the war in Vietnam was certainly the focus of protest, causes also included the rapid expansion of and changes within industry, education and the cities. There was a massive migration of black Americans from the rural south to northern and coastal cities. The Spanish-speaking population of the United States also grew rapidly within the cities. The continuing exodus of the middle class from the inner cities to the suburbs often led to situations similar to those which had bred nationalism in former colonies—a poor, recently urbanised ethnic population ruled by, and increasingly in confrontation with, a financially better off, culturally 'alien' establishment. Affluence and the need for more trained specialists led to an extremely rapid increase in university education, a drop in standards, and dissatisfied students, many of whom had enrolled solely for the purpose of avoiding military service. Not only did the circumstances approximate those from which the new nations were emerging, the rhetoric and strategies of the Third World were seen by the younger intellectuals and protoelites of the minorities as applicable to the United States. Minority and various ethnic groups rejected the dominant culture and began to demand recognition.

While the rise of the use of drugs, especially among the well-off, was a consequence of affluence, social disorganisation, the rejection of dominant cultural values and the adoption of supposedly foreign and Third World models, it should be remembered that LSD and its effects were recent discoveries. If a romantic streak within modern culture has often viewed the irrational and paranormal as a source of vision and transcendence, the wide-spread availability of the means to the hallucinatory was the result of modern technology and mass culture. A form of modernisation, reflected in the 'generation gap', had once more turned into a supposed reaffirmation of the primitive, natural, organic, and other notions associated with the rejection of modern urban society.

The breakdown of the dominant cultural tradition and the prestige associated with it was a continual theme during the rapid changes in sensibility of the 1960s and '70s. If within Britain the emergence of 'pop' culture and Carnaby Street fashions reflected the affluence of the period and the recognition of a new mass market among the young, it also expressed the continuation of the rebellion against older cultural and class values. But alongside, and as a result of, the cultural fragmentation of the 1960s, there was a desire for communality, ethnic and regional authenticity and other social structures to replace the anomy produced by self-liberation and revolt. Americanisation, like other forms of modernisation, produced a reaction, especially among those in transition between classes and radically different ways of life.

The rise of various smaller nationalisms is not, of course, only a phenomenon of the English-speaking world. In Belgium, France, Germany and Spain there are separatist and micro-nationalist movements wanting education in their own regional languages, recognition of local culture and political independence. The combination of affluence, liberal ideals, mass culture and the centralisation of power in the modern state creates such tensions and demands. Liberal ideology produces guilt when its ideals of freedom and self-determination are confronted by the reality that the centralised modern state is based on repression as are all forms of society.

Although the sensibility of the late 1960s temporarily threatened established governments and modified prevailing social values, it produced no British or American literary classics that directly express the era. Perhaps this is because the emphasis on immediacy, orality and *praxis* led to the ephemeral. The literary works that were popular during the late 1960s and early '70s, however, reveal a sense of cultural breakdown and personal isolation. The novels of Joseph Heller and Thomas Pynchon and the second and third generation of absurdist plays are expressions of a sense of cultural dislocation and social fragmentation. Unlike earlier absurdist literature, which draws upon an awareness of an indifferent universe, or a world in which God and man are not linked by a providential order, the supposed existentialism of the late 1960s was rather a reflection of a social and cultural discontinuity than of philosophical thought. The common progression of the time was from anxiety to alienation and absurdity, which resulted in anarchy. Confidence in the cultural order was lost, rapidly followed by rejection, a sense of discontinuity, a demand for the immediacy of a different reality, and a rage with the lack of viable alternatives. The demand to tear down existing structures while having no alternative models in view was an expression of bewilderment and frustration that resulted from the loss of faith first in a central British cultural tradition, then in the new American order. With the loss of belief in such sequential middle-class values as education, career, family and property, the young turned to the new nations of the Third World to offer alternative views of community—tribe, ethnicity, revolutionary movements, slogans. Those works of literary value that reflect the period are, oddly, not the expression of such feelings but, rather, more conservative reactions to the mood of the times. The later novels of Saul Bellow portray fears and bewilderment which contrast remarkably to the optimism of his earlier writing.

The most analytical and best expression of the mood of the 1960s comes rather from authors identified with the new national literatures than from the older metropolitan powers. Perhaps this is only to be expected. The ex-colonial, the outsider, is more likely to be shocked by change and disorder than the insider. But whether or not this is so, the fact that authors from the new nations wrote best about the period is additional evidence that the new literatures are themselves a product of international cultural and political developments, and that the increasing acceptance of writers from the new nations as some of the best authors of our time is because the problems of the new nations reflect, or serve as metaphors for, the cultural confusions and anxieties of the West in recent years.

To show what I mean I want briefly to look at novels by a West Indian, a New Zealander, and a European long resident in India—V. S. Naipaul's *Guerrillas* (1975), Janet Frame's *The Adaptable Man* (1965) and Ruth Prawer Jhabvala's *Heat and Dust* (1975). That the writers are expatriates of one kind or another may suggest that they are in fact reporting upon their own sense of dislocation, which happens to echo that of others, or it may suggest that—like such previous expatriates as Conrad, James, Joyce, Eliot, Hemingway and Nabokov—they are in a privileged position to record the social and cultural anxieties of their time.

While V. S. Naipaul's *Guerrillas* is based on the Black Power riots in Trinidad and Jamaica during the period 1968–70, it also makes use of events that occurred in the Caribbean when a returned London Black Power leader murdered an English woman. The plot concerns Jane (the name is ironic and reflects the Tarzan–Jane movie relationship—a cliché of the 1960s for white women who sought excitement from black men), an English woman who goes to the West Indies in search of the stimulus and drama that she cannot find at home. Peter, whom Jane has followed to the West Indies, is a representative white liberal who has a reputation from the South African resistance movement. He wants to do good, but depends on the established order to be able to help what he considers those who need help. His link to the Third World is Jimmy, who created a reputation as a Black Power leader in London among fashionable society and in the liberal press, but who, deported to his home island, can only mouth metropolitan slogans which have no relationship to the local reality. His commune is pathetic, he is distrusted by the poor blacks, and when a Black Power strike does occur it is unconnected to his efforts despite his subsequent attempts to assume leadership. It is soon put down as a result of the threat of American power, thus showing the new indirect neo-colonial world order which has replaced the Empire.

The novel's focus, however, is on individuals and how they play their roles against the back-drop of the Third World. Jane, an upper-middle-class English woman, having lost her class privileges in the little England of the post-colonial period, turns nihilistic, raging against the pettiness of her life and society. To her the new nations offer excitement, a new order, a centre of the world to replace what her class has lost. The discovery upon arriving in the West Indies that it is on the fringes, not the centre, of world power, her subsequent boredom with Peter and seduction of Jimmy, follow from her lack of real involvement. She uses a cigarette lighter filled with butane gas from the Sahara, symbolical of the real relationship of the developed countries to the new nations. To Jimmy, however, Jane represents the colonial past that has humiliated him. Despite national independence, he remains a colonial. His house has English furniture, he reads English books and dramatises his importance to London journalists to whom he still writes. He envies Jane's Englishnesss while hating it. He fantasises raping and then chivalrously helping white women. But at the same time he loves Bryant, a deformed black youth who represents the authenticity and poverty of which Jimmy is not part. At the novel's conclusion he sodomises Jane and offers her to Bryant who, insane at what he understands as Jimmy's betrayal, hacks her to death. Peter flees the island, destroying what evidence remains of Jane's having been there. The fragmentation of narrative with its shifting points of view communicates a sense of social disorganisation, a community in which everyone is fighting a private battle and in which everyone is a guerrilla. The Black Power riots against which the individual lives are portrayed are rather an expression of resentment than politics. Although the local government quickly collapses, it is brought back into power by the display of a few American helicopters.

Naipaul has shown a former colonial society in which the only social and moral authority was the Empire and British culture. After independence a local elite was left in power over an impoverished society without the resources to build a new nation. The withdrawal of Empire meant social chaos and the coming of American-style neo-colonialism in which the new nations have the appearance of power but are in fact dependent upon foreign business interests, usually present for raw materials. The Americans have brought no new cultural order, but they prop up existing governments. The masses of the Third World are frustrated, resentful and live by fantasies of religion, Africa, or revolutions which explode into acts of anarchical revolt. Lacking the resources, social structure and foundations that provide for authentic nationalism, the nations of the Third World appear in Naipaul's novels as doomed to despair.

Janet Frame's early novels were concerned with her sense of alienation in New Zealand. Having been raised in a family that was poor but in which literature was devoured, she felt an outsider to a bourgeois society in which eccentricity and the artistic were not acceptable. Suffering from repeated nervous breakdowns, Frame in her work reflects her personal sense of stress, of discontinuity. But it is just those feelings of isolation, of fragmentation, of approaching disaster, that have made her novels seem metaphors for the modern world. Rejecting contemporary middle-class society, the artist usually creates a myth of order or the authentic nation—Soyinka's Ogun myth, Achebe's tribal village, the Australian 1890s, Naipaul's nostalgia for a unified high culture—but Frame has consistently refused to create such myths. Her novels are notoriously fragmentary and elliptical, the narratives often concluding with disaster. The lack of horizontal unity reflects the disorder of reality, especially for those who have gone beyond the dead sensibility of social convention. Esssentially such a narrative method is a criticism of conventional ways of perceiving and a rejection of those who claim to see purpose in life. Frame's style, however, is poetic and makes use of symbols, puns, word-play and other devices which give an artistic unity to her fictional world. Whereas others would use such techniques of association and language games to show that the imagination can impose order on the chaos of life, Frame subverts such romantic claims for the artist by pointing to the discrepancy between the world of her narrators and what the narrator-artist creates.

If Frame's novels record the neurosis of the non-conforming individual in a conformist society, where the ability to adapt is necessary for survival, she has recognised that alienation is the essential modern condition. In her later novels it is not only the artistic and sensitive who are outsiders; modern bureaucratic, industrialised society has made everyone feel uprooted and under pressure to adapt to an order which lacks any stability or centre. The conformist is a prisoner in a civilisation where patterns are illusions.

The Adaptable Man (1965) is set in Little Burgelstatham, an old country village in England. Instead of the organic, harmonious village community of modern nostalgia, we are shown a group of alienated individuals, each an outsider to what they imagine to be the real natives, the farmers. The Reverend Aisely Maude has lost his faith but cannot adjust to a modern Christianity with its celebration of a new existential religion based on the death of God. Freedom leaves him lonely, confused, in a world without explanation. Russell Maude hates the present and withdraws into contemplating the past. His wife Greta longs for the excitement of contemporary life and hopes to achieve it through her son Alwyn. Alwyn accepts all prevailing fashions, but his frenzied adaptation results in unmotivated murder, incest and expatriation. Vic Baldry, a farmer, wants to emigrate to the unbounded space of Australia. His wife Muriel feels lost in her own house. Ruby Unwin, an elderly farmer's widow, dreams of returning to her childhood home at Stanford where, in the past, people had taste, manners and dignity. Her son, Lex Unwin, is obsessed by a lost inheritance and petty grievances. His wife Dot feels captive and wants to escape to London and excitement. Each character is maladjusted, an 'I' believing life is, was, or will be better elsewhere. There is no unity, pattern or purpose to their reality, and their attempts to adjust to or to escape from their situation only lead to further frenzy. Even Alwyn, the completely adaptable man, ends in 'bitterness', feeling trapped in his own age with its pressure to conform to the present.

Little Burgelstatham may appear to the city-dwellers, with their pastoral nostalgia, as a harmonious social community, but it originally was dark, isolated, impoverished, and now has joined modern culture with its electric lights, television, up-to-date comforts, mobility, jet airplanes and government regulations. It is increasingly a suburb of Greater London. The contemporary world destroys any remaining patterns; it creates greater alienation which results either in withdrawal into nostalgia or in a frenzy to conform.

Modern life has none of the organic relationship to the seasons, to ritual, to a natural order that primitive man may have had or that animals still have. (The imagining that such order once existed is the closest Janet Frame comes to creating a nostalgic myth of a golden past.) In the novel even the flowers are 'all insect-bitten, or they've been affected by spray'. Frame writes that 'human beings have little to impel them from century to century'. Man makes his own sun which guides his movements. 'This everlasting movement back and forth in time without the stability and guidance of a visible world, recognized seasons, shared sun, is enough to make a man mad with the thought that he is not a migratory bird.'[1] Reality is always an illusion, a projection of the individual's own psychology.

Ruth Prawer Jhabvala is a European who married an Indian, settled in the country and has written of Indian life and the English in India for over twenty years. *Heat and Dust* (1975) concerns an English woman who visits India during the 1970s to trace the history of a relative, Olivia Rivers, who in the 1920s left her civil servant husband for a local ruler. The two stories are intertwined with the past and present made parallel as the narrator presents letters from fifty years ago. The novel contrasts an earlier period of British culture, when involvement with natives was to be avoided and when it was romantic to defy such social conventions, with the present, when hippies and drop-outs litter the Indian scene and when independence has left both those formerly colonised and the coloniser disillusioned and soiled. The nameless narrator (the granddaughter, through a second marriage, of Olivia's ex-husband) speaks flatly about and records objectively the romance of colonial India and her own grey, apparently purposeless existence there. She wears Indian clothing, eats the local food and drifts into an affair with her landlord. Pregnant, she ascends into the holy, mist-covered mountains where Olivia's final years were spent. Although she seeks to understand what the undocumented conclusion of Olivia's life was like there is an obvious parallel to herself. Is she ascending towards a spiritual understanding of India, towards being another romantic drop-out in search of a guru, or towards a mental breakdown and loss of contact with reality? As we see events through her eyes and as the style is flat, understated, and fragmented, there is no positive evidence of which significance is correct, although there is a little textual evidence for each interpretation.

While *Heat and Dust* is another modern novel with a possibly unreliable narrator and with an ambiguous conclusion, its presentation of characters is related to various traditional images of India and its culture. These are set against the reality of India in the modern world. The romantic image of India is shown to neglect the poverty and injustice caused by its local feudal princedoms. Even the heroic past is suspect. If the modern descendants of the Nawab live decadently in London from smuggled state treasures, it is possible to see the Nawab himself as nothing more than a privileged bandit. The Nawab may have provided a romantic attraction to Olivia with her liberal notions and boredom with colonial life, but we are given a glimpse of the 'devastatingly handsome' prince, flabby and fat, prematurely aged at fifty, stuffing himself with cream cakes in London while seeking money from the Foreign Office.

If the romanticisation of the past is questionable, the present provides even more problems. Is the narrator simply another of the neurotic European women, often found in Jhabvala's novels, who have sought in the myths of India a solution to their own emotional disturbances? The very flatness of the narration may be a sign of objectivity and common sense or an indication of a deadness of personality and character. The narrator has rejected Europe and hoped to find a 'simpler and more natural way of life' in India. She contrasts the loneliness of her isolated London life with the 'happiness' she feels in India where sleeping in the open air she experiences a sense of community with the town. She speaks of herself as shy and to Indian eyes a male eunuch, but she casually goes to bed with one of the foreign derelicts who has come to India on a spiritual quest, and she becomes pregnant by her landlord, a rather unlikeable person. Indeed, by any commonsense standards she has been driven to India by failure and inadequacy, and the novel shows her disintegration as she confuses romantic myths with the poverty, indifference and cruelty of actual Indian life. Is her quest for spiritual enlightenment to end any better than that of the various hippies and other western derelicts she meets who also are a feature of modern India? Perhaps in the snow-covered mountains she will find *sanyasi*, that fourth stage of life which to Indians is to be granted after withdrawal from the heat and dust of worldly activity.[2]

The three novels I have discussed are written by authors from Trinidad, New Zealand and India. They appeared within the decade that spanned the mid-1960s to the mid-1970s and each has gained an international reputation. Each is written in a fragmentary, selective narrative manner to suggest ambiguity and disorder and each reflects our contemporary sense of cultural disorganisation. Each is concerned with the relationship of the past to the present. Naipaul's novel alludes to a colonial past which, filled with prejudice and injustice, has bred a sense of humiliation in the new nations of the Third World. The withdrawal of Empire has resulted in imitation nations without the resources and cultural cohesion of authentic societies, and subject to the less direct but even more powerful influence of international American business. The instability and rhetoric of the new nations provide vicarious drama to developed nations. Janet Frame's *Adaptable Man* is set in the English countryside which has proved a myth of home, of stability and of an organic community to those who live in the cities and those of English descent who live in the new nations. But isolation and grey purposelessness which express the lack of pattern and harmony in human life are the actuality presented in the novel; it is part of our condition that there is no wholeness to be found by adapting to any reality. Ruth Prawer Jhabvala's *Heat and Dust* presents an ironic and ambiguous portrait of the myth of the colonial past in India and of contemporary attempts to find spiritual satisfaction in the supposedly simpler ways of undeveloped countries and in Hindu mysticism. It is possible that the European fleeing the alienation and isolation of western cities makes a myth of India which if indulged will result in greater alienation and in disintegration of personality.

Writers from the new nations have been particularly sensitive to the cultural changes of our era and have both contributed to the establishment of new cultural myths and to the criticism of such myths. For every Achebe, Soyinka, Wilson Harris, or Edward Brathwaite who has attempted to assert an authentic community in the past or find in ritual and myth a basis for conduct, or who claims that social fragmentation can be overcome through the creative and sympathetic imagination, there is a Naipaul, Frame or Jhabvala aware that colonialism left the new nations without a sense of order, that idealisation of the new nations can destroy an individual's sense of reality, and that there is no ideal city or harmonious organic community to be found anywhere. Significantly, Naipaul, Frame and Jhabvala all record a sense of isolation, alienation and greyness of life in England. In each of the three novels London is mentioned as not offering satisfaction to its inhabitants and as a place where people dream of better, more vital, more natural lives in the countryside, in India, or in the Third World. Dissatisfaction with our lives is general in our time.

It is often felt that the world has changed from an older culture, in which there were few social roles and in which relationships were established through family and custom, to a culture of individuals in which roles are specialised, where there is more social distance between people, and where relationships are established through work and group interests. Instead of communal solidarity, little division of labour and the simple legitimacies of the past, modern society is threatened by anomy which results from its complex division of labour, mobility and urbanisation. This creates a desire for national legitimacy. The village novels of Achebe, the nostalgia for a traditional communalism in Soyinka's recent work, the past in Lamming's *In the Castle of My Skin*, the myth of the 1890s in Australia, the search for African roots in the West Indies, the quest for identity in Canadian literature, are all variations of a reaction against industrialisation and the dominance of the city in modern life. The same factors that emancipated man from the stable obligations of the past created a sense of fall which has been particularly acute in the new nations, where the social and economic forces that created nationalist movements have alienated the writer both from the tastes of the middle classes and from a sense of belonging to a stable community.

One appeal of modern nationalism is that it attempts to recreate in the secular, rapidly changing modern world the social and spiritual stability that supposedly existed in the past. As the modern world has become complex and the individual disoriented, there is an urge to simplify, to lose the sense of personal significance and find purpose in an ideology, a myth of the past, the folk or the authentic nation. By crossing traditional barriers between tribes, ethnic groups and isolated communities and by creating a common culture, modern mass communications contribute to the increased rapidity of social change and, paradoxically, to the desire for stable values. Where centralised government, democracy and modern industrialism are impersonal and have created a feeling of distances between the masses and their rulers, nationalism has held out the hope of mass participation, an access to influence by the common man. The longing for identity, community and participation undermines institutions which are looked upon as unauthentic. The writers from the new nations are particularly sensitive to the crisis of legitimacy and often portray or record a quest for origins, for alternatives to modern society, for an authentic national culture. The government in power and established society, regardless of its kind or nature, is usually criticised as false, unrepresentative and lacking genuine local roots.

The continuing attack on the middle class in the new English literatures can be explained by associations between the dominant society and colonialism. But it should also be seen as part of the modern culture's inheritance from the Romantic movement, with its rejection of conformity. The dissatisfaction of writers with their own background and education paradoxically reflects the values of the middle class, a class which is never settled, cherishes mobility, believes in progress, is dissatisfied with itself, and usually wants more from life. Whereas the aristocrat and peasant supposedly have fixed social roles, middle-class economic and status aspirations easily transform into spiritual dissatisfactions and the desire for a higher or more authentic way of life.

Creative writing in the new English literatures has often dealt with aspects of authenticity and the problems arising from it. In Nigeria Ekwensi's fiction treats mostly of the process of urbanisation, especially of the rural masses moving to cities, which is an early stage of the rise of nationalist movements. Achebe's village novels reflect the search for a usable cultural past; his *No Longer at Ease* portrays the confusions of the proto-elite between rural and urban, ethnic and foreign values. *A Man of the People* reflects the disillusion of the intellectual elite with the actual societies produced by new nations. While the work of Wole Soyinka criticises both simplistic forms of nationalism and the imitation of foreign behaviour, it attempts to create a more profound view of authentic African culture which, having its origins in universal ritual, will bypass the conflict within nationalism between the past and modernism.

The above summary might be applied, with some local modifications, to the literature of India, Canada, New Zealand, Australia and the West Indies. The nationalism of *The Bulletin* and the 1890s in Australia could be seen in relation to the following social changes: the sheep stations of the outback were no longer a frontier, Australia had started to become urbanised, Melbourne in particular had become one of the main cities of the Empire (many of the early radical nationalists were from Melbourne and moved to Sydney), immigration was creating competition for land and jobs, and the growth of the idea of imperialism threatened to strengthen English colonial power. Most shades of Australian intellectual opinion, from Vance Palmer's radical nationalism to A. D. Hope's reintegration with western culture, have been against the prevailing Australian middle-class suburbia. Writers have sought myths of national authenticity in the deserts, the Aborigines, in the station hands, in transported convicts, or, in the case of Martin Boyd, in a cultured aristocracy, but few writers have examined or celebrated the actual realities of Australian urban life.

There is, however, a reason why creative writing and nationalism usually only meet as ideals, reactions and protest. The writer is part of international culture. The language, conventions and *genres* of his work have been shaped by tradition, by past art, by centuries of European culture. His work is an evolution from such a heritage. Local culture can provide subject-matter, themes, myths, a perspective and speech as a basis for a new style, but cannot offer an alternative to what are essentially forms of communication that have been developed by western culture. The linguistic distinction between *langue* and *parole* is relevant. Western culture provides the language of the writer, local culture shapes his personal speech. The movement back and forth between the two, and the reasons for movement, is the inner history of the new national literatures.

Notes

Chapter One

1. Lotika Basu, quoted in John B. Alphonso-Karkala, *Indo-English Literature in the Nineteenth Century* (Literary Half-Yearly, University of Mysore, 1970), p. 106.
2. The standard history is W. David McIntyre, *The Commonwealth of Nations: Origins and Impact 1869–1971* (University of Minnesota Press, Minneapolis, and Oxford University Press, 1977). Useful introductory histories of the Commonwealth include Sir Ivor Jennings, *The British Commonwealth of Nations* (Hutchins University Library, London, 1961); John Bowle, *The Imperial Achievement* (Penguin Books, Harmondsworth, 1977); Michael Crowder, *The Story of Nigeria* (Faber & Faber, London, 1978); Gordon K. Lewis, *The Growth of the Modern West Indies* (MacGibbon & Kee, London, 1968); Kenneth McNaught, *The Pelican History of Canada* (Penguin Books, Harmondsworth, 1969); Roland Oliver and J. D. Fage, *A Short History of Africa* (Penguin Books, Harmondsworth, 1975); W. H. Oliver, *The Story of New Zealand* (Faber & Faber, London, 1960); Percival Spear, *A History of India*, vol *II* (Penguin Books, Harmondsworth, 1973). Also useful is Parker Thomas Moon, *Imperialism and World Politics* (Macmillan, New York, 1963).
3. J. E. Clare McFarlane, *A Literature in the Making* (The Pioneer Press, Kingston, Jamaica, 1956), p. 94. Una Marson's poem can be found in the *Yearbook of the Jamaica Poetry League 1939* (The New Dawn Press, Kingston, 1939).
4. Alfred H. Mendes, 'A Commentary', *Trinidad*, I, 2 (Easter, 1930). Reprinted in *From Trinidad*, edited Reinhard W. Sander (Hodder & Stoughton, London, 1978), p. 21.
5. 'Author's Note' to *A Literature in the Making*.
6. *A Literature in the Making*, p. 28.
7. *The Beacon*, II, 12 (June 1933). Reprinted in *From Trinidad*, p. 31.

Chapter Two

1. Geoffrey Serle, *From Deserts the Prophets Come: The Creative Spirit in Australian Literature 1788–1972* (Heinemann, Melbourne, 1973), pp. 151 and 180.
2. Quoted in David Thomson, *England in the Twentieth Century* (Penguin Books, Harmondsworth, 1977), p. 213.
3. Doris Lessing, *Ripples From the Storm* (Michael Joseph, London, 1958), p. 251.
4. Derek Walcott, 'What the Twilight Says: An Overture', *Dream on Monkey Mountain* (Farrar, Straus & Giroux, New York, 1970), p. 4.
5. Pennsylvania State University Press, University Park and London (1975). Critical studies before 1970 mentioned in this chapter can be found in New's bibliography.

Chapter Three

1. Various comments in this chapter have been particularly influenced by Joshua A. Fishman, *Language and Nationalism* (Newbury House, Rowley, Mass., 1972); Anthony D. Smith, *Theories of Nationalism* (Duckworth, London, 1971); Everett E. Hagen, *On the Theory of Social Change* (Dorsey Press, Homewood, Ill., 1962); D. Lerner, *The Passing of Traditional Society* (Free Press, New York, and Collier-Macmillan, London, 1958 and 1964). Also see my 'Thoughts on African Literature', *West African Journal of Modern Languages*, I, 2 (1976), 11–17.
2. My comments on education have been influenced by Geoffrey Serle, *From Deserts the Prophets Come: The Creative Spirit in Australia 1788–1972* (Heinemann, Melbourne, 1973).
3. For a useful discussion, see Kenneth Ramchand, *The West Indian Novel and its Background* (Faber & Faber, London, 1970).
4. My remarks on Haliburton are indebted to Fred Cogswell, 'The Maritime Provinces (1720–1815)' and 'Haliburton', in Carl F. Klinck, editor, *Literary History of Canada*, vol. *I* (University of Toronto Press, 1977), pp. 85–97, and 106–15.

Chapter Four

1. J. P. Clark, *The Example of Shakespeare* (Northwestern University Press, Evanston, 1970), p. 43.
2. For the war and post-war years, see Michael Crowder, *The Story of Nigeria* (Faber & Faber, London, 1978).
3. Ghaṇa Publishing Corporation, Tema, Ghana (1971; originally published 1941).
4. E. N. Obiechina, editor, *Onitsha Market Literature* (Heinemann, London, 1972), p. 3.
5. Lutterworth Press, England. I am indebted to Ernest Emenyonu's *Cyprian Ekwensi* (Evans, London, 1974) for the details.

6. *People of the City* (Dakers, London, 1954; revised edition, Heinemann, London, 1963), p. 3 and p. 5.
7. Ayọ Bamgbose, *The Novels of D. O. Fagunwa* (Ethiope Publishing Corporation, Benin City, Nigeria, 1974), p. 5. Fagunwa's first story, *Ògbójú Ọdẹ*, was published by the C.M.S. Bookshop, Lagos (1938). Wole Soyinka's translation, *The Forest of a Thousand Daemons*, was published by Nelson, London (1968). It is of interest that Fagunwa's father was an Ifa priest who was converted to Christianity. Fagunwa was educated, and himself taught, at various mission schools.
8. *The Palm-Wine Drinkard* (Faber & Faber, London, 1952), p. 35.
9. See Martin Banham, with Clive Wake, *African Theatre Today* (Pitman, London, 1976), pp. 8–13.
10. *This Is Our Chance* (University of London Press, 1956), p. 38.
11. *Morning Yet on Creation Day* (Heinemann, London, 1975), p. 70.
12. *Things Fall Apart* (Heinemann, London, 1976), p. 3.
13. *One Man, One Wife* (Nigeria Printing Co., Lagos, 1959; Heinemann, London, 1976), p. 3.
14. *No Longer at Ease* (Heinemann, London, 1975), p. 68.
15. *Arrow of God* (Heinemann, London, 1977), p. 189.
16. *A Man of the People* (Heinemann, London, 1975), pp. 148–9.

Chapter Five

1. For factual details, I am indebted to Gerald Moore, *Wole Soyinka* (Evans, London, 1971).
2. *The Lion and the Jewel*, in *Collected Plays, 2* (Oxford University Press, London, 1974), p. 9.
3. *The Swamp Dwellers* was performed in London in 1958.
4. *Camwood on the Leaves* (Methuen, London, 1973), p. 31.
5. *A Dance of the Forests*, in *Collected Plays, 1* (Oxford University Press, London, 1973), p. 11, p. 29.
6. *Myth, Literature and the African World* (Cambridge University Press, 1976), p. 1, p. 27.
7. *The Strong Breed*, in *Collected Plays, 1*, p. 129.
8. *The Road*, in *Collected Plays, 1*, p. 149. The Agẹmọ cult on which *The Road* is based and which appears to have influenced Soyinka's interpretation of the Ogun myth is supposedly peculiar to Igebu. Soyinka's father is from Igebu. See Ebun Clark, 'Ogunde Theatre', *Black Orpheus* 3, 2 & 3 (Oct.–Dec. 1974/Jan.–June 1975), p. 84, footnote 43.
9. *The American Scholar*, 32, 3 (Summer 1963), 387–96, p. 392.
10. *African Forum*, I, 4 (1966), 53–64, p. 53, p. 62.
11. *The Interpreters* (Heinemann, London, 1970), p. 235
12. *Ibid*, p. 9. Sekoni's stutter effectively reveals his character but annoys many readers. I have therefore edited the stutter from his speeches.
13. *Kongi's Harvest, Collected Plays, 2*, p. 60.
14. *Idanre and Other Poems* (Eyre Methuen, London, 1969), p. 88.
15. *The Man Died* (Rex Collings, London, 1973), p. 33.

16. 'Conquering the Abyss of the Crypt', *World Literature Written in English*, 16, 2 (Nov. 1977), 245–55, p. 246. My understanding of *Shuttle* is indebted to this article.
17. *A Shuttle in the Crypt* (Rex Collings/Eyre Methuen, London, 1972), pp. 38–9.
18. *Season of Anomy* (Rex Collings, London, 1973), p. 282.
19. *Ogun Abibimañ* (Rex Collings, London, 1976), p. ii.

Chapter Six

1. Early Jamaican literature is discussed in J. E. Clare McFarlane, *A Literature in the Making* (The Pioneer Press, Kingston, 1956). Trinidadian literature is discussed in Anson Gonzalez, *Self Discovery Through Literature*, five radio scripts (St Augustine, Trinidad, 1972); and Anson Gonzalez, *Trinidad and Tobago Literature on Air* (National Cultural Council of Trinidad and Tobago, Port of Spain, 1974). Also see Robert E. McDowell, *Bibliography of Literature from Guyana* (Sable Publishing Corporation, Arlington, Texas, 1975). The two most useful books on West Indian literature are Kenneth Ramchand, *The West Indian Novel and its Background* (Faber & Faber, London, 1970); and Bruce King, editor, *West Indian Literature* (Macmillan, London, 1979).
2. See Reinhard W. Sander, editor, *From Trinidad: An Anthology of Early West Indian Writing* (Hodder & Stoughton, London, 1978).
3. *In the Castle of My Skin* (Longman Caribbean, London, 1970), p. 299.
4. A useful book is John La Guerre, editor, *Calcutta to Caroni: The East Indians of Trinidad* (Longman Caribbean, London, 1974).
5. Edward Brathwaite, *Contradictory Omens* (Savacou, monograph no. 1, Kingston, Jamaica, 1974).
6. Republished with an introduction, to which I am indebted, by V. S. Naipaul as *The Adventures of Gurudeva and Other Stories* (André Deutsch, London, 1976).
7. Naipaul's works, published by André Deutsch and also available in Penguin editions, include: *The Mystic Masseur* (1957), *The Suffrage of Elvira* (1958), *Miguel Street* (1959), *A House for Mr Biswas* (1961), *The Middle Passage* (1962), *An Area of Darkness* (1964), *The Loss of Eldorado* (1965), *The Mimic Men* (1967), *In a Free State* (1971), *The Overcrowded Barracoon* (1972), *Guerrillas* (1975), *A Bend in the River* (1979). A useful study of Naipaul's work is Landeg White, *V. S. Naipaul: A Critical Introduction* (Macmillan, London, 1975).
8. *Palace of the Peacock* (Faber & Faber, London, 1960; 1968 edition), p. 152.
9. *The Whole Armour*, 1962; published with *The Secret Ladder* (Faber & Faber, London, 1973), pp. 17–18.
10. *The Secret Ladder*, 1963; published with *The Whole Armour* (Faber & Faber, London, 1973), p. 144.
11. *Tradition, the Writer and Society* (New Beacon Publications, London, 1967), p. 20. Also see Harris's *The Far Journey of Oudin* (Faber & Faber, London, 1961); and *The Sleepers of Roraima* (Faber & Faber, London,

1970). Useful books on Harris include: Michael Gilkes, *Wilson Harris and the Caribbean Novel* (Longmans, London, 1975); Hena Maes-Jelinek, *The Naked Design* (Dangaroo Press, Aarhus, Denmark, 1976); Anna Rutherford and Kirsten Holst Petersen, editors, *The Enigma of Values* (Dangaroo Press, Aarhus, 1975).

Chapter Seven

1. Useful historical and critical studies, anthologies and volumes of West Indian poetry include: Norman E. Cameron, editor, *Guianese Poetry: 1831–1931* (Argosy Co., British Guiana, 1931); John Figueroa, editor, *Caribbean Voices*, 2 vols. (Evans Brothers, London, 1966, 1970); J. E. Clare McFarlane, *A Literature in the Making* (The Pioneer Press, Kingston, 1956); J. E. Clare McFarlane, editor, *A Treasury of Jamaican Poetry* (University of London Press, 1949); Edward Baugh, *West Indian Poetry: 1900–1970* (Savacou Publications, Kingston, n.d., reprinted 1977); Edward Brathwaite, 'Creative Literature of the British West Indies during the Period of Slavery', *Savacou* I (June 1970), 46–73; O. R. Dathorne, editor, *Caribbean Verse* (Heinemann, London, 1967).
2. Martin Carter, *Poems of Resistance from British Guiana* (Lawrence & Wishart, London, 1954). Republished with one additional poem as *Poems of Resistance* (University of Guyana, Georgetown, 1964). *Poems of Succession* (New Beacon Books, London and Port of Spain, 1977) includes work from Carter's various publications.
3. Kenneth Ramchand, 'Parades, Parades: Modern West Indian Poetry', *Sewanee Review*, LXXXVII, 1 (1979), 96–118, pp. 110 and 104.
4. Derek Walcott, 'Meanings', *Savacou* 2 (Sept. 1970), 45–51, p. 45.
5. *Another Life* (Jonathan Cape, London, 1973), p. 3.
6. *Epitaph for the Young* (Advocate Co., Barbados, 1949), pp. 6, 9 and 10.
7. *Poems* (The City Printery, Jamaica, n.d.–1952), p. 42.
8. *Selected Poems* (Farrar, Straus & Company, New York, 1964), p. 3. The New York and London volumes of Walcott's work are often different. *In a Green Night: Poems 1948–60* (Jonathan Cape, London, 1962) includes work from three privately published books. *Selected Poems* includes 'In a Green Night'. Most of the new poems were included in *The Castaway* (Jonathan Cape, London, 1965). The New York edition of *The Gulf* (Farrar, Straus & Giroux, 1970) includes poems from *The Castaway*. Consequently the dates given for Walcott's poems in this chapter should be treated with caution.
9. See Rhonda Cobham, 'The Background', in *West Indian Literature*, ed. Bruce King (Macmillan, London, 1979), pp. 9–29.
10. *The Castaway and Other Poems* (Jonathan Cape, London, 1965), p. 35.
11. *Ibid.*, p. 52.
12. *Dream on Monkey Mountain* (Farrar, Straus & Giroux, New York, 1970), pp. 9–10.
13. *Sea Grapes* (Farrar, Straus & Giroux, New York, 1971; new edition, 1976), p. 21.

14. I am indebted to J. Michael Dash's essay, 'Edward Brathwaite', in *West Indian Literature*, pp. 210–28.
15. *Savacou*, 2 (Sept. 1970), 35–44, p. 38, p. 44.
16. *The Arrivants* (Oxford University Press, London, 1973), p. 18.
17. *The Arrivants*, p. 271.
18. *Mother Poem* (Oxford University Press, 1977), p. 25.
19. 'The Love Axe/1: (Developing a Caribbean Aesthetic 1962–1974)', *Bim*, 16, 61 (June 1977), 53–65, pp. 53–4.

Chapter Eight

1. I am indebted to Joan Stevens, *The New Zealand Novel: 1860–1960* (Reed, Wellington, 1961, revised 1966), and E. H. McCormick, *New Zealand Literature, A Survey* (Oxford University Press, Oxford, 1959), for observations on early writers. Also useful is Wystan Curnow, *Essays on New Zealand Literature* (Heinemann, Auckland, 1973).
2. *Collected Stories* (MacGibbon & Kee, London, 1965), pp. 33–5.
3. *I Saw in My Dream* (John Lehmann, London, 1949; reprinted Auckland University Press and Oxford University Press, 1974), edited by H. Winston Rhodes, p. 3. Useful studies are H. Winston Rhodes, *Frank Sargeson* (Twayne, New York, 1969), and R. A. Copland, *Frank Sargeson* (Oxford University Press, Wellington, 1976).
4. If I understand the parallels to *Pilgrim's Progress*, the Merry-go-round at the auction is the 'Holy City' and the death of the Macgregors is the final judgement and damnation of those who attempt to enter the New Jerusalem on false pretences.
5. For a study of Janet Frame, see Jeanne Delbaere, editor, *Bird, Hawk, Bogie: Essays on Janet Frame* (Dangaroo Press, Aarhus, 1978).

Chapter Nine

1. Australian National University Press, Canberra (1976). Useful studies of the nationalists can be found in Chris Wallace-Crabbe, editor, *The Australian Nationalists* (Oxford University Press, Melbourne, 1971). Also see H. M. Green, *A History of Australian Literature*, 2 vols (Angus & Robertson, Sydney, 1962); Geoffrey Dutton, editor, *The Literature of Australia* (Penguin Books, Harmondsworth, 1964).
2. *Images of Society and Nature: seven essays on Australian novels* (Oxford University Press, Melbourne, 1971), p. 173.
3. *Voss* (Penguin Books, Harmondsworth, 1960), pp. 28–9.
4. See Thelma Herring, 'Odyssey of a Spinster: A Study of *The Aunt's Story*', in *Ten Essays on Patrick White*, edited G. A. Wilkes (Angus & Robertson, Sydney, 1970), pp. 3–20; and J. F. Burrows, '"Jardin Exotique": The Central Phase of *The Aunt's Story*', in the same volume, pp. 85–108.
5. 'Northern River', in *Collected Poems* (Angus & Robertson, Sydney, 1975), p. 6.

6. See, for Furphy, Richardson and Boyd, A. D. Hope's *Native Companions* (Angus & Robertson, Sydney, 1974), which republishes previous essays and reviews.
7. *Collected Poems: 1930–1970* (Angus & Robertson, Sydney, 1972), p. 12.
8. 'Vivaldi, Bird and Angel', in *Collected Poems*, p. 276, p. 278.
9. 'Letter from Rome', in *Collected Poems*, p. 144, p. 146.

Chapter Ten

1. For nineteenth-century Indian writing, see John B. Alphonso-Karkala, *Indo-English Literature in the Nineteenth Century* (Literary Half Yearly, University of Mysore, 1970); and K. R. Srinivasa Iyengar, *Indian Writing in English* (Asia Publishing House, New York, 1962, republished 1973).
2. For Anand, see Krishna Nandan Sinha, *Mulk Raj Anand* (Twayne, New York, 1972); and M. E. Derrett, *The Modern Indian Novel in English* (Université Libre de Bruxelles, Brussels, 1966), which contains good material on the development of writing in English and on the style of the Indian novel.
3. A good evaluation of Rao's novels is C. D. Narasimhaiah, 'National Identity in Literature and Language: Its Range and Depth in the Novels of Raja Rao', in *National Identity*, edited K. L. Goodwin (Heinemann, Melbourne, 1970), pp. 153–68. Also see M. K. Naik, *Raja Rao* (Twayne, New York, 1972); and Una Parameswarah, *A Study of Representative Indo-English Novelists* (Vikas, New Delhi, 1976).
4. Meenakshi Mukherjee, *The Twice Born Fiction* (Heinemann, New Delhi and London, 1971), includes good discussions of myth and style in Narayan and other Indian novelists.
5. Ved Mehta, 'The Train Had Just Arrived at Malgudi Station', in *John is Easy to Please* (Farrar, Straus & Giroux, New York, 1971), pp. 133–71, p. 141. I am indebted to Mehta's interview with Narayan for the biographical facts and some insights. Also see R. K. Narayan, *My Days* (Chatto & Windus, London, 1975). Many of the characters and incidents in his novels can be found in his autobiography. Narayan's use of spiritualism is discussed in William Walsh, 'The Spiritual and the Practical', *The Journal of Commonwealth Literature*, 5 (July 1968), 121–3; and V. Panduranga Rao, 'The Art of R. K. Narayan', *The Journal of Commonwealth Literature*, 5 (July 1968), 29–40.
6. George Woodcock, 'Two Great Commonwealth Novelists: R. K. Narayan and V. S. Naipaul', *Sewanee Review*, LXXXVII, 1 (Winter 1979), 1–28, p. 19.
7. *Mr Sampath* (Eyre & Spottiswoode, London, 1949), republished under the title *The Printer of Malgudi* (Michigan State University Press, East Lansing, 1957), p. 164.
8. The myth upon which the film is based: 'Shiva is in a rigorous meditation, when his future bride, Parvathi, is ministering to his needs as a devotee and an absolute stranger. One day, opening his eyes, he realises that

passion is stirring within him, and looking about for the cause he sees Kama, the Lord of Love, aiming his shaft at him. At this, enraged, he opens his third eye in the forehead and reduces Kama to ashes.' In the printer's seduction of the actress and Ravi's absurd attempt to win her by abduction, we are also reminded of Ravana's abduction of Sita from Rama in the epic *Ramayana*. The first myth is retold in Narayan's *Gods, Demons and Others* (Heinemann, London, 1965); the second myth is included in Narayan's version of *The Ramayana* (Viking Press, New York, 1972).

9. *Waiting for the Mahatma* (Michigan State University Press, East Lansing, 1955), p. v.
10. *The Man-Eater of Malgudi* (Viking Press, New York, 1961), pp. 74–5.
11. *My Days*, p. 148.

Chapter Eleven

1. MacLennan is judiciously discussed in Edmund Wilson's *O Canada: An American's Notes on Canadian Culture* (The Noonday Press, New York, 1966). Also see Carl F. Klinck, editor, *Literary History of Canada*, 3 vols (University of Toronto Press, 2nd edition 1976).
2. If the parallels to *The Tempest* are not always clear—and it should be remembered that these are somewhat humorous analogies and not allegorical symbols—it is because by a further irony Robertson Davies has drawn upon situations in Thomas Shadwell's late seventeenth-century version of *The Tempest*, an adaptation which includes additional characters, a double set of lovers and comic situations.
3. Davies has often written on Leacock. See his 'On Stephen Leacock' in *Masks of Fiction*, edited A. J. M. Smith (McClelland & Stewart, Toronto and Montreal, 1961, 1969), pp. 93–114; and Davies, *Stephen Leacock* (McClelland & Stewart, Toronto, 1970).
4. Donald Cameron, *Conversations with Canadian Novelists* (Macmillan of Canada, Toronto, 1973), pp. 32–3.
5. *Tempest-Tost* (Clarke Irwin & Co., Toronto, Vancouver, 1951. Paperback format, 1965), p. 16.
6. *Leaven of Malice* (Clarke Irwin & Co., Toronto, Vancouver, 1954. Paperback format, 1955), p. 301.
7. *World of Wonders* (Macmillan of Canada, Toronto, 1975. Penguin Books, Harmondsworth, 1977), p. 225.
8. Marq de Villiers, 'The Master's World', *Weekend Magazine*, Montreal (15 November 1975), p. 8.
9. *Conversations with Canadian Novelists*, p. 85.
10. *Eleven Canadian Novelists*, interviewed by Graeme Gibson (Anansi, Toronto, 1973), p. 22. See Margaret Atwood, *Surfacing* (Simon & Schuster, New York, 1972); and *Survival* (Anansi, Toronto, 1972).
11. *Eleven Canadian Novelists*, p. 172.
12. *Ibid.*, pp. 161, 155, 156.
13. *Ibid.*, pp. 11–12.

Chapter Twelve

1. *The Adaptable Man* (George Brazillier, New York, 1965), p. 4.
2. See Yasmine Gooneratne, 'Irony in Ruth Prawer Jhabvala's *Heat and Dust*', *New Literature Review*, No. 4, pp. 41–50.

Index